FURTHER ALONG THE PATH

by

H. A. Owens

To Tom Carey
1996
Many Thanks
H A Owens

ISBN 0-9510640-1-0

Published by
H. A. OWENS,
~~1 Eva Road~~, Cheadle Heath, Stockport, Cheshire, SK3 0SX.

Printed by
Douglas Printers Ltd. Woodhouse Drive, Wigan, Lancs., WN6 7NT.

Contents

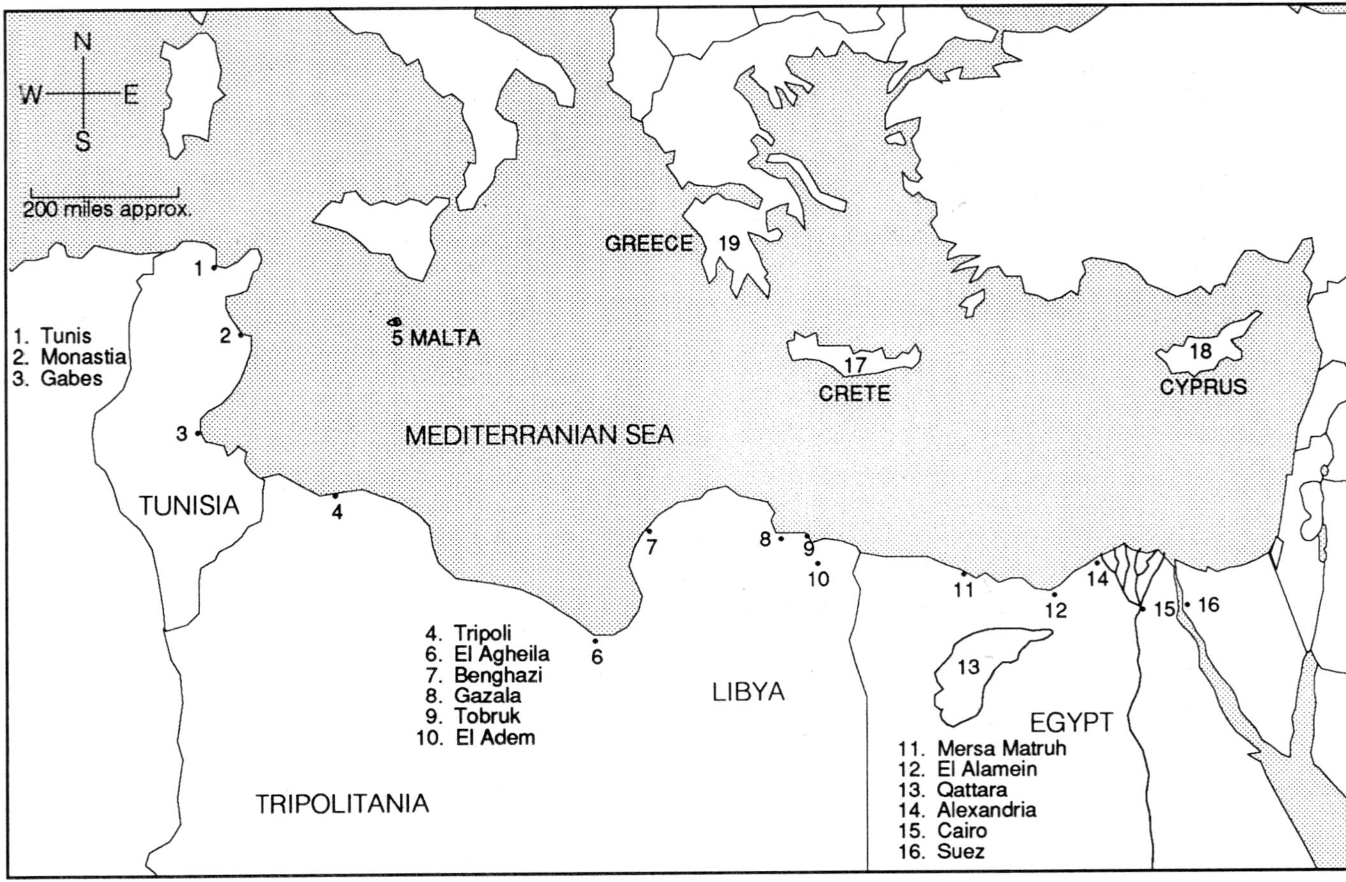
N
W
E
S
200 miles approx.
1. Tunis
2. Monastia
3. Gabes
TUNISIA
5 MALTA
MEDITERRANIAN SEA
GREECE
19
17
CRETE
18
CYPRUS
4. Tripoli
6. El Agheila
7. Benghazi
8. Gazala
9. Tobruk
10. El Adem
LIBYA
TRIPOLITANIA
13
EGYPT
11. Mersa Matruh
12. El Alamein
13. Qattara
14. Alexandria
15. Cairo
16. Suez

Introduction

Let not the TRUTH be withheld from YOU.

That remark just about sums up both of my books. For instance, how many know the Fighter and Bomber Squadrons of the Desert Air-Force consisted of very large numbers of men from South Africa? Likewise, both titles of my books were suggested by spirit friends who not only saved my life many times in the desert but, also helped me to write the books.

This help was given to me for a very good reason which I thank them for, because it will help all mankind in the very near future.

There have been hundreds of books written by outstanding air crews but, how many have been written by the R.A.F. ground staff?

These often nameless fitters etc., performed near miracles in keeping the aircraft flying, not quite with sealing wax and string but, very nearly so. Then again, not many people realize that the Salvage Units of the Desert Air-Force, picked up over 3,000 crashed or shot-down aircraft. Many of which came down behind the enemy lines or in mine fields.

Now I must thank all the people who have helped me to put this book together, especially my two daughters, Patricia and Jean. Not forgetting my dear friend Winifred, who corrected so many of my mistakes. Finally, I dedicate this book to my son David, who passed to the world of spirit at the age of 25. But I must not forget the many R.A.F. pals who never had the chance to even reach that age.

Chapter 1

Reaping the whirlwind

This book is a continuation of my first book, 'Nightmare towards the path'. In anticipation of requests to continue the series of adventures, I feel I must try to do something about it. Actually, I had no intention of writing any kind of book, but if I tell you that I was gently persuaded to do so, then those of you who are psychic will understand.

The first book covers part of my life in the R.A.F. during World War II from the end of the Battle of Britain in 1940 to the commencement of the Battle of El Alamein.

The mystery began to unfold in Egypt, it was as if I was led step by step towards the path which I could not see, nor did I know existed at that time. I was still only twenty when the incidents began and my life was saved, not once or twice, but four or five times, all within the space of about twelve months.

Some of the adventures were most unusual and I learnt something each time, but likewise, my psychic faculties were stimulated and aroused from their slumber, so that I became aware of many things which I had not noticed before. Later, I could feel a presence with me and, although I could not see anyone, I knew that I was not alone. Gradually, my eyes opened to the greater reality, which was there all the time, but I could not see it until circumstances made the darkness visible.

Years later, as the last pieces of the jigsaw began to slot together, I felt compelled to write it all down and pass it on to anyone who is ready to receive it. So you understand that my first book is a 'must' if you wish to satisfy your curiosity and not feel frustrated, wondering what the devil was in - 'Nightmare towards the path'. But for those of you who cannot possibly get hold of a copy, I will try to give you an idea of what the situation was like in the Egyptian Desert on the 26th October, 1942. Then come with me across the world's largest desert to Tunis, and back again to Egypt.

The battle of El Alamein had started on the night of October 23rd, 1942. It was now into the third day, so there were eight more days and nights of hell to go through before the British 8th Army overcame the last defences, and hammered their way along the coast road to begin the chase which would eventually end in Berlin. No one knew at that time how long the battle would last, neither did we know that this was to be the turning point of World War II.

At that time I was on the largest airfield I had ever been on, either before or since, and soon you will get some idea of the tremendous size. It was one of a number of airfields on the edge of the Western Desert of Egypt. This is where I found myself after the massive retreat earlier in 1942. First, from near Benghazi, then from El Adem, where the cauldron bubbled over after the Gazala line was by-passed and we had lost four hundred tanks in a whirling battle. Three hundred more of our tanks were decimated a few days later and all the forward airfields were captured, so there was nothing left but to make a run for it and hope that the shattered remains of the 8th Army could make a last stand, somewhere.

Regarding the landing ground I was now on, it was just one of many, hastily hacked out of the desert and not a blade of grass grew on it or near it. I still do not know the exact location, but approximately fifteen miles to the east of us, the lush green delta area of Egypt abruptly stopped and the desert began. So, if you then flew due west you would fly for over four thousand five hundred miles across the continent of Africa, and see nothing but burning desert. If you force landed anywhere and had no water, then you only had forty-eight hours left to pray and scream in!

But returning to the landing ground once more, I estimate and try to remember that Alexandria was about thirty-five miles behind us, as the crow flies, and the front line was about twenty-five miles in front of us. Say, seven minutes by Stuka dive bombers and six minutes for the ME 110. They all came over to bomb and machine-gun us almost every day.

All around the perimeter of the airfield were tents, slit trenches, machine gun pits, anti-aircraft guns and the usual bomb dumps and petrol dumps. There were also the fighter squadrons aircraft of Spitfires, Hurricanes and Kittyhawkes, with one American fighter group of P40 fighters who had come to help us about eight weeks before and they still had a lot to learn. In addition, there were squadrons of South Africans, with Bostons and Baltimores twin-engined medium bombers. Then came the Salvage Unit, which I belonged to, equipped with mobile cranes and workshops, because we also repaired many of the aircraft after we had brought them back from wherever they had been forced down. Recovering them was quite a job, sometimes the pilots did not have much time to choose a place for a belly landing, and often they landed behind the enemy lines, or worse still, between the lines in a mine field.

They were the most awkward ones to recover, and many of my pals never returned from those trips. Here, was a ready-made baited trap which would not be missed by the enemy. The foreseen tragedy would be set in motion by some over-zealous officer or N.C.O., who would often remain in the rear. The chosen ones would be briefed. "There is one of our fighters down about thirty miles away, just in front of the Australian lines, go and bring it back!"

So a party of about six fitters with a three-ton truck was loaded with tool boxes, food, water, petrol and bedding. A mobile 'Coles' crane and driver would be going along also, along with a salvage truck and driver. I was not chosen this time, so the rest of this little episode comes from one of the three men who came back on foot about four days later. An N.C.O. gave them their last orders. "The Australians will show you a gap through our mine-field and they will cover your movements, but once in the mine-field, you are on your own and must come back with the aircraft the same way. Just lift it right onto the truck and get out fast. You can take the wings off when you get to a safe place!".

So that was that. They shouted cheerio and set off in the small convoy. Five of my pals were already dead men but they did not know it yet. They soon got to the sector where the Australians were well dug in, keeping their heads down, as they waited for the next skirmish which may start anytime. The tough Aussies stopped the small party at a safe distance, then took them on foot and belly, to point out the way through their mine-field. They told them it was suicide to attempt it, but the salvage crew had had their orders, which must be obeyed! The Aussies mentioned that the pilot had crawled to their lines the day before, miraculously missing the mines and leaving a trail of blood back to the aircraft. He was a Rhodesian, and was now in a field hospital nearby. Now, it was time to go in regardless. The three-tonner lead the way with the crane and salvage truck in the rear.

The enemy watched and waited for the signal. An 88mm dug-in gun had already got the range worked out to a yard. The Salvage Party unknowingly gave their own signal as the jib was raised up over the aircraft and the slaughter began. The first shell screamed over and knocked the crane into a twisted heap. Two more shells and the other two trucks were smashed to pieces, and as the smoke curled upwards, three men crawled away on their bellies. The Soldiers dragged them into the safety of their trench, and said, "We told you it was suicide!".

This is just one of many such incidents which were happening all the time. It had happened to me a few months before, and later I would be sent into the trap again. The Officers and N.C.O.'s were told to curb their zealousness, because we were losing too many valuable mobile cranes; but it still went on, although, to a lesser degree. The pawns could be replaced comparatively easily, but the cranes were getting difficult to replace; everything had to make the long sea journey round South Africa. A convoy of ships could take ten weeks or more running the gauntlet of the U-boat packs.

But now, everyone was feeling optimistic, the Army had got new tanks and we now had plenty of Spitfires, also a large percentage of us had had a week or more leave in either Egypt or Palestine, to recover from the thrashing we had received on our thousand miles retreat. Now, we were talking of going twice as far. Of course, there were a few old sweats who had been all the way to Benghazi and back, twice since 1939. They had had a bellyful and now they kept silent, perhaps, remembering the early days when the Gloucester Gladiator bi planes were the front line fighters in the desert.

The Army and the R.A.F. had waited since July 1942, to be strong enough to win the El Alamein battle, and to make sure this time that we would have the power to carry on the chase. For over three months we had built up our strength behind the front line, time after time the Germans and Italians had tried to break through. They hurled themselves onto the defences, preceeded by waves of dive bombers and tanks, and each time they were thrown back in baffled amazement.

How could we hold them off when we had lost so much equipment and men in the last retreat? Surely, we must be on our knees after losing every battle since Christmas! It certainly seemed unusual, we had been absolutely shattered and disorganised when the 8th Army turned at bay to make a last desperate stand at El Alamein.

Everyone in the Salvage Unit had lost all, or most of their kit, including tool boxes and rifles; many like myself had got back with only the clothes we stood in. The front line fighter squadrons had been overrun and torn to pieces, men and aircraft on the ground had been decimated. As for the Army, only those soldiers who lived to talk can tell you. Thousands were sacrificed on the long road back, so that others could live to fight and hold the last line of defence. But we had lost so much, hundreds of tanks had been knocked out, thousands of guns and trucks had been abandoned in twisted heaps, littering the coast road and open desert.

So what was the secret of the only line that could not be penetrated nor by-passed by the masters of Blitzkrieg? The so far invincible enemy who had overrun Europe, adding Greece, Crete, Cyranica, Libya and half of Egypt, had now come upon a line of shattered, ill-equipped soldiers, yet they could not pass!

For what it is worth, I will tell you of the mysterious rumours which were whispered amongst some of the so-called crack pots in those desperate days.

Could there be any truth in the stories of the mysterious power emanating from the only surviving wonder of the old world, 'The Great Pyramid'? Was it still active, or, had it been re-activated, to beam out an occult power to the four corners of Egypt? Or, was it the British soldiers and the soldiers of the old empire, along with a few free French and Greeks who, weary as they were, stopped running and turned at bay?

So now you can form an idea of the desperate situation in which the whole Middle East was in, and yet I never saw any real panic amongst the soldiers or airmen I met. Men went on leave to Cairo or Jerusalem, others played cricket near Alexandria, and danced in the night clubs. It was as if we knew we were safe behind the El Alamein line, and it was true that many civilians had fled across the Suez Canal, and that the bridges over the Nile were made ready for blowing up.

But now, on the third day of the battle, the enemy were beginning to fall back, Hitler had told them not to retreat, but die where they stood for the fatherland. Many of them did just that, and the rest learnt what Blitzkrieg really felt like on the 'receiving end'. They were reaping the whirlwind and they knew it.

It meant that all their successes over the past three years would eventually be set at naught, and all they had gained would be taken from them. But it was still 1942 and the future was a closed book, only after this ferocious battle would we catch a glimpse of the light glimmering at the end of the blackness.

Now, the darkness descended suddenly and completely, the last fighters and bombers had landed about one hour before sunset, so that the fitters etc. could prepare them for first light.

In the west, the sky blazed with gun flashes and bomb bursts, as the night bombers took over from the day bombers. There was no rest for the soldiers of both sides, they hammered away at each other, whether it was night or day.

Sooner or later, one side or the other will become exhausted or run out of ammunition. My God! what must if be like for them!

If only we could get some proper news. Are we really winning or are we going to have to pull back across the Suez Canal? Of course, we got no newspapers or radio news in the desert, only rumours passed from man to man as we stood in groups, watching the western sky-line erupt in sheets of fire.

Chapter 2

The morning of the fourth day

At this time I had been in the Middle East for about twenty months, and most of that time I had been eating and living rough in the desert. About four months ago I began to reap the effects in the form of desert sores and constipation. The so-called desert sores were festering after any kind of cut or knock, and we got plenty of those; they took months to heal, which meant I constantly had bandages on either my hands or legs.

The constipation in my case was due to the lack of fruit and vegetables, I had always needed plenty of those. The result was haemorrhoids. I had suffered in silence long enough, now I was very concerned because I knew they were getting worse, and if we did have to start on the chase up the desert, I also knew that the further we got from the base hospitals, the more primitive the field hospitals became. So my mind was made up, I would report sick the next morning and see if any ointment or medicine would help me.

The morning of the fourth day found me in a queue of airmen outside the camp medical tent. An orderly was stood in the doorway of the tent, busy dishing out aspirin in water or No. 9 pills, with the usual blarney thrown in. "Where is the Medical Officer?" I said, when my turn came. That request immediately had the wrong effect, producing a hard-boiled look on the orderly's face. "The M.O. is not available" he snapped back, and in the next breath, "What is wrong with you?". I told him what was wrong and how long I had been suffering. Embarrassment now flushed my face as I expected him to say, 'drop your shorts and let me see'. But no! He just said "I suppose you want me to give you some cotton wool and ointment". I said "yes, anything which may help". "We have none", he barked, "you will have to go to the Army field hospital, over there". He pointed to a group of tents which appeared to be about six miles away on the distant horizon. "You will have to walk" he snapped, answering the question which was still forming in my mind. I turned away, disgusted at his manner, moving off in the indicated direction before I lost my temper.

The first fifteen bombers of the South African airforce were already running up their engines at the far end of the runway, ready to start the first bombing raid of the day. The next fifteen would take off thirty minutes later and so it would go on all day, as it had done so for months. About thirty fighters had already taken off at first light and others were warming up on the edge of the runway, waiting their turn. I had to walk round the end of the airfield and could now see that I was going to be caught in the man-made sand storm when the bombers began to roll, so I increased the pace and with it the discomfort.

I had got about three quarters of the way past the end of the airfield, when the thirty engines opened up and blotted out the sun with stinging sand. All I could do was crouch down and clamp my handkerchief to my nose, and wait with my eyes screwed up tightly. It took about ten minutes before the cloud of dust dispersed sufficiently for me to see where to walk.

I must have been walking for over an hour, the sun was mounting higher and I had left my hat and water bottle behind in my tent, not expecting to be away for very long. Now, I could see it was going to take me till nearly midday to get to the hospital tents, as gradually the pace became slower as the sun rose higher. The weather was still hot during the midday periods, but it cooled off rapidly at sundown. No! I do not think I will get sunstroke at this time of the year.

I stopped for a rest and a cig, cursing myself for not bringing my water bottle. Now, I was trying to calculate the time by the regular take-off of the bombers. Was it four or five groups which had shattered the peace and stirred up the sand as they took off in line abreast? Get going again, it must be only another two or three miles by now, but distance was very deceptive in the harsh desert.

I looked again at the groups of marquees dancing in the heat haze and could now make out the huge red crosses painted on the side. But what is going on! There are only four, I am sure I saw five not long ago, and as I watched, another began to sink slowly to the ground. My God! They are pulling them down ready to move, have the soldiers broke through at El Alamein?

I tried to quicken the pace, but the weariness and discomfort would not let me, and by the time I was within half a mile, there was only one tent still standing. A battered Army truck stood nearby, half loaded, whilst two men sat at a bare table in the door-way of the tent. They looked up and watched me cover the last hundred yards, as they sat drinking mugs of tea and smoking. At last, I stood in front of them, my eyes searching the shoulder straps for the badges of rank, there was none, so I did not salute.

"What can we do for you soldier?" One of them said. I explained my situation, adding I was R.A.F. as I looked longingly at the half empty tea mugs. One of the medical orderly's produced a folding canvas chair and invited me to sit down. I thanked him, and the other orderly said, "We are moving up right after dinner, the enemy is falling back". I was pleased to hear the good news, then he said, "We will have a look at you in a few minutes, we cannot pull this last tent down until he has gone". He indicated towards a man in the far corner of the tent on a stretcher "He is an Arab, stood on a mine!"

The information was given crisply in a matter of fact way, and I realised that I was in the presence of another hard-boiled one. I left them to finish their tea and cigarettes as I went over to the Arab on the stretcher. I wanted to speak words of comfort, but what could I say, the only Arabic phrases I knew at that time, were - 'hurry up, do this or that', 'come here', 'you are beautiful' or 'go away'. My shadow, cast by a hissing lamp hanging from the tent roof, aroused him from his agony as I approached. His jet black eyes were hostile, mixed with pain and fear, so I moved slowly forward and whispered "Sa i i da", as I ran my hand over his steaming forehead. Slowly the hostility and fear disappeared from his eyes, but the agony remained, as he struggled to return my greeting. He was obviously a Bedouin, as tough as nails, but his legs and stomach were no match for an anti-personnel mine. Slowly he spoke in Arabic, gasping each word out. I could only understand one or two words, he was asking for water. Quickly I went to do his bidding and returned with one of the soldiers mugs full of water. The Arab's eyes showed his thanks as I held the mug to his lips.

"Come on, we will have a look at you now", one of the orderlies was saying, so I left the Arab with a last farewell, and walked up to the table. "Take your clothes off and get onto the table". I thought, my God! what have I let myself in for! As I undressed, the soldier said, "that was a waste of time giving him water, he will be dead within the hour." You can leave your boots on, was the next request; minutes later, I lay on the table feeling very embarrassed. "Yes! we will have to do a bit of cutting there," he said! "What about some kind of ointment?" I replied, hopefully! "No! it's no good, he snapped back.

Meanwhile, the other man had got a small bowl of water and a towel. "Here! stand up and wash yourself." I stood in the doorway of the tent, next to the wooden table and washed myself, thinking, shall I say no! and look a fool in front of these soldiers. "Are you ready?" the other soldier said. "Yes! I am ready", I replied.

My mind was made up as I got back onto the table, saying a silent prayer to the Great Spirit, as a mask was placed over my nose and mouth. One soldier was saying, "Breathe deep", as I drifted down into the valley of shadows. My sense of hearing seemed to be the last of my senses to succumb, but I could still think, my thoughts racing in a jumble, as unfamiliar voices babbled in the mists. Shall I snatch the mask off now! Hope they don't start cutting yet, I am still conscious, then the blackness swallowed me up.

Someone was shaking me by my shoulder and I could hear a cup rattling on a saucer, I must be on leave and my mother is bringing me a cup of tea in bed. I stared up at the roof of the tent, billowing in the breeze, a soldier was kneeling down at my side helping me to sit up, as the cup clattered in his free hand.

Slowly, it all came back, I was on a stretcher on the sandy floor of this huge empty tent. "Drink this," he said, "and have a fag, then you will have to go." I murmured "thanks" in a dreamy kind of way, I was going to say more, but a sudden stab of pain shut me up. He stuffed a lit cigarette in my mouth and handed me the cup and saucer which now danced in my hand, then he was gone to continue packing.

I noticed that I was fully dressed and bandaged up under my shorts. The next moment, one side of the tent walls were untied and rolled up, to disappear into the waiting truck. The other stretcher with the Arab, had gone. I drank the tea and finished the cigarette in stunned silence, as the desert breeze wafted a cloud of sand into my face. Perhaps, they are going to send me to a proper base hospital to recover, I thought, and an ambulance will be here soon.

Another wall of the tent disappeared into the truck, then the soldier came across to me. "Can you stand up now?" I thought, you must be joking, but he was already lifting me onto my feet. I felt weak and unsteady, but said, "I was O.K." because his stale sweat was reaking in my nostrils and I already felt like vomiting. He held me up and I shuffled my legs, as he steered me towards the open door of the tent. "There you are, over there, can you make it?". I whispered, Yes! and thanks for the tea, then I shuffled away before he could see my eyes glazing over. I thought it is all a dream and I will wake up soon, surely this cannot be happening to me.

It took me hours to fumble my way back to the airfield. The sun had already set whilst I was still two or three miles away, but I had got a fix on the setting sun before the camp was swallowed up in the darkness.

At last, I got back to my tent. I had missed both dinner and tea and there was nowhere to go and buy anything, and even if there was a canteen, I had no money, because no one bothered drawing their pay in the desert. I did have my water bottle and cigarettes but I felt terrible and tossed and turned all night long, but the real agony had not even started yet. How I got through the next month, I will never know. I still had to go on parade and carry on my work as an airframe fitter as if nothing was wrong.

Next day, I collected a supply of bandages from the hard-boiled medical orderly, and changed the dressing every second or third day. The dread of going to the toilet became a nightmare, and I soon stopped visiting the communal toilets. I wanted to be alone, far in the desert where I could groan to myself without being heard.

My faith in human kindness and consideration had received a severe blow. The primitive field hospital had shocked me, if it was like that on the edge of the desert, what was it going to be like when we moved up deep into the empty quarters, a thousand miles from nowhere? Henceforth, my pity and compassion would go out to any poor beggar who was taken to the field hospitals. I know the medical people were operating under appalling conditions, but did they have to be so hard-boiled about it?

But, I had learnt another lesson, which was going to be severely tested in the weeks of agony to come. I could not sit down, all day long I was on my feet, whether I was working or eating. Walking was hell, and jolting along on the back of a truck was just as bad. My weight dropped to just over seven stone in a matter of days, but whatever happened, I must guard myself from becoming hard-boiled.

Chapter 3

The Advanced Party

The morning of the fifth day started just like all the other days. A crescendo of noise shattered the silence as ten fighters took off in line abreast before the sun had cleared the distant horizon. Out to the West, the desert was already seething and boiling into an inferno, a killing ground for mad-men and those who survived of both sides would never be the same again. God! how can anyone stand it any longer!

Minutes later, your eardrums vibrated as a dozen fighter bombers screamed down the runway together. More fighters followed in quick succession, clawing at the air like fiendish vampires out for blood. Then the twin engined bombers of the South Africans, turned the day into a hideous vibrating madness, as fifteen roared down the runway together, blotting out the sun in a swirling dust storm.

Now, there was a bit of peace for about half an hour, and the ground staff could concentrate on repairing damaged aircraft until the first wave of fighters returned. Soon the news spread from the pilots that the enemy were fleeing in disorder, our soldiers are leap-frogging forward and cutting them to pieces.

Hitler, must have tore his hair at the news. "They have disobeyed my orders." But his troops had fought bravely till they ran out of ammunition. Then there were two choices left, either put your hands up, or make a run for it, and if you had no transport and your water bottle was empty, then you would not run far in the desert.

They put their hands up by the hundreds, and then by the thousands. The Italians swarmed out of their holes with their hands up, many had no choice because the Germans took their petrol and trucks, or so the story goes.

But, by the evening we heard that the line still held, although we had moved forward a few miles here and there. So it went on, day and night until the evening of the eleventh day, There was just one hour of daylight left, when a sergeant came bellowing along the row of aircraft which we were repairing.

"There is a meeting outside the cook-house tent in five minutes, so you can knock off now." A surge of excitement swept through us. What is happening, must be something big because we could already see an R.A.F. staff car ploughing through the soft sand towards the cook-house.

Two high ranking officers got out, and we formed a ragged circle round them; we must have looked a right shower, unwashed, unshaven, and no hats or socks on. The senior officer started to talk.

"The 8th Army have broken through the last defences, and the enemy are on the run all along the front. General Montgomery sends his congratulations to all men of the Desert Air Force, for putting up such a good show, and he knows that you will carry on in the same spirit. Back home they are ringing the church bells for the first time since 1939. Keep the enemy on the run, you may be home by Christmas. And good luck."

The officers got back into their staff car and disappeared in a cloud of dust. "You may be home by Christmas," but which one?

An N.C.O. took over. "Right you shower, you should all be on the peg for being improperly dressed, but I am letting you off, you lucky people." He then produced a sheet of paper, answer your names as I call them out, you will be the "Advanced Party" and move up at first light. You are not taking the big tents, from now on you will have the small 'two man' tents, so choose your friends carefully." A ripple of laughter was silenced as he bellowed out the list of names and followed with a smaller list of drivers.

I was not surprised to find my name on the last list, tomorrow I would have to sit down, whether I liked it or not. The N.C.O. still shouted on. "Your new tents will be in the trucks which should arrive very soon." He started to say something else, when his voice was drowned in a sea of noise, as about twenty of our fighters came sweeping in to land.

The fighters landed in groups of four or five at a time, but three of them still circled round at about two thousand feet. Two of them were coughing and spluttering and all three still had their wheels up. "Get going, what are you waiting for?" The N.C.O. bellowed. The duty crew ran for the mobile cranes and salvage trucks. A fire tender and an ambulance were already creeping down the side of the runway.

Suddenly a plume of smoke streamed out from one of the fighters. In seconds it was upside down and diving, as the pilot jettisoned the canopy and kicked himself out. The parachute opened at about five hundred feet - he would live to fight another day.

Meanwhile, the other fighter with engine trouble was approaching for a belly landing. The flaying prop struck first and folded backwards along the fuselage, then the belly ploughed a furrow in the sand for two hundred yards or thereabouts. As the light faded, the last fighter came in ploughing another furrow in the sand. All three pilots were O.K. so within fifteen minutes both aircraft had been moved from the runway and we went for our tea.

Something like that happened nearly every day, but this was a bad day, because ten more fighters never came back at all, so shortly we were going to be very busy looking for them.

As I have already mentioned, there were many other airfields or landing grounds strung along the edge of the Egyptian desert, and I have no doubt that life was very similar for them as it was for us.

I was glad to get to bed that night, I felt weary and in a run down state. How much blood I had lost I do not know, because every time I went to the toilet it opened up the cut and I lost more blood, at the same time the pain sapped my strength.

Next morning on parade after breakfast, the Sergeant continued his interrupted talk. "You, of the 'Advanced Party' especially, be on the look out for booby traps at all times. They could look like a fountain pen, or a flask of tea, even dead bodies are being used to set off mines when they are moved. The enemy have sewn mines everywhere. Many of them are anti-personnel mines and when you step on them you trigger the mine, so that when you move your foot, the thing shoots out of the ground and explodes at a height of about three feet, sending the shrapnel horizontal all round, which can cut you and your pals to pieces at a hundred yards, or more. It is estimated that there are over five hundred thousand mines, not counting booby traps, which roughly means there are about twenty mines for each Army and R.A.F. Truck. So you have been warned, keep to the lanes which the soldiers have cleared through the mine fields."

About one hour later the party of sixty men on four new trucks set off, followed by a mobile crane, mobile workshop, two special salvage trucks, a jeep and caravan for the boss, not forgetting another truck carrying a field kitchen and tins of food with a water bowser in tow. We shouted our goodbyes and set off for the coast road which would, eventually, take us all the way to Tunis. Some of us would never get there, and of those of us who did, only a handful would come back.

I must say more about the cookhouse truck. The information may be useful to anyone who believes in fair play, and may wish to suggest ways and means of implementing a fair system of ration distribution, especially in any advanced party of air-men during war time, and most certainly in an empty place, where it is impossible to scrounge food off the land.

The cookhouse truck was loaded with iron rations, tins of corned beef and large hard square biscuits to break your teeth on later. There were also tins of margarine, jam, bacon, fruit and vegetables, plus tinned milk, sugar, tea, etc. But unless you were very lucky, or friendly with the cook, you would never see the tinned fruit from South Africa.

These things happened when you moved up into the empty places, and unfortunately, other things happened of a like nature so that life became unbearable for the lower ranks, as you will see in due course. This was one of the reasons why I was suffering after the operation, because the tinned fruit was not shared out properly.

Another sore point with the lower ranks, was the special hardship money paid to the officers when they moved up with us into the desert, but our money remained the same!

Now I had to concentrate on driving the three ton truck. I had taught myself to drive in 1941 at Heliopolis, but I had only driven about sixty miles on proper roads, and perhaps forty miles on desert tracks. But it was easy enough to keep my place in the small convoy whilst a friend of mine stood on the passenger seat, swinging the machine gun round which poked through the cab roof. I was glad he was doing that, because I knew he could not see my face, which was screwed up in agony every time the truck bounced over some rough ground.

We had been ploughing our way through the sand for about twenty miles, when my pal suddenly bent down and caught me wincing with pain. He wanted to know how to load the machine gun, but now he stopped and stared. I had been trying to sit on one cheek to ease the pain, and he had seen a patch of blood on my shorts. Quickly and briefly I told him of my predicament, his eyes softened with sympathy. "You should be in hospital" he said.

The compassion and understanding touched me deeply, and I knew that I had found a true pal. I had almost forgot there were people like that around. He had only been out in the Middle East for three months, and was still, at eighteen, three years younger than me. "Can you drive?" I said.

"No, I have only driven a dodgem car on the fair ground!" He answered,

"But I have always wanted to drive a car or truck."

"Watch me closely and I will take over the gun, it is less painful for me to stand up."

He was in full agreement and watched every move, and listened to my comments of what my feet were doing, and why. A few more miles of bouncing and we reached the edge of the coast road. Now I hoped that it would be a bit easier for me, but later, I found out how wrong I was to think such thoughts!

The Redcaps (Military Police) stopped us at the edge of the road. "Stop there, and have your dinner, later we will squeeze you into the line of trucks moving up." He explained that replacement tanks were needed up the road. The chase was on in earnest.

So we all got down to stretch our legs, go to the toilet, and light the petrol fires to brew tea. I took the opportunity to go behind the nearest sand dune to change my bandages and shorts. Then just before the water boiled on the smoky fires, I showed my pal how to fix a pan of ammunition onto the machine gun, and I fired a short burst, which had the Redcaps ducking instinctively.

Yes! I would teach my pal all I knew of how to survive in the desert. I told him, "Never let your water bottle become empty, and always be on the look out for a hole to dive into." I would point out the pole-star, which would guide him to the coast road, if he ever got lost in the desert. Next, we brewed the tea and opened tins of bully beef to eat with the hard biscuits, after banging the biscuits on the sides of the truck to break them into smaller pieces.

The convoy of Army trucks continued to grind past us in an endless line, nose to tail, as we finished our dinner and lounged in the shade, smoking cigs.

Suddenly, the Redcaps shouted for us to get going. As the traffic came to a halt, we began to merge into the line of trucks until we became part of it. They shouted instructions to us. "Don't drive or walk off the road until you are told it is safe to do so."

That was blunt and clear enough, it meant that if we were dive-bombed, we had nowhere to run; we would all have to squirm under the trucks and hope for the best.

Soon the pace dropped to a ten m.p.h. crawl, with constant stopping and starting, which gave me a chance to let my pal have a drive whilst I got a little comfort, standing in the gun position. I had a good view all round, and the gun was loaded ready, but no enemy aircraft came over; they were too busy retreating to other airfields further back.

Just before tea time, the endless convoy began to crawl past an area where there were no mines. In this area were thousands of prisoners lounging about in separate groups. Some were sullen, dispirited or bomb happy, whilst others were laughing and joking. Still cocky and arrogant, but never-the-less, glad to be out of it. We laughingly gave them the Nazi salute, like we had done to others the year before.

Another mile or so, and we drove past huge stacks of captured arms, rifles, machine guns, field guns, anti-tank guns, and half tracked personnel carriers, which looked old fashioned but were very useful in the desert. Then we saw the skull and crossbone signs at both sides of the road, which meant we were once more confined to the narrow strip of road flanked by mine fields.

The sun was sinking fast now in the west, and the convoy gradually ground to a dusty halt on the road. It was an incredible thought. Here we were in the worlds largest desert, and yet we could only move twenty paces north or south.

The petrol fires were lit between the trucks to get the tea brewing quickly before the darkness drops like a blanket. After tea when all the fires were extinguished, you could go to the toilet on the road, but be careful because you also had to sleep on the road! The nights were getting chilly now and you needed both blankets, even though we slept fully dressed. By about 8.00p.m. most of the talking had stopped, and an almost full moon had risen like a silver ball, flooding the desert with light, so that you felt naked under the trucks.

Everyone was hoping that no enemy aircraft would come over because we were trapped on the road, and dare not run into the desert to disperse. The warm tarmac gradually lost its stored heat, and the breeze sighed through the wheels of the trucks, making us wriggle closer together.

The dawn was cold enough for greatcoats to be worn, and everyone bustled about loading the trucks as we waited for the petrol fires to boil the water for a welcome mug of tea. Breakfast was bully stew and biscuits, which we had to finish off as we drove along, because the convoy had started to move.

Squally rainclouds filled the sky in the west, something we had not seen for eleven months. Behind us, the sun sent out golden shafts of probing light which appeared to prod the rain clouds further westwards, so we did not see any rain that day.

By about ten o'clock, it was hot enough to change back into shorts and shirts, which we quickly accomplished during one of the many stops. It was during one of these stops that we managed to get a bit of news of what was happening at the front.

An Army unit was pulling back for a rest and refit, and when they had to stop, we were shouting questions across the road, the soldiers responded.

"Enemy trucks are going like mad, about thirty miles in front of you. They are driving eight deep in the desert, because the R.A.F. have cut the road for miles, but our tanks are bogged down in a sea of mud. It's raining like hell up there!"

So the enemy were getting away and no doubt digging in here and there to try to hold up the advancing whirlwind.

My pal was still driving as the convoy crept forward once more, and I was standing at the machine gun position. Now I could see the soldiers sweeping the edge of the road with cumbersome metal detectors, whilst Indians carefully lifted an assortment of mines and stacked them in huge dumps at the edge of the road.

On our left and right, as far as I could see, were massive tangles of barbed wire twisted into knots where shells or bombs had landed, and here and there were shattered tanks with dead bodies all around. The horrible smell suddenly made your nostrils twitch in protest and the ghastly sights assaulted your eyes, searing into your mind, to be pigeonholed for future nightmares.

Now the convoy stopped again, and the sights made your blood run cold. We were in the midst of an area where a ferocious battle had taken place. All around us were the shattered remains of our own, and the enemies tanks, guns, trucks, many still burning, and perhaps, fifteen enemy tanks in twisted heaps. Whilst here and there the remains of smashed Stukas and R.A.F. aircraft littered the ground in grotesque jumbles.

The carnage was indescribable. There were areas of desert so littered with debris of all kinds that you could not see the sand. My God! how they must have fought and suffered here, what agony could the bloated corpses tell you if they could only speak!

On the right-hand side of the road, where the blue Mediterranean gently lapped against the sand dunes, the burial parties were busy. I could see they were Australians going about their gruesome task. Whilst on the left, the scavenger birds were waxing fat on the easy pickings. Many were so loaded, they could not take off when we threw stones at them, they just flapped about with a satisfied gleam in their eyes. Now they would have to wait for nature to do its work, before they could catch the last thermals back to their roosting places in the minarets of Alexandria or Cairo.

At last, the convoy began to move again at about 10 m.p.h. What we had just seen was obviously only a fraction of the front line, which had extended about thirty miles to the Qattara depression in the south.

For the next few miles we drove past hundreds of knocked out trucks, armoured cars, field guns, self propelled guns, and shattered tanks, just about everything was there. Now it became obvious that thousands of enemy soldiers must have been running on foot, desperately trying to get away from the advancing tidal wave of death. First they had discarded their packs and webbing equipment all over the place, then their bandoleers of ammunition and gas masks were strewn everywhere. Finally, their tin hats and rifles littered the ground along with the dead and wounded begging for water and help.

At last we came to a safe area, where we could pull off the road and have our dinner. Later, we went scouting around for souvenirs. I picked up a German helmet and mauser rifle in beautiful condition, but what was the use, I already had my own rifle and tin hat, plus all the rest of my stuff to look after. Other chaps came back with iron crosses, wristlet watches, and God knows what!

Part of the 51st Highland Division, was resting nearby, and later they began forming up in full regalia, squeezing 'Scotland the Brave' out of their bagpipes, which brought a lump to your throat, even if you were English or Welsh. Their knees showed white under their swaying kilts, proclaiming that they had not been in the Middle East very long.

Suddenly, out of the inferno ahead of us came a convoy of over-loaded ambulances. They lurched and swayed slowly past the pipers who had now gathered together at the edge of the road. It was a sight I shall never forget, because the convoy of ambulances was the largest I had ever seen. Now, it was time for us to get going, and we had just found out that there was very little water left, the trucks had taken much more than normal during the slow crawl. Squeeze back into the endless line of trucks once more, and start the slow crawl westwards. Don't go off the road again, because of mine fields right up to the edge of the crumbling tarmac.

Once more, I was having a reasonable rest standing in the gun position, and my pal was getting plenty of practice stopping and starting as the convoy slowly crept forward. How many miles had we covered I do not know! We had obviously passed the place of destiny, El Alamein, where the desert had been churned up for square miles. It was so littered with carnage that it would have been impossible to walk on the sand for more than two paces.

We must be getting near the first airfield at, El Daba, but now we were carefully squeezing past a long line of enemy trucks, which had been shot up on the road. Some were still smouldering and half full of reeking, bloated corpses.

My God! I never knew that a corpse could swell up to almost twice the size. The uniforms were bursting at the seams.

I lost count of the number of shattered trucks when I had reached fifty five. They completely blocked the road, and our troops had to clear a path through the mine field to get round them.

Once more, we were back on the road crawling slowly forward, when suddenly the hairs on the back of my neck began to prickle. Immediately I recognised the feeling of imminent danger. The warning sign had developed slowly from June 13th 1942. Now I was fully alert, my ears straining above the noise of the grinding convoy.

"There, over the sea," I shouted so that the others could hear me as I swung the machine gun round. Three twin-engined aircraft were coming right at us, in line abreast, skimming over the waves like flying fishes. They must be ME 110's. That meant twelve cannons and six machine guns would rip the convoy to pieces any moment.

For a second the earth stood still as we waited for the attack, but what is happening? Before they opened up on us, they suddenly veered to the west with their engines screaming as they hugged the ground in a frantic swoop.

A shattering noise of aircraft now rent the air. The whole truck vibrated like a living thing as dozens of our fighters swept over the convoy from the east. They were stepped up from three hundred to five thousand feet, sweeping the skies of any enemy aircraft.

We had been very lucky, it must have been one of those coincidences. The ME 110's could have wiped out a dozen trucks in seconds, and then dived back and forth three or four times onto the sitting ducks.

We spent another uncomfortable night sleeping on the road under our trucks, and the next morning we reached the first captured airfield of, El Daba.

Chapter 4

Mutiny

What a sight El Daba was, there were bomb craters all over the place, and the carnage of smashed enemy aircraft was unbelievable. Some of my pals said they had counted sixty wrecks, whilst others said it was eighty or more. We were put to work at once, filling in the bomb craters which the pattern bombers of the S.A.A.F. had made days and weeks before.

Just before sundown we pitched our two-man tents, either near an abandoned slit trench, or, a bomb crater on the airfield edge. Other airmen had unloaded the field kitchen and rigged up a cook-house tent.

The cooks had done well, we had potatoes with our stew, but the water rations were low, so we only had a half mug of tea each. Search parties had been out looking for water, but they came back empty handed, so the situation was becoming desperate.

Round about 8.30p.m. we were all in bed, whilst nearby packs of wild dogs howled and fought amongst themselves as they scratched around for dead bodies. I hoped there were no wounded soldiers lying around. The thought sent an uncontrollable shudder through me as I tried in vain to banish *the horrible memories crowding in. My pigeon holes were overflowing as my pal snored by my side.

Just before dawn the rain came down, and I tossed and turned as I listened to the wind throwing sheets of water onto the sides of the tent.

At first light we were up, as a river of water swept through the tent, soaking our blankets and clothing. Now everyone was busy filling their water bottles from the puddles, and drinking the water by the mugful! Before lunch the sun evaporated all the water in clouds of steam and, in no time, it was as if the rain had never been.

Later, that same day a number of our fighters landed. They were hoping

*See Nightmare Towards The Path

to get ammunition and petrol, but as yet, there was none. The petrol bowsers and ammunition trucks were still struggling to get through, miles away. Everybody wanted priority through the gaps in the mine-fields. We were bogged down by our enormous number of trucks.

The Army needed their petrol, ammunition, water and food, to carry on with the chase and, we wanted the same. So our initial success was slowing us down, the enemy were slipping away and finding time to sow more mines or dig in here and there. On top of that, there were thousands of prisoners milling around, many of them wounded and all wanting our water and food.

Now, we were beginning to lose count of time, it was about the third day at El Daba, when the R.A.F. Regiment arrived. We had heard about this new Regiment being formed months ago, but we had never before met them.

The Regiment was formed to take some of the duties off our shoulders. At last! Someone had woke up to realise that we ground staff could not be repairing aircraft, if we were already busy repairing, or, even making landing strips and then guarding them day and night. We were very pleased to see these new chaps. Now we could go scouting around for our crashed aircraft and bring them back for repair again.

It was getting near to dinner-time, the sun was in the right place, but not overhead at this time of the year, and I felt a bit keyed because we had not been attacked at, El Daba, yet.

As I walked towards our cookhouse tent, I passed a newly made machine gun post which was manned by the R.A.F. Regiment, when it happened! I was rooted to the spot for a moment, as six ME110s suddenly appeared on the western edge of the airfield. They were at about five hundred feet, with bomb doors open as they swept in. The Regiment chaps were already on their bellies in the dust, so I dived onto the twin machine guns which were fully loaded on a tripod. I swung them round and up, cocking them as I did so. My God! I could not miss at this range. The nearest aircraft was already over the middle of the airfield with bombs cascading down. I took aim and squeezed both triggers, within five seconds the guns jammed, so I dived for cover on top of the chaps already there.

The pattern of bombs shook the ground and made more craters to be filled in later. Seconds later, the six aircraft came back from the east, skimming the ground and spewing cannon shells all over the place. I was a bit late for dinner but the tension had gone now and I was wondering if I had hit one of the damn things.

As I ate my dinner in the open, a truck slid by full of wounded airmen going back to look for the nearest field hospital. Poor beggars! I thought of the ordeal they had still to face when they get there!

That same evening, just after sundown, before the moon had risen, we suddenly got the shock of our lives. We did not know that various 8th Army units were dug in all round us until they all opened up together. Every kind of gun was firing away towards the west. What the hell is gong on? The whole sky was lit up all round us for about ten minutes, then it abruptly stopped and someone said. "It's November the 5th." It may have been the 5th of November for all we knew, but I do not think the barrage of gun-fire was to celebrate that, because it was repeated every hour throughout the night.

My pal and I had very little sleep when the first shafts of sunlight woke us up. Normally, we would be up with the sun, but now we just lay there staring at the tent roof, about three feet above our faces. Next moment, we heard a peculiar clicking sound, it was like someone gnashing their teeth. We immediately sat up and moved the kit bags (used as pillows) to reveal a huge tarantula spider. We stood up as one man, lifting the tent out of the ground as we did so and, my pal grabbed his bayonet and chopped up the spider. We had a good laugh as we re-erected the tent.

I had stopped keeping a diary after losing all my kit in the last retreat from Benghazi, and we never saw a newspaper or heard any news because we had no radios. We were cut off from civilization and soon lost all track of time. Weeks merged into months and, exact dates and place names became a jumble, but nothing mattered as long as you survived each day and night. We never knew when it was pay-day, because no one bothered to collect any pay and, we never knew when it was Sunday, because we never saw any ministers of any denomination!

Likewise, the aircraft fitters did not have maps, and you would need many of those things to cover an area so large that the whole of Western Europe and the U.K. could fit in with ease. Later, I did manage to take two very good maps off a dead German soldier, but, of course, the writing was in German. Never-the-less, the maps were helpful and interesting. Many times I was amazed to see the name of a place on the larger map, which I thought would be a small village, only to find later that the place consisted of three date palms and a dried up well. Or, at other times, a magical sounding name turned out to be a five foot out-crop of rock in a flat stoney area, which Wales could have disappeared in.

I was still suffering after my episode in the field hospital, my supply of bandages had run out and all my clothes were blood stained. There was still not enough spare water to wash in, let alone washing clothes, and now the food supplies were running low. But what was much more serious, all the fighters at El Daba, were still grounded, waiting for the petrol and ammunition to get through.

What we did not know and did not find out until months later, that we were not the most Advanced Party of the R.A.F. in the Western Desert.

Some fighter bomber Squadrons had been secretly moved up, deep into the desert, out of sight, but opposite the head of the fleeing enemy convoys. The ground staff with petrol, food and ammunition, had been airlifted into position by R.A.F. transport aircraft. So now, our fighters and fighter bombers were annihilating the enemy transport seven hundred miles in front of us. Then our aircraft disappeared back into the empty quarters, hiding in the vastness of the desert.

After breakfast the next morning, we had a pep talk from one of the new N.C.O's whose proper name and rank I am not revealing. This was the first time I had seen him at close quarters and, I was not amused. Here, was the face of a man whose features were moulded to read - 'Do not trust me, neither expect fair play from me.' You have met them, the type of person who stands on the heads of his fellow men and disregards the rules of common decency to get what he wants.

When the talk was over, we all went about our different jobs, but a peculiar atmosphere was slowly building up. We resented some of this newcomers's remarks, especially those of us who had first formed the Salvage Unit, the year before. But not only that, we were running out of cigarettes as well as food and water.

The shortage of cigarettes did not affect me a great deal, because I had only started smoking the year before to keep the flies away. I was satisfied with the fifty free issues per week which we received whenever we were in the desert. But for those who had been smoking for years found it very distressing, there were no corner shops here. We were cut off, on our own with no beer, women, cinemas, cafes etc.; and now no cigs. On top of that, we were sleeping and eating rough, with sudden extermination shadowing us night and day.

So you can imagine the feeling of those who were really hooked on cigarettes, how they must have felt when their only pleasure was with-held from them and I mean 'with-held!' The cigs were there, in the boss's caravan - cartons of them!

An ugly situation was developing fast and it boiled over on parade for work the next morning. We waited in silence as the various jobs were allocated, and then the N.C.O., the one whose face told all, said, "Go, get on with your work." It was then I got the surprise of my service life, someone had organised a very strong protest.

The circle of airmen around the N.C.O. stood still. My God! This was mutiny whilst on active service. The N.C.O.'s face changed colour, and he barked out. "Get on with your work." But the circle closed tighter around him, hemming him in. He looked from left to right, now visibly shaken and squirming for a way out. "What's the matter with you, have you all gone crackers?" "You can be shot for this."

Some brave person spoke up. "Give us our cig. ration and we will go to work." Now the silence could be felt. What would he do now and what would he say, as he glared at the spokesman, who was now a marked man, so others began to shout. "Give us the cigs. Give us the cigs." until we were all shouting to cover the marked man. Silence again, and then he spoke. "I have not got any!" Then a voice from the rear, out of sight, said, "Your bloody caravan's full of fags.".

The atmosphere was electric, anything could have happened, especially when those at the rear began to squeeze the circle inwards. That was it, he was squirming like a cornered rat now. "All right." He blurted out, "I will dish them out at dinner time." Now the chorus joined in. "Give us the cigs. now or we are not going to work."

We knew he was weakening, but what would the consequences be for us afterwards? We had put our very lives in jeopardy for the sake of a smoke. The circle closed tighter, the inner circle of men were eyeball to eyeball, close enough to 'sock him one.' The situation was very tense, even if he cracked now, we could all be doomed later. Then he spoke. "All right, come to the caravan and you can have your cigs, but you will all work twice as hard to make up for the lost time!"

His empty threats meant nothing, we got our cigs. and just worked normally, wondering what would happen next. The days slid by and nothing happened, I think he was glad to forget about it. But within six months, I was dragged into another mutiny of a far more serious situation, when pistols were pointed at our heads by our fellow men, and neither of these incidents got into the newspapers, as far as I know.

The next day we received orders to move up. The airfield at, El Daba, had been fully operational for some days now and we had eventually heard the good news that British and American forces had made landings at

Casablanca, Oran, and Algiers. We heard that they were going to try and take Tripoli before us, but they had to think again when they met up with some of Rommel's panzers!

Some days later we heard that four hundred ships had sailed from Britain, and about one hundred from America, to make the landings in Morocco. We were all very pleased to hear this good news.

As we moved up, by-passing the next airfield at Fuka, on the coast, we travelled about forty miles inland, hoping there were no mines in our path. We must have advanced one hundred and fifty miles by now, from our starting place near the delta, and any aircraft we picked up as we moved from El Daba, were sent back to Fuka, for the rear party to repair.

Many of the aircraft were not worth salvaging, just a twisted heap of molten metal in the rough shape of a cross, slowly disappearing in the shifting sand. Others had made perfect belly landings, and then the pilots had died of gun shot wounds where they sat. We buried them nearby and marked the graves with twisted propellers, and heaped up rocks to stop the wild dogs digging them up!

Meanwhile, to our right along the coast road, the enemy rear guard were putting up a stubborn resistance to the 8th Army, who constantly chopped off the tails of the fleeing convoys of trucks. Whilst in front of everyone, seven hundred miles west, the R.A.F. wrought havoc to the head of the enemy convoy, who thought they were out of range of air attacks.

We made camp in the open desert, somewhere south-west of Fuka, and I was chosen to go with a party to try and find a Hurricane which had forced landed further south. The information was vary vague. 'Drive south for a hundred and fifty miles, then start searching east and west.' He has been down for two days already, so he would either be dead or a raving lunatic if we found him.

The Hurricane was very important as it was one of the 'Tank Busters' which had been hastily modified to carry a Bofor's gun under each wing, firing armour piercing shells. 'Just bring the wings and guns back if you bring nothing else.' The message said. Eight of us were going right after breakfast the next day and, as usual, we would be taking a mobile crane, salvage truck and a three tonner.

We loaded the three tonner up with a week's ration of food and water, plus gallons of petrol in forty gallon drums. Next morning, we loaded our tool boxes, rifles, blankets and kit, then disappeared into the empty quarters.

We were all glad to get away from the 'task master' for a few days. The three tonner carried a compass, so he lead the way, going south in a straight line. We were already forty miles south of the coast to start with, and by about 9.00a.m. we had left the sand dunes behind. Now we were in a flat stony area, which was so vast the horizon merged with the sky in every direction.

The temperature mounted with every mile we drove south, and I began to wonder how such a place could be formed. It was so flat and so big, and yet every square foot was occupied by about six stones some three inches across and almost of equal size. It was uncanny, we drove for hours in a straight line over the stones, and nowhere were the stones bunched together or thinned out

Eventually, we stopped for a brew of tea, and realised we were in a suffocating furnace of radiating heat which hammered on our heads and glared back from the ground. The whole horizon in every direction shimmered and danced as if it was alive, yet only us and the flies moved. There was no sign of vegetation of any kind, and even the wind stood still, so that the deathly silence made you talk in whispers. I, and some of the others had seen flat stony places before, but this was unreal. Surely, only optical instruments and a swarm of steam rollers could have got this place so level and flat. I picked up a small red-hot stone and then let it drop onto the others, and it sounded like a boulder falling onto a metal plate.

One of the drivers said, "Come on, let's go, if the pilot is still alive, he will be praying for us to find him." So we all piled into the trucks and set off once more, but this time I climbed up into the crane driver's seat, I could get more breeze up there, once we were moving again in a straight line, at about 25 mph. I could also see a lot further and I got some peace from the flies, they had settled on the truck and on the back of my shirt!

I decided to have a cigarette, which burst into light as soon as I focused my magnifying glass on the tip. The driver must have seen me in his mirror, and to my surprise he began to climb out of the cab and make his way along the side of the crane towards me, and asked for a light. The mobile crane kept on going at the same speed, only veering slightly to one side. We exchanged a few words, then he leisurely climbed back into the cab; I knew he must have set the hand throttle before performing his trick.

I was keeping a sharp look out, we must be getting near the hundred and fifty mile mark by now, and I knew exactly what it was like to be on your own, on foot, in the middle of nowhere. It was not long after, when the leading three tonner stopped and the other two trucks pulled up at either side. "This is it" the driver said, "shall we go east or west now?" We soon decided to go east for about fifty miles, the sun would be setting behind us and the view in front would be better.

The flat stony place was exactly the same as before, we saw nothing for another fifty miles due east. Now, it was time to stop and make camp, tomorrow we would drive south for ten miles and then drive west for one hundred miles.

Round the petrol fire after tea, we sat talking and smoking leaving the fire to act as a beacon, just in case the poor fellow was on his hands and knees out there somewhere. No enemy aircraft could creep up on us, we would have heard them miles away, there would be plenty of time to get the fire out and merge into the blackness.

Eventually, the fire died away, and the magic of the twinkling stars focused our attention as we lay back on a cleared patch of sand. Soon, all the talking stopped and the stars appeared to reach down as if they were only a few miles above us. The silence wrapped itself around us, it was as if we had passed through a secret door which lead to a time when the earth was young and only we had been created.

After a hasty slipshod breakfast, we all piled into the trucks and the three tonner with the compass, lead the way south for about ten miles, then in a straight line due west. Everyone kept a good look out, occasionally talking or lighting cigarettes as we drove hour after hour. At last, we stopped for dinner. The drivers checked their trucks for water and petrol etc. whilst the rest of us made the petrol fire and warmed the bully stew. Now, get into the shade under the trucks, but keep away from the tyres because they were like balls of fire.

This was the worst part of the day to stop, the heat hit you in sickly waves, radiating from the ground, whilst above, the sky looked like molten lead, heavy and oppressive. In fact, the source of all life pressed you into the ground and you knew it was now a killer.

The rest of the day and all the next day, we drove up and down in the frying pan, but there was nothing but the leaden sky and stony ground. We could do no more, we had to get out whilst we still had enough petrol and water left to reach our camp. It must have been about the fifth day when we got back to report that we could not find the hurricane. The whole Advanced Party of the Salvage Unit were waiting for us to return, before we all moved up another seventy miles, or so.

All the next day, we churned our way through soft sand dotted with small dunes. We were still about forty miles from the coast, going more or less parallel to it. My pal was driving one of the trucks and he was doing very well, learning fast, except for clashing the gears now and then.

Suddenly, we came upon two huge, three engined Italian bombers, which had crashed landed on very rough ground. One was on its nose, the burnt out skeleton looking like some prehistoric monster bleaching in the sun. The other was torn in half, upside down, whilst swarms of flies indicated the position of the trapped crew who would not be going anywhere.

Another twenty miles and we had to turn north to avoid some very rough ground, consisting of rocky outcrops and dry river beds, which may have held water from time to time. Later that day we made camp, just south of Mersa Matruh. This was one of the places where the British rear guard had made a stand for a few days in June or July, 1942, so that the rest of us could flee to the safety of El Alamein.

Chapter 5

Kilroy was here

We made camp near Mersa Matruh, for a few days. Here, we managed to wash our clothes in buckets of petrol which we collected from our smashed aircraft. Water was too precious at the moment and the petrol killed off all the lice, bugs and fleas in fine style.

At last, I was beginning to feel a little better, the pain was not quite as bad and I was eating more, but I still felt only half alive and was longing for just one day's rest. But there was no chance of a rest for us at the moment, the chase must go on. We did manage to get some news from a passing Army convoy, which had just come from the delta, and they told us that the coast road was packed solid all the way back to Alexandria, about two hundred miles away.

The enemy had lost over fifty thousand men with the dead and prisoners, not counting the wounded who were still being found dazed and shattered.

But, the 8th Army had lost over five hundred tanks in the first fortnight, they had been shot to pieces as they battered their way through the mine fields and defences.

Whilst the R.A.F. had already lost over two hundred aircraft, mostly fighters and fighter bombers, since the battle started. Now, in front of us up the coast road, a strong enemy rear guard were putting up a stiff resistance, trading their lives for time.

They were fighting like fanatical madmen, because a hundred miles farther west at the deadly *Halfaya Pass, a huge bottleneck of trucks was forming. Thousands of trucks were bunching together, waiting their turn to grind their way round the hairpin bends of the Pass, and the queue stretched back for forty miles, as the Desert Airforce took a terrible toll of them.

We moved up the next day deep in the desert, by-passing Halfaya Pass, and travelling eighty miles inland with a massive convoy of Army trucks,

*Hellfire Pass, as we called it

driving four deep, creating a blinding sandstorm.

For two days we drove in this huge convoy of trucks. The soldiers were going to seal the road behind another fanatical rear guard at Bardia. It was very tough going where we were, the sand was finer than flour and many trucks were floundering up to their axles. When we got out to push, our feet disappeared below the surface and each step created a billowing cloud of dust which clung to everything. Everyone had wrapped handkerchiefs round their mouth and nose, and most of use wore anti-gas goggles to protect our eyes; so that we all looked like bandits or workers who had worked all day in a flour mill.

Now the four-lane convoy was being funnelled into a marked corridor through a minefield, so the pace dropped to a crawl as the trucks jockeyed themselves into a single line. Ahead, we could see the frontier wire which stretched from the Mediterranean Sea in the north, to the Sudan, fifteen hundred miles to the south. Redcaps shepherded us through a gap which had been cut in the wire fence. In a few minutes we would be back in the Libyan desert. This was no ordinary wire fence, as you will see when I explain what the cross-section was like.

It was composed of barbed wire formed into loops, each loop or circle was approximately three feet in diameter. Now, imagine ten such loops laid side by side like drain pipes, that was the base. Nine more circles were laid on top until you had a pyramid-shape in the cross -section, which was thirty feet high and thirty feet wide at the base. The whole lot was bound together with crisscross barbed wire, so that only a cat could have got through.

Very soon, we came to Fort Capuzzo, an outpost of the Italian Empire, miles from nowhere. There had obviously been a terrible battle here, dozens of corpses were already bleaching in the sun, and the holes blasted in the walls were large enough to drive a tank through. We did not linger long, the place reeked with that nauseating smell which was becoming all too familiar.

Just before we got back onto the coast road, a large section of the Army convoy turned eastwards to attack the fanatical rear guard from their rear, whilst the rest of us sped west to attack and harass the tail of the fleeing Germans and Italians.

Our small convoy stopped for dinner on the edge of the coast road as the airfield at Gambut, about twenty miles to the west, had not yet been captured, so we had to wait for a few more hours. It was quite a nice place to linger, the blue Mediterranean was just in sight over the sand dunes; the dunes themselves were dotted with clumps of camel thorn bushes. It was very pleasant to rest our screwed up eyes on a bit of green and see a group of sparrows darting about to remind you of home.

About two hours later, we were still waiting for news regarding the fighting up the road, and I was trying to foresee what may happen if the enemy rear guard behind us, suddenly broke out to make a running fight right through our position. My mind was working overtime, I could just imagine an armoured column of desperate fanatics brushing us aside in a fighting retreat.

Fortunately, nothing happened, the rear guard were encircled, but they managed to hold out for a few more days before they were compelled to give in, or be wiped out.

Suddenly, lurching towards us came three captured Italian trucks full of German and Italian prisoners who were singing 'Lily Marlene,' but to our surprise in each cab were two or three girls alongside the British drivers. They stopped to ask us if the coast road was clear. We all gathered round staring at the girls with unbelieving eyes, and explained to the drivers that they would have to take the desert track inland because the coast road was still blocked. It was only when they had gone that I found out the girls were ladies of the oldest profession who had been doing 'their bit' for the fatherland, just behind the lines.

Eventually, an Army dispatch-rider on a Norton, came to tell us we could now move up to Gambut; so about one hour later, just as we were approaching, a swarm of Hurricanes, Kittyhawks and Spitfires, beat us to the landing ground. We had advanced about four hundred miles by now, but probably clocked up two thousand with all the diversions to bring in crashed aircraft.

We, of the Advanced Party of the Salvage Unit, had already salvaged about thirty-five of our fighters since the El Alamein battle and, no doubt, the rear party had done the same. But that figure would reach two thousand plus between us before we got to Tunis, and those would be all fighters; so it gives you some idea of what was going on in the waste lands. Then if you count the one thousand plus we salvaged on our last trip to Benghazi, and the fact, both then and now, we never found them all, nor bothered with many which were almost unrecognisable. What amazed me, was the small number of multi-engined bombers we found, I can only remember seeing about sixteen wrecks, the rest must have limped back to base on one or more engines.

The next day an R.A.F. transport aircraft landed at Gambut, it had brought about a dozen replacement fitters for us. They were all new to life in the desert, but one of them had a most unusual story to tell.

He had been in Turkey, for the past twelve months, along with many more

R.A.F. ground staff, all in civilian clothes, but with no aircraft. Turkey, had remained neutral and each side had tried to persuade them to join their side, so the German Luftwaffa were there, also in civilian clothes, but with no aircraft. The R.A.F. chap said. "That at night time both sides met each other in the bars, but they all had to act like tourists, because of Turkey's neutrality."

Gambut, was familiar to many of us and we soon found our old dug-outs or holes in the ground. It was about this time, mid-November, 1942, we heard that the British and Americans in Algeria, had got within two hundred miles of Tunis, and it certainly looked as if they were going to get there, and then on to Tripoli, before us, as we had about one thousand six hundred miles to go to Tunis.

We stopped at Gambut, for about a week, salvaging our fighters and patching them up as best we could, then we had to move up again.

Tobruk and Gazel, had already fallen to the 8th Army, who were, even now, at the gates of Benghazi.

Tobruk, was a battered looking place, it had certainly received some hammering. There was hardly a building which had not got a shell hole through the walls, or, a bomb through the roof. I was surprised at the carnage in the harbour, there must have been at least, ten ships with just the funnels showing. In the bay nearby, were three German troop-carrying gliders, slowly breaking up where they had landed.

We did not stay long in Tobruk, our objective was a landing strip near Gazala, which we reached just before sundown.

We stopped at Gazala, for a few days, then it was down with the tents and load the trucks, and move up towards Benghazi, which had now changed hands for the fifth time. We followed the coast about forty miles inland, making our own tracks through very difficult country. The flat desert was to the south of us, whilst we were in very rough hilly country, and soon we got fed up repairing the track and re-building makeshift bridges across dry river beds.

Progress was very slow, we were lucky to do thirty miles in a day, and we were exhausted carrying boulders and any rubbish to repair the rough track. The task master drove us like slaves, and many of us thought 'why does he not let some other group take the lead for a while, to give us a rest'. We realised this was revenge for daring to demand our cigarette ration, a few weeks back.

I noticed some Roman ruins surrounded by olive trees not far away, but we had no chance to go and look at them. Dotted around were Italian villas and farmhouses surrounded with date palms and other tropical plants, where birds flitted about and sang their love songs, which to our weary eyes and ears was paradise.

At last, we reached Benghazi, or, what was left of it. Our small convoy stopped near the shattered Cathedral, and on a ruined wall nearby, some twelve month's ago, a British soldier had written - "We will be back!" whilst underneath, a message said that 'Kilroy was here!' We could not linger very long, especially when crowds of starving civilians surrounded us to beg for food.

About one hundred miles to the south, was an airfield at Agedabia, which had just changed hands; this was our next destination, so we moved off along the coast road leaving the hills and bits of green behind us. The next day we reached the airfield and I had not seen any town or village, just a huge airfield carved out of the desert.

At this time, the front line was about seventy miles away at El Agheila, here, the enemy were putting up a very stiff resistance, as his reinforcements flowed in from Tripoli. Behind us on the coast at Barce, about one hundred and fifty miles to our rear, another strong rear guard were fighting to the last. Within a few days the airfield was crowded with fighter squadrons, including the one American group, which again was opposite to us across the runway. Agedabia, had suddenly become a prime target, so we dug in deep and mounted all our machine guns in pits.

The next day, to everyone's surprise, an R.A.F. transport aircraft landed, and out got four nurses. All work stopped, we could not believe our eyes as we stood around the perimeter transfixed to the spot. There they were in crisp white uniforms, an unbelievable sight, which made us feel very conscious of our unwashed, tramp-like appearance. A large staff car materialised from no where and they were quickly whisked away. The rumours said they were going to a hospital in Benghazi, to try to help the thousands of wounded of both sides, who were suffering terrible hardship.

It was after we had been at Agedabia, about three days, when we got up one morning to find the whole area covered by thick low cloud. Today, I would see something I would never expect to see, as the cloud was unusual to all of us who had been in the Middle East for some time; it hung like a blanket about three hundred feet up, and probably was a few hundred feet thick. There was no flying from our airfield that day, so everyone was busy tuning up the fighters or repairing them.

Suddenly we could hear a dog-fight going on above us, screaming engines and burst of machine-gun and cannon-fire filled the air above the cloud. Then, to everyone's surprise, a large twin-engined German bomber suddenly burst through the cloud, right over the airfield. He was only about fifty feet up and smoke was coming from one engine, everyone opened up with machine-guns and rifles, and I could see more holes appearing in the fuselage. Now, flames were pouring out of the one engine as he made a forced landing at the end of the runway. I saw two or three airmen scramble out, rolling in the sand to put out the flames which covered their flying suits, when it happened!

I just could not believe it, two Spitfires dived through the cloud and shot them up where they lay. But, of course, I must not pass judgment on my view of the last act in the drama, who knows! The bomber crew may have shot a Spitfire pilot off the end of his parachute, perhaps, minutes before!

The German bomber was now a blazing inferno, the ammunition exploding in all directions like a display of fireworks. An American and R.A.F. truck rushed round the airfield to try and rescue any survivors. But whether they managed it, I do not know, because I was suddenly ordered to go with a Salvage Party to try and find a Spitfire which had been shot down somewhere out in the desert.

We returned with the Spitfire the next day, and now we listened to the stories of a terrific air attack which had been mounted on the airfield whilst we were away. An R.A.F. field hospital had also arrived and set up their tents a few miles away from the airfield. It was already full of wounded airmen after the raid.

Everyone was busy digging deeper holes to sleep in, and moving further away from the edge of the airfield. My own two-man tent had disappeared, but my pal had been safe with me. Now, we rummaged round trying to salvage some of our belongings, then we went looking for a better hole three hundred yards away from dispersed aircraft on the edge of the airfield.

We found a suitable slit trench, but it was only about two feet deep, and when we tried to dig it deeper, we struck solid rock. From past experience, I knew it was not deep enough for safety, so we scrounged around for sand bags, then, after much sweating and filling sand bags, we built a wall of bags round the hole and then rigged up part of an Italian tent over the top. Now, we hoped to be comparatively safe and dry if it rained.

About three hundred yards away were two Hawker Hart biplanes and a Lysander of the Communication Squadron, and the very next day I was put to work on one of the biplanes. Some pieces of shrapnel had gone right through the fabric of the lower wing without causing any internal damage. I had almost finished the repair, when a Sergeant pilot came to check it over and take the aircraft up on a test flight.

The chance of a flight was irresistible, so I asked him if he would take me with him. He readily agreed and, although I had no parachute, I eagerly climbed into the open cockpit of the rear gunner's position. It had been quite a few months since I had had a flight of any kind, and now I could feel the excitement rushing through my veins as we roared down the runway. This was real flying, with the familiar smells from a hot engine, rushing past my face as the wires and struts sang in my ears.

It reminded me of R.A.F. Cranwell, where I often flew in Hawker Harts, and Avro Tutors before the war, except that now there was no patchwork quilt of green below us, only the burning desert shimmering in the noonday sun. The pilot threw the aircraft around the sky, and I suddenly realised that we were a sitting duck for any ME 109 which may be scouting around as there were no machine guns on our aircraft.

Next moment, the pilot turned his head, and waved one arm to attract my attention; now he was pointing to the air speed indicator which was stuck at zero. I knew what that meant, a tricky landing for the pilot as we came in, trying to judge what speed we were doing as he touched down. If we came in too fast, we could sheer the undercarriage off, or run out of runway. On the other hand, too slow in the approach and we could get into a fatal stall and dive into the ground.

I quickly checked that I was properly strapped in and braced myself for a heavy landing, or worse. Fortunately, we got down safely, after a very fast approach and a couple of heavy bumps to the undercarriage. Later, the aircraft was checked over for any damage, and the airspeed indicator was replaced.

After tea that same day, we all eventually left the cookhouse tent, and made our way to our various holes in the ground as the sun dipped below the horizon. It must have been about midnight when I was suddenly made wide awake by the rocky ground vibrating beneath me. The thud of heavy bombs blasted through the air, at the same time, the flash enabled me to see easily through my tented structure.

I got up quickly, and once outside I could see the hospital tents on fire and people running to and fro. One or more large bombers were circling over the airfield, and now that the whole place was lit up, they came lower, machine-gunning everything. Seconds later, a petrol bowser which was dispersed with the two bi planes and the Lysander, about three hundred yards away, blew up, sending rivers of blazing petrol towards the aircraft.

My pal and I, and a number of other airmen, ran to push the aircraft out of the way before they went up in the blaze. We only managed to save one of them, the others disappeared in balls of fire thirty yards away. Now, it was like daylight, and with the machine-guns turned on us, we could see the tracers squirting at us like deadly hosepipes of spitting lead as we dived for cover, clawing at the ground to try and bury ourselves in the sand. I thought it was the end for me as I dug at the ground with my bare hands, but now they had passed over to circle round again. We all ran for better cover not knowing that we were running into the path of the next shower of screaming bombs.

My pal and I, got to our shelter and dived right in, only to land, unexpectedly, on four or five airmen who had got there before us. So instead of us being below ground level, we were above it, as a shower of bombs came whistling down.

The screaming shrapnel and jagged rocks tore through the sand bags, and a red-hot piece of metal twanged onto my backside and stuck there sizzling, until I clawed it away. Moments later, a lone Hurricane night-fighter screamed overhead, with its eight machine-guns blasting away, like a demon out of hell.

There was no more sleep that night for us, we were too busy counting the cost in burnt-out aircraft, trucks and tents. How many wounded airmen had been burnt to death in the hospital tents, I never found out, no one bothered to go and see. My God! Were we all becoming hard-boiled now?

At dawn, we had the roll call, and miraculously, no one was missing on the Salvage Unit this time. We had been very lucky, and I was not surprised to see that the nearest bomb crater to our slit-trench was less than ten feet away. The rocks had been gouged out to a depth of about five feet, so we moved our kit into the hole and rigged up what was left of the tent over the top.

At tea time that same day, I noticed some of my friends were absent, but they turned up later well pleased with themselves. They had made friends with some of the American fitters who had invited them to their mess, then they said, "We actually sat down on chairs at a table and had a damn good meal, but wait for it, we finished the meal with fruit and ice-cream." Now, they dished out queer smelling cigarettes and were full of praise for the Yanks. Ice-cream in the desert, we had never heard of it before, and chairs and tables in the mess, My God! we were behind the times.

Chapter 6

Court Martial

We were still at Agedabia, but where our rear party were, I had no Idea. The bitter fighting in El Agheila, was still holding up any further advance. Remember, it was here, about twelve months before that Rommel and his panzers turned at bay and thrashed us all the way back to El Alamein.

The 8th Army were getting bogged down and waiting for their supplies to catch up, which were being dragged through the desert for about one thousand, two hundred miles. But whereas, certain Army units were pulled out of the thick of it every few days to rest and refit, we never got any rest! You would have thought that our rear party would have taken over for a few days and go in front of us to give us a break, but it never happened. So we were becoming fed up with constant air attacks, lack of both water and proper food, plus no rest days.

At last, the mail arrived to save our sanity. Most of us received about ten letters each, but the news from home was already four months old, therefore anything could have happened to our families since they wrote the letters. One chap suddenly mentioned that it would be Christmas in ten days and, of course, there was no sign of any snow. A few days later we prepared to move up once more as we would be by-passing the fighting at El Agheila, by going deep into the desert.

After breakfast the next day we moved westwards, and some joker said, "Every mile west is a mile nearer home." But soon we turned south into the empty quarters. Here, no birds sang, nor was there any sign of green, as the trackless desert swallowed us up. We ploughed through the shifting sand for hours, our small convoy of about eight trucks and a mobile crane all hoping that the driver in the first truck knew where he was leading us.

Eventually, we must have been over one hundred miles south of the Gulf of Sirte, and we still could not turn west because of impassable stretches of soft sand. It was then we saw something very puzzling, we drove past a huge pool of oil, as large as a village duck pond. Everyone thought it must have been an underground oil dump that had been bombed. It was years later that I realised we must have seen natural oil seeping up through the sand.

Finally, we got back onto the coast road after a detour of two hundred and fifty miles, or thereabouts. Then we had another unusual experience, one of our trucks came back to camp one day with a live pig in the back. What a nice surprise for us because it would be Christmas in two days time. The cooks soon got busy on the pig, and I must say, I had my best Christmas dinner for many years, and everyone had a good laugh when the boss found the pig's tail nailed to his caravan door!

It was round about New Year's Day 1943 that we eventually got to an airfield which had been christened 'Marble Arch', as nearby was this huge arch, built across the road by the Italians. We were now in Tripolitania, and what money we had, had to be changed into Liras, although there would be no chance to spend it until Tripoli was captured.

Marble Arch airfield had been well and truly sown with mines, someone had ploughed it up and sown anti-personnel mines like seed potatoes. Almost every day a luckless airman trod on a mine with devastating results, because they were also sown at the perimeter where we had our tents.

Two or three days later, after the landing ground had been cleared of mines and rolled flat again, the fighter squadrons began to land. Later, the same day, half a dozen C47 Dakotas of R.A.F. Transport Command, began to arrive; they brought all kinds of goods as well as ground staff for the fighter squadrons.

The twin-engined Dakotas, parked into wind, at the end of the runway just in front of us. We were in a very dangerous position, it meant that any aircraft taking off, were only a hundred feet up when they passed overhead. It appeared to me that the Dakotas could not park anywhere else, and we could not move to a better place because all the mines had not yet been found. So the scene was set for us and it only needed destiny to say when.

I remember working in the open on a bench, behind me were the two-man sleeping tents and a larger cookhouse tent, whilst in front was the end of the runway. Every few minutes four or five fighters would charge down the runway together and skim over our heads. Then it had to happen, the next group of fighters screamed towards us and, at ten feet up the undercarriages were folding into the wings, when suddenly, the centre one began to cough and splutter. He sank towards the ground, chopped off the tail of a Dakota, ran up its back, chopping the fuselage up as it did so, then bouncing off the top, it came right for us. The three bladed metal propeller had now become three bent scimitars thrashing the air and shaking the aircraft to pieces. I was already flat on my face as it missed the bench by inches, then flattened the cookhouse tent and spun to a hissing stop between two more tents. In less than five seconds, the dazed pilot was dragged out of the cockpit as other airmen came running with fire extinguishers which were not needed.

A few days later it was time for us to move up, it must have been mid-January and we were all glad to get away from our dangerous position. We had heard that the forward troops were already probing the outskirts of Tripoli, as we got to a place called Misurata, on the coast. We made camp in the sand dunes about fifty yards from the Mediterranean sea.

None of us had had a proper wash or changed our clothes for about five weeks, so it was not long before we were dashing into the sea, only to dash out again minutes later. Someone had seen a mine bobbing in the surf! We had just got back to our tents when the thing went off with the loudest bang I had ever heard. The sand dunes saved us from the blast, but the shock wave through the ground lifted us into the air. When we thought we had got away with it, a shower of red hot metal rained down, but luck was still with us, none of us were hit.

Later that day, I was thinking about our lucky escape, to think we had come about one thousand, four hundred miles up the desert to this particular spot, and if we had been a couple of minutes later, the mine may have gone off as we approached the waters edge. I was thinking back in time off all the other lucky escapes I had had. It was then I realised that I had just had my 22nd birthday about seven days back, it had slipped by with New Years Day also, and I never knew.

As the 8th Army closed on Tripoli, my run of good luck changed for the worst, I knew it was partly my own fault, but I was getting fed up, the war was going on too long and I had been in the R.A.F. since 1938. But one particular N.C.O. was making my life miserable for some reason, only he knew. He had ordered me to clean out the latrine buckets twice in one week, a thankless job which normally only came round about once every two months.

When he told me to do it again a few days later, I said, "No It's not my turn!" I found myself on a Court Martial right away. I thought, My God! I have obeyed ten thousand orders in the past, but refuse one because it was unfair and I am for the 'high jump!'

The next day we had to move up, Tripoli had been captured and our destination was the airfield at Castel Benito, about five miles south of Tripoli. My Court Martial could not take place just yet. Two day's later as we entered the airfield, a most unforgettable sight met our gaze. There were abandoned aircraft everywhere, all around the perimeter and in the hangars. I counted about seventy-five bombers and fighters, mostly Italians, but inside one hangar were three German Fiesler Storches, in various states of repair.

Myself and half a dozen other airframe and engine fitters were immediately set to work on the Fiesler Storches. "Get one of them flying as soon as you can." We were told. That was easier said than done, because none of us could read German and the aircraft were most unusual; not only that, we had no idea what was wrong with them.

It must have been about three days later, after we had been on 'pay parade', when I was Court Martialed on the spot! The C.O. appeared sympathetic as he gave me twenty-eight days in the cooler. He said, "You can do fourteen days field punishment on the camp, because the 'glass house' is not ready yet!"

This was a turning point of my life, henceforth I would never volunteer for anything, I would get what I could out of the R.A.F. and keep my mouth shut.

For fourteen days I worked all day on the aircraft and after work I had to tie two blankets round me and run up and down whilst holding a rifle over my head. My webbing equipment had got lost somewhere, so the two blankets replaced my full pack. All my pals had two days leave in Tripoli, but I got none, only more work and more drill!

Two of the Fiesler Storches eventually flew away, one of them going to Montgomery for his personal use, to visit the forward troops. These remarkable aircraft could land and take off between the goal-posts of a football pitch. In the next hangar some Americans were still working on a three-engined Savoia Marchetti, which they eventually flew back to Cairo for a leave period.

Chapter 7

We were manacled together hands and feet

On the thirteenth day of my punishment, the Medical Officer sent for me. He said, "You are going to the cooler tomorrow, strip off and let me check you out." I moved towards his tent to strip off when he stopped me at the door, saying, "Do it here, in the open." A few minutes later he said, "I was fit enough for more punishment." So the next day I had to load all my kit onto a truck and, accompanied by an armed guard, we set off south.

After driving for about two hours, we eventually climbed over a ridge of sand dunes, and there in front of us stood an old Italian Fort, isolated and grim looking. This Fort had only been captured a few days before, and now the Army Redcaps had turned it into a punishment centre.

From the moment I got out of the truck, everything was done 'at a run,' even though I was carrying all my kit! The huge double gates clanged shut, and an armed guard blasted out an order. "Empty both bags on the floor and take all your clothes off." He was not giving me a medical examination, just searching me and my kit, looking for cigarettes and money etc: but he did not find the five pounds worth of liras I had hidden!

Before I had actually gone through the gates, I had noticed that the walls were about 20ft. high, topped with barbed wire, whilst soldiers with rifles patrolled around the walls.

It must have been dinner-time when I arrived, so I was hurried along a concrete corridor inside the walls and given a 6ft by 3ft space on the floor. "This is where you sleep, drop your kit and run into this queue. Keep running on the spot until you get a thick lump of dry bread in one hand, and a tin of water in the other. Now run back to your space on the floor."

My God! what a place this is! I sat on the floor in the middle of some of the toughest looking soldiers I had ever seen. I noticed that the two on either side of me were not looking at me, they were looking at the lump of dry bread in my hand. Next day, I would understand why, but now, as they had guessed, I could not eat all the bread, and as soon as I started to break the lump in half, it was snatched out of my hand.

There were no cigarettes in this place, everyone stopped smoking whether you wanted to or not. We had become zombies or mindless robots almost, but not quite, as you will see later. Next moment, a shrill note on a whistle had everyone on their feet, now busy putting on all their equipment and full packs, whilst I wrapped the two blankets around my shoulders. In a moment we were out in the noon day sun, lining up on a sandy parade ground.

We lined up in three rows, perhaps, two hundred men of assorted regiments with 20% R.A.F. from different squadrons mingled here and there. The next moment a huge Redcap bawled out an order and we divided into four groups with an armed 'task master' for each group. One group collected pick-axes and spades as they had to dig a long trench six foot deep, and then fill it in again! Whilst another group had to carry and run with large boulders and stack them in a corner, then run back with them to their original place!

My group, and the remaining group were drilled at the double, running backwards and forwards until you felt like screaming. When my group ran one way, I was behind an R.A.F. chap, and when we about turned, I was behind a New Zealander, who was old enough to be my father. I felt sorry for him, his hair was already silver, and the next moment he fell flat on his face. The R.A.F. chap behind me, and I, went to drag him into the shade of a wall. But before we could do so, the guard came up and ordered us to leave him and get back in the line!

I was absolutely disgusted with what was happening, the poor fellow was lying in the sun, and if he was not already dead, he would soon have sunstroke!

After a short break we were given the shovels and picks. The picks we did not need, because it was just soft dry sand which slid back into the trench as fast as you dug it out. All the time the guard stood shouting, "Dig, dig faster, I want to see your heads disappear. Right! get out and fill it in now."

Hell! I am glad I have only thirteen days to go, the thought shot through my mind as I lay on the concrete floor after tea. I was exhausted like everyone else, we were too tired to talk until about eight o'clock that night.

There must have been about fifty men in each sector of the walls, but we could not pass from one section to the other, we were locked in, what I can only describe as a concrete tunnel with slits facing outwards, which were too high to see through. There must have been a wooden bench along one side when the place was used as a Fort, then you could stand on it and shoot through the 3" slits.

I moved along the tunnel, towards half a dozen R.A.F. chaps. "What are you in for?" I said. One of them told me they had got twelve years for smuggling captured 'small arms' to the Jews in Palestine. I was amazed, they were all aircrew, and had flown the arms in their bomber from the fighting area back to base, and got caught doing it again.

One of the aircrew was from Dublin, he had volunteered to fight with the R.A.F. but now he was busy doing something with his kneecap, and I am not saying what! When I spoke to him about it, he said, "They are not having me running around like a pack animal any longer." Such was the desperation of many of us!

Later, I spoke to some of the soldiers. One of them told me he had deliberately done something to get away from the front line. "I had had enough," he said, "It's tough going here, but at least you are not being shot at." I could see his point.

At breakfast the next day, I realised why the soldiers had been looking at my crust of bread the day before. After eating my watery porridge and drinking half a mug of weak tea, I was still hungry, even though I weighed less than eight stone. We were all slowly starving. So this was it, they run us off our feet and kept the rations low, someone did say they could not get the rations through to us, but we did not believe them.

All that morning till dinner-time, my group ran about moving the rocks from one place to another, and I never saw the New Zealander again. In the afternoon after our dinner of watery soup, I was separated into a small party of about a dozen. We were double marched, still with our packs on and me with my two blankets, out through the gates to a group of tall trees next to a villa, about half a mile from the Fort.

Some kind of irrigation system was in operation nearby, and signs of cultivation near a group of almond and olive trees, which were watered by a windmill pumping water out of a well. I do not know why we had come out of the Fort, unless it was sympathy of the guard, who now let us stand in the shade of the trees.

A number of soldiers promptly began to reach up to pick the green almonds off the trees and ate them at once, whilst I joined others plucking small tufts of grass and eating it as fast as we could. Then the guard turned round, he had been talking to an Italian man and woman over the fence; immediately, he had us running to and fro as he walked back to the Fort. Later that evening the soldiers who had eaten the green almonds were writhing on the floor in agony. Eventually the guards took them away and I never saw them again, but I did hear that the next day they had been taken to hospital in Tripoli, and once in the city, two of them jumped off the truck and escaped.

It was about the fifth day when I decided to go sick. One of the desert sores on my leg had become inflamed and very painful, I just couldn't run about all day any more, or so I thought. There were about fifteen of us on sick parade but no doctor to see us, so we had to go to a tented hospital on the edge of Tripoli.

In the truck I got the shock of my life, I just could not believe it, we were manacled together, hands and feet. Only one soldier was not chained up, because he was not going to run anywhere, he had put a pick through his foot; I'll leave you to guess whether he had done it accidentally!

It was dinner-time before we reached Tripoli, this was the first time I had ever seen it. For over two weary years, I, with many thousands more, had tried our utmost to get there, and now I arrived in chains!

Tripoli was a shimmering jewel carved out of the harsh desert, an oasis of over two million date palms to rest your eyes on. The truck pulled up in a tented compound, it appeared to be a public park with a busy road cutting it off from the centre of the city. Here, in the park, the grim looking field hospital looked out of place. A harsh command from the armed guard and we climbed off the truck. Now the usual waiting began but not in a waiting room, we stood in the midday sun and waited!

How long does it take for the doctor to have his dinner and then decide he is ready to see us? We waited and swayed, many of us were really ill, but we stood there and waited; at last, he started to see the first one. We stood still chained, hands and feet, and the passing crowd stared in wonder, "Who are these poor chaps, are they British soldiers?" Stop a bit longer and we will see them fall over, one by one!

At last, it was all over, three of the men would remain in the hospital, the rest clasped pieces of paper which said, "Medicine and duty," which meant you carried on as before, and don't argue with the doctor because he is 'hard-boiled.' So we rattled and clanked our way back onto the truck, the crowd of onlookers dispersed, knowing that they would see a similar spectacle the same time tomorrow and the next day, etc.

Finally, we arrived back at the Fort, we had missed dinner and no one even offered us a cup of water as we stood in the sun, waiting. I must not let the anger get me down, I must fight the bitterness gnawing with hunger in my stomach, I must keep my sense of fair play, knowing that kindness and understanding can still be found in some of my fellow men.

Teatime could not arrive quick enough, and now I found myself staring like an animal at the crusts of bread in the newcomers hands. I looked around the concrete tunnel after tea, everyone looked haggard and drawn, except the newcomers who had been squeezed in whilst I was away. Eventually, I crept back to my space with one blanket to lie on and one to cover me. In minutes I was in dreamland, that was the only place you could find happiness, at least, you had a fifty-fifty chance.

The crack of a rifle shot brought me back to reality, two or three more followed quickly. What the hell is going on? Then in the pitch darkness of the tunnel, whispering voices, shuffling steps, creaking, now hurried whispering, all at the far end where the door was. Next moment the lights were switched on, guards shouting and swearing whilst counting heads. No one was missing anywhere, so go back to sleep now, if you can.

Next day, I and everyone else except the guards heard a most amazing story. A number of soldiers had managed to unlock the door of the tunnel, get out of the Fort and past the armed sentries patrolling outside. Now wait for it, you will not believe it, but it is a fact. They then walked through the night to a cross-roads and stopped an army truck, begged, yes! begged them for Army Biscuits and came back with them. But as they climbed the wall to get back in, they were fired on by their fellow soldiers who thought they were trying to escape.

Now remember, I smuggled £5.00 in Italian money in with me, well, I gladly gave it to one of the soldiers for four biscuits. I asked him why they bothered coming back, and he said, "What's the use, you cannot live in the desert, sooner or later you would have to creep into Tripoli, to steal food, and then you would be a thief as well as a deserter, and you know what happens to deserters whilst on active service."

Yes, I understood, I knew the desperation and agony which had driven them to risk their lives for a few biscuits. But I also knew I was talking to a real man, not a zombie. Here, was a man who not only had courage but wisdom also, the sort who wins medals before breakfast. Our conversation was cut short, it was time for more punishment, by this time I thought I had seen everything and nothing would surprise me anymore, but I was wrong, as you will see.

Remember, we were isolated here, no welfare visitors or kindly parsons came to talk to us. You could not write to your M.P., or ask for a lawyer, we were cut off and treated like wild animals in a cage.

Now, we were all lined up in full marching order, but we would not be marching, only running. I was towards the middle of my group of fifty men, but we were still in the larger group of something like two hundred men. Heads were counted, orders to form four separate groups were barked out and no one moved! Again, the orders were shouted, and no one moved. My God! this is mutiny, someone had organised the most dangerous protest any soldier could make. Obviously some bunch of tough nuts had planned it, but I, and many others who had only a few more days to do, knew nothing.

By this time, the Parade Ground was full or armed Red-Caps and a Sergeant Major took over, who was going to stand no nonsense. "Parade, right turn." A cloud of dust rose up as we all turned in perfect order. "Double March," he shouted, and no one moved. Hell! we had gone beyond the point of no return, we were finished and I had only four days to go. "Drag the first three men away," the Sergeant Major bawled out to a bunch of Red-Caps, "Put them in the 'sweat boxes' and you all know what 'sweat boxes' are, don't you!" "Double March," he screamed again, and no one moved. "Drag them three away, about turn," He thought he would try the other end. "Double March," he yelled again after we had all turned, but still no one moved, and three more men were dragged away.

Now, the Commanding Officer came out of his office, looking full of pomp and bluster. The atmosphere was like a simmering volcano, as he ordered the guards to draw their revolvers out and move in menacingly. Then the C.O. began to read the Riot Act, reminding us that we could be shot for mutiny, or, get twenty years if we were lucky. For the next half hour the same procedure went on. A soldier next to me said, "I hope someone starts to run soon, I have only got one day left to do."

Now, the group of men left was getting smaller and smaller. Soon I would be put to the test of loyalty and I did not want to show myself up, and yet, on the other hand, was it worth it. At least thirty men had been dragged away by now, and what was happening to them made me shudder.

Suddenly, the C.O. showed a bit of sense. "What's the matter with you, are you all mad?"

"No! we are starving!" someone shouted back.

"Give us the proper rations and we will do the punishment."

"Give us some cigs: also." someone else blurted out.

Then the C.O. said, "Alright, I will look into the rations and try to increase them, but you don't get any cigs: here." Then it was all over, but they ran us into the ground every day after that. We did get more watery food but they made us suffer for it, and what happened to the thirty men who had been dragged away, I never found out!

At last, the time came for me to say cheerio to the poor beggars I was leaving behind, but the memories would come with me forever. A crowd of us, soldiers and airmen, climbed into the waiting truck. We were all changed men, bitter with the seeds of revenge growing in many of us, which would not be satisfied until someone had paid the price. The 'bastards' how could they treat us like they had.

Chapter 8

'Sabratha' the beautiful

We were taken to a large tented transit camp, just outside Tripoli, here, we waited with six thousand others until we could be sorted out. But first we were asked to volunteer to give a pint of blood each. What a laugh! We were all determined not to volunteer to do anything, then they told us we would get a pint of beer in exchange, so we changed our minds.

This transit camp was full of Army and R.A.F. chaps who had lost touch with their regiments or squadrons somehow, or they were the only survivors when the rest of their units had been wiped out. I was very surprised to meet a lot of the 51st Highland Division, but most of them spoke with Lancashire or Yorkshire accents, and when I asked them how this came about, they said, "There were not enough Scotsmen left to replace the original division after the losses at Dunkirk."

After we had given our blood and then had a very good meal, washed down with our beer, we were told that we could go out of camp until 23.59 hours. This was very welcome news, but then we were told that Tripoli, was about six miles away and no transport was available. However, six miles was nothing to us we must have ran that far every half hour with a full pack on when in the 'Glass House'. I managed to borrow some Italian money off one of the R.A.F. chaps who had also smuggled some money in and out of the Fort.

Now, we set off for Tripoli, twelve soldiers and three R.A.F. including myself. Six of the Army chaps went looking for Red-Caps, and if they found one or two from the Fort, they intended to sort them out. I did not wish to get mixed up with that, so when we got to the city I drifted away on my own. Peace and female company was what I wanted, someone to talk to who was kind, sympathetic and understanding. I looked in vain. But I did find a Forces Canteen run by the Y.M.C.A., or Salvation Army, I forget which one. Here, I could sit in the garden in peace drinking a proper cup of tea whilst sat on a proper chair.

Nearby, was the harbour with the masts and funnels of about three dozen assorted ships showing above the water. Along the promenade, Italian and Arab men and women strolled with their children running to and fro. I felt at peace, life was not too bad after all. At the far end of the promenade stood a massive Fort, with the Union Jack proudly flying on the highest tower. Everyone appeared to be drifting towards the Fort, so I finished my tea and followed them. I knew something was about to happen, but I was not sure what!

Suddenly, a Scottish pipe-band in full regalia came marching down a road at the head of a troop of very smart looking soldiers, rifles at the slope and bayonets glinting in the sun. I felt another foot taller as hundreds of people pressed forward to watch the changing of the guards at the Fort.

Later that evening, after a damn good meal in the Forces Canteen, I strolled along the water front which was now almost deserted. Immediately I was alert, it was such a nice evening yet there was hardly anyone about, something was wrong, the local people knew something which I did not! The next minute as I started off back to camp, I heard the unmistakable throbbing of German bombers: immediately a dozen searchlights lit up the sky over the harbour. I could see a bomber already caught in the cone of light and as I moved quickly away, the bomb doors opened and a shower of bombs came whistling down. At the same instant, the most concentrated and ferocious barrage I had ever seen opened up. Now, I was running for the shelter of a clump of date palms, knowing that at any moment there would be a shower of shrapnel blanketing the place.

The date palms were still twenty yards away when I heard the familiar crump, crump, of a stick of bombs which appeared to be chasing me up the road: it was like some firery monster leaping forward a hundred yards at a time. Now, I was in the ditch, grovelling under a hedge of prickly pear, as the crump, crump, leap-frogged past me in a shuddering screaming hell of flying chunks of metal. Next moment, I was running steadily up the road and the whole area was lit up by the searchlights and flashing anti-aircraft guns. Twenty minutes later, I was well out of the danger area, now, I could walk and have a smoke as I removed a load of prickles from my side and back.

I remained at the Transit Camp for about four days, I think it was February or March 1943, but I had lost track of time. Whilst I had been at the punishment centre, it appeared that the Salvage Unit had moved up about forty miles.

Now, they had been located on the coast beyond Tripoli, and I had to wait until they picked me up. Eventually, a truck from my Unit came into Tripoli, for rations, and called for me on its way back. I was glad to get back to my pals who had made camp near an Italian fishing village on the coast.

The place was 'Sabratha', one of the best camp sites we had been on, and we could swim in the sea nearly every day. I noticed about half a dozen German twin-engined bombers parked under a group of eucalyptus trees. They were dying for want of water, because the wind-driven pump was blasted and twisted into a heap. On closer inspection of the bombers, I noticed they had been shot up where they stood. "But where was the airfield?" I asked my friend. He said, "The Germans must have been using the main road for a runway, because there was no sign of a normal landing strip or airfield." I could see the possibility of taking off on the road because it ran straight and flat for about a mile or more, like a Roman road.

As a matter of fact, there were a large number of what looked like Roman ruins nearby, these I was going to explore later. But first I must explain the situation, the Salvage Unit had been here for about nine days, and most of my pals had had a day or more in Tripoli: we were actually resting, something I could hardly believe! The front line was bogged down in Tunisia, near the Mareth mountains, where the enemy had dug in.

Now the 8th Army and R.A.F. were building up their strength again, before they tried to drive a human wedge through the fortification. The First Army in Algeria, which was composed of something like 75% British and 25% Americans, had twice been severely mauled at the gates of Bizerta and Tunis, before they were thrown back in disorder: so we still had a chance to get to Tunis first.

I had missed nine days of easy going in Sabratha. Of course, we were not resting completely, the trucks were worn out and needed thoroughly overhauling, so there was some work to do. Later that afternoon, I noticed that groups of my pals were making boats from anything they could get hold of; it was then I found out there was going to be a regatta in about three days time.

All the best materials, such as, long-range drop tanks, wood and canvas had already disappeared, but as I was scrounging around near the German bombers, I suddenly got an idea, the leading edge of the main plane would make a nice canoe. All the next day I was busy hacking-sawing the leading edge off. At last, it was lying at my feet; now I only had to seal both ends with wood and well doped fabric, and I had a twelve foot canoe. Next, I made a double-ended paddle out of a tent pole and cut and shaped duralumin blades to fit, then screwed them on.

Round about tea time, I carried the canoe to a small jetty and lowered it into the water, but as I gently lowered myself into it, disappointment hit me, as it fell over on its side and sank beneath me. I swam to the beach with the canoe in tow under the surface, then dragged it clear and emptied the water out. Some pals of mine were roaring with laughter at my predicament, but I knew exactly what to do because my mind was leaping ahead as I visualised the wing tips of the bomber making perfect outriggers!

The following morning I found that the wing tips were only attached with a row of screws. In no time I had them off and screwed on to a cross-member which I had already fixed on the canoe, now I sealed them with more aircraft fabric and dope. The whole contraption was so light I could run with it under my arm to the waters edge.

There were already about twenty make-shift boats being tried out as I climbed into mine feeling very pleased with myself now, because it sailed perfectly. I paddled away along the coast for about two miles: this was great, the hot sun shone, the blue sea sparkled and the war was forgotten for a while. Now, I could see the Roman ruins very clearly: a small town half excavated and nearby an amphitheatre, just beckoned to be explored. Yes! I will go there tomorrow before the boat race the following day.

Suddenly, three or four loud bangs out at sea disturbed the peace, but it was only the local fishermen about a mile out, fishing the easy way, with hand grenades tossed into the water.

The following day, a small group of us set off to explore the ruins. One chap brought a paraffin lamp as he had been to the ruins before and seen a long dark tunnel going under the town. It was another glorious day, and soon we came to the first ruins. Fantastic looking buildings poked out of the sand dunes, along with the beautiful carved and graceful columns pointing to the sky. Soon we came to the pitch dark tunnel, and at the entrance we lit the lamp: now we were whispering and keeping close together as we proceeded under the town into the catacombs.

We could see stone coffins on either side in nitches cut out of the rock walls. Someone had been here before us because many of the stone lids had been moved sideways. One chap stuck his hand in, "feeling about for jewels," he said! The next minute he had both hands in the coffin rummaging among the dry bones until he came up with a skull. As he showed it to us, saying, "I will keep this as a souvenir," it suddenly crumbled to powder in his hands and the teeth dropped onto the floor! That seemed to be the signal for us all to start running for the daylight: we emerged a few seconds later feeling a bit scared and, perhaps, a little guilty.

I have no doubt that if we had gone back and opened some untouched coffins, we would have found some proper souvenirs, but we just could not bring ourselves to do it. After exploring the well preserved theatre which looked like the one in Rome, only not as big, we returned to our tents.

The next day was boat-race day, and even a few Italians from the village turned out to watch. Soon we were all lined up near the jetty with the oddest looking assortment of boats you ever saw, one fellow even had a sail rigged up. The C.O. was going to give the signal and, the first one back to the jetty after rowing round a buoy half a mile out, would be the winner.

There must have been about two dozen boats all waiting to go, the C.O. gave the signal and we were off. At once, I was in front paddling like mad: I believe I was the first round the buoy, and to my surprise leading by about fifty yards. The other boats were mostly heavy and clumsy, except for two of them made from wing drop tanks. With only a hundred yards to go, one blade of my double ended paddle broke off: now I was handicapped and slowing down. I could hear the crowd shouting 'Come on, come on!' but the two were gaining on me: now I was paddling like a maniac, swinging the paddle from one side to the other, until there was no time for me to turn alongside the jetty, I just rammed it at full tilt and sank on the spot. Eager hands hauled me out of the water, I had won the race, and minutes later the C.O. the one who had given me twenty-eight days, now gave me first prize! I was more than satisfied. Later, I salvaged my boat and after repairing it, I spent many happy hours exploring the coast line near Sabratha.

Chapter 9

The Baited Trap

The few happy days at Sabratha, were coming to an end, there was just one more pleasant surprise before we moved to a terrible place in the desert. The next evening, one of those concert parties we had heard so much about, but never seen, were going to give a concert in the old amphitheatre. Some chaps even shaved off their beards and sorted out clean shirts for the occasion, but when we arrived it was a little disappointing as there were only three girls and about six men on the stage. The place was full of soldiers and airmen from miles around, tier after tier of them sat where the ancient Romans had sat years ago. The acoustics were perfect, no mike was needed when the girls sang and the jokes came across very well.

Next day we packed up all our gear onto the trucks and moved off south-west into the desert. We were all sorry to have to leave the seaside and, especially, the boats we had made. Although, it was only the middle of March, we were very surprised how hot it became with every mile as we moved away from the coast.

Eventually, we came to a huge low lying flat valley surrounded by hills, and in the centre was an air-strip. I noticed we had just passed a small village called, Azizia. After the war I was reading a book which mentioned that the highest temperature ever recorded anywhere was at, Azizia, the shade temperature was 136° in 1932. Here, the hot winds seared into your body, burning through our cotton shirts and shorts, and drying out the moisture in our mouth and eyes, so that our eyeballs felt sluggish and our tongues became like hot cinders in our mouths. Each searing gust of hot wind seemed to be blasted out of hell itself. It sapped your strength and made you cringe as you felt the hairs on your legs and private parts being scorched off. The searing heat bounced back from the surrounding hills, swirling round and round the low valley, so that we felt as if we were in a cauldron which was ready to boil over at any moment.

What a place this was, it reminded me of, Wadi Halfa, in the Sudan, and we had no sooner got our tents up when twenty brand new Spitfires started to land. Where the hell had they come from? No one told us anything, only that everyone had to be jacked-up and the undercarriages tested. I think they must have flown right off an aircraft carrier in the Mediterranean, which had brought them straight from England; but on the other hand, they could have come across from Malta, which was almost due north.

That night it was so uncomfortably hot we could not sleep, even when we moved out of the tents and lay in the open with just our shorts on, it was still boiling. I began to wonder if the surrounding hills were the walls of a huge crater and we were in the centre of a volcano, as I remembered having seen boiling water blowing out of the ground and smelling of sulphur, just outside Tripoli.

Next day we finished inspecting the Spitfires and they all flew away, only to be replaced by another batch which needed the same inspection. It was a good job we had plenty of water as we were emptying our water bottles almost every hour. I had never known anything like it. The last batch flew away the next day about dinner-time, and no more came until the following day. Once more we jacked them all up and tested the undercarriages, I don't remember finding anything wrong with them, but they all had to be checked.

'Pack your stuff tonight', we were told at tea time, 'we are moving after breakfast'. "Thank God, for that" someone said, "this heat is a killer." So the next day we pulled out of the valley, now, we moved north-west, to hit the coast at Zuara. Here, it was much better, dinner being served amongst a group of date palms. After dinner we crossed into Tunisia, and stopped at Bengardin, on the coast again. Immediately we were surrounded by Arabs, who wished to buy anything such as, food, clothes or blankets and they waved fists full of Tunisian French notes in our faces. Of course, we did not know that the money was worthless but everyone sold anything they could get their hands on. I received the equivalent of £20 for a towel and shirt, and thought I was a millionaire. The crunch came later, especially for the chaps who had sold all their kit except the clothes which they stood in!

Now, we were busy again salvaging our shot down fighters and repairing them, or, if they were in a very bad state, we sent them to the rear. Meanwhile, the 8th Army probed and shelled the extensive fortification in the Marath mountains, whilst a strong force of mostly New Zealanders, Maoris and

Gurkhas, vanished into the empty quarters to try and get round the mountains, to surprise the enemy from their rear.

The following day, as I was helping to repair one of the Spitfires, which we had inspected a few days before at, Azizia, we saw a group of soldiers walking towards us. At first, we could not make out what they were doing, they looked like a real tough bunch, moving from one group of camel thorn to another. As they got nearer, we stopped work to watch them, now we could see they were members of the Foreign Legion, picking snails off the bushes to supplement their rations. We tried to make conversation and offered cigarettes, which they almost snatched out of our hands, then they offered us some juicy snails which we had to refuse! We found out that they had been moved up from Lake Chad, about 1,500 miles south, and what they did not know about life in the desert was not worth knowing. You could see that they were as hard as nails, heads shaved, and skin like burnt teak, the sort of fighting men whom you were glad were on your side.

Meanwhile, the Germans and Italians were pouring troops and equipment into Tunisia, and they were coming across in anything which would fly or sail. We also heard that thirty junkers transport aircraft, full of soldiers, had been shot down by the Desert Airforce in one day.

Things were hotting up now and desperate hand-to-hand fighting was taking place in the mountains. The enemy were being hemmed into a smaller and smaller pocket, with their backs to the sea, desperately fighting a ferocious rear guard action on all fronts, throwing in some of their best troops, regardless of casualties. But the more they sent across from Italy and Sicily, the more men and equipment they would lose.

For many days we were hard pressed to bring in all the shot down aircraft, we worked from sunrise to sunset every day. Our hair and beards grew longer, our clothes grew dirtier and shabbier. At one particular time, I remember we had brought in so many wrecks there was no time to repair them. Something like forty assorted fighters were lined up on their bellies in rows, and then a photographer came round who actually had to ask us if we were R.A.F. because we looked like tramps or wild men, then he took photos of us and the wrecks. I am still hoping I may see them one day.

A few days later the 8th Army had hammered a human wedge down one of the passes in the Marath line, and a signal came to us that three fighters were on their bellies in a salt-marsh. The Sergeant immediately picked a group of us to go and bring them back and I was in the group selected. The mobile crane, three salvage trucks and a three tonner were loaded up with a dozen men, food and tool boxes. Eventually, our small convoy was stopped by Redcaps, near the salt-marsh which was part of the Marath Mountains that jutted up beyond the marsh, about a mile away. The Redcaps told us to be careful because two 88mm guns were hidden half-way up the mountains, dominating the marsh and the road. They also suspected that heavy machine-guns and, 'do or die' Germans were dug in to protect the guns.

The situation was tense, we could see two Kittyhawks and one of the special Hurricanes with two bofor guns fitted. They had each ploughed a furrow in the marsh and now it only needed a hot-headed N.C.O. to order us to certain death. Here, was the baited trap once more. Go and get them, what are you waiting for?" The order came. Someone said, "The trucks and crane would sink in the marsh," and he walked forward on the soft ground to demonstrate. "All right," the N.C.O. said."You three walk out to the nearest aircraft and see what the ground is like and get the pilot out, if he is still there!'

The three chosen ones set off, each one walking up to his knees in slime towards the first aircraft. We all watched holding our breath, knowing what was going to happen before our eyes. When the men got to the aircraft, we could see them wrenching the canopy back and reaching inside, endeavouring to get the pilot out. Then the sudden crash of shells as three came screaming over and the aircraft and men disappeared in a whirl of smoke and fire. It was then I noticed an R.A.F. signal truck nearby, and the officer who had pinpointed the guns was already on the radio talking. Ten or fifteen minutes later a dozen Kittyhawkes came screaming out of the blue, diving to the attack with bombs thudding down, then riddling the area in turn with their six machine guns.

After a few minutes, all was quiet and the rest of us were ordered to see if we could get the other two pilots out. We crept forward, hoping that the guns had been knocked out, wondering if our number was up, as our feet squelched in the mud leaving our shoes behind. At last, three of us got to the next aircraft; we bounded onto the wings in bare feet and peered inside, it was empty. At that moment the other aircraft disappeared in a whirling blinding flash. Instantly, a group of our field guns opened up behind us, the shells screamed overhead as we scrambled away in a mad dash for safety. Most of us managed to get back round a bend in the road and we were fuming as well as shaken, knowing that we had been used to draw the fire and show up the gun positions.

Finally, the last 88mm gun was silenced, but we had already abandoned the attempt to salvage any part of the aircraft as they would slowly sink down into the salt-marsh. A straggling line of infantry now moved slowly up the road prodding with their bayonets for mines and anything else. We returned to the rear empty-handed and five men short, only to find that everyone was preparing to move up the next morning.

Gabes, on the coast, had just been captured, the enemy were being squeezed into a smaller and smaller pocket as we moved up all the next day. Towards evening, we passed by a walled town called, Medina. It looked a very interesting medieval place, flat roofs and date palms poked above the walls, but I noticed the huge wooden gates were locked, probably because it was almost sunset. We made camp for the night, forming up the trucks into a circle and sleeping under them after a rough and ready tea. Water and food were getting short, we were either moving too fast or the supply ships were being sunk at Tripoli!

Next day, we pushed deeper into the wild rugged country, quite a nice change from the desert; there were patches of course grass here and there and wonderful wild flowers delighted our eyes. But the going was tough and slow, especially, when we had to start remaking the battered track and gathering rubbish to fill in dry wadis before we could cross. There was plenty of rubbish about in the form of wrecked trucks, enemy aircraft, shattered guns and God knows what!

As we rounded a bend between steep cliffs, we perceived a beautiful view, a valley dotted with outcrops of rocks spread before us. Masses of wild flowers grew between the rocks and birds flitted from bush to bush, whilst here and there grew carpets of blood-red poppies. But, do not look too close under the bushes because bloated bodies lay and the red scars on the ground were not all 'nodding poppy flowers'. Yes, there had been a bloody battle here, the entrance to the valley had been stubbornly defended and just as stubbornly overcome.

Towards tea-time, we were back on a proper road, a signpost said we were approaching Gabes, a small town on the coast. It looked very nice except for black smoke rising up and drifting over the sea. We made camp near the remains of a shattered farm just outside the town and immediately went foraging for food, anything to supplement our rations which were now running out. Water was another problem, we searched in vain for a tap or well in the shattered farm, only to find the pump wrecked in the farm yard.

But nearby was a pool of stagnant water half covered with green slime and a mangy looking horse lay dead, half-way in the pool, its bloated stomach appeared ready to burst! Quickly, we moved the slime to one side and dipped our empty water bottles into the water. Now, we sat back and emptied the bottles down our throats! I suppose we should have boiled the water, but we could not wait or care any more.

Later, we dined on fried eggs and hard biscuits, and to our surprise the stagnant water never affected us. We stopped at the farm for two days waiting for orders to move up again. The end was near in Africa. Sfax had just fallen, so get going and wait near Sfax for further orders and for the rations to catch us up. It was some date in early April 1943 when we got to Sfax. Tunis, was only one hundred and eighty miles away and our next destination was an airstrip scratched out of the scrubland, south of Monastir.

We arrived at the new airstrip the following day. Now, we were existing on half rations and stretching them out with roasted pigeons which we had shot with our rifles; you can imagine what a pigeon looked like when brought down with a 303 bullet! About four days later we got our proper rations through from Tripoli, which was now, approximately, four hundred miles to the rear. The countryside was much better here, we had left the desert behind at Azizia, but you only had to go about two hundred miles south and the Sahara Desert was waiting to swallow you up.

It was about this time, mid-April, that two of my pals got yellow jaundice and to everyone's disgust, they were given two days rations and told to hitch-hike back to Tripoli! Only one of them made it, the other was buried at the roadside, whilst still a hundred miles short of the hospital in Tripoli!

The rest of us were as busy as hell again, once more we were bringing the shattered aircraft back so quickly it was impossible to repair many. We stacked them side by side in a huge dump, rows of Spitfires, Hurricanes and Kittyhawkes, until there must have been over a hundred. I was given three men and put in charge of the scrap-yard. It was now our job to lift the aircraft with the crane and help any fitters from the different Squadrons to remove whatever spare parts they wanted. Everyone who came seemed to want propellers more than anything else and, there was not one straight one in the whole dump.

Meanwhile, we started to get odd days off and were taken by truck about ten miles to Monastir. Here, we could swim once more in the Mediterranean, or drink cheap wine in the cafes. Eventually, my turn came for a days rest in Monastir. I had already shaved off my beard and washed my clothes the day before, now, three of my pals and I climbed onto the open truck along with about twenty more chaps. One of my three close friends had been to Monastir before, and he was going to show us around. He was carrying a 45 colt revolver hidden in his pocket and I had my trusty luger inside my shirt with a spare clip in my pocket, whilst one of the others had a 38 revolver in his trouser pocket.

Eventually, the truck pulled up on a small promenade near the sea, in the centre of the town. "Don't forget," the driver said, "be back here at 10.30p.m. or you will have to walk back." It was then we remembered we had not brought our swimming gear with us, as most of the others ran off to the beach, so we strolled round the town; two of us looking reasonably smart but the other two had dressed anyway they could, in the only clothes they had left and none of us had hats on. Soon we came to an open market in a large square, the stalls were just old pieces of canvas laid on the ground and most of the stall holders were Arabs. There was quite a large variety of fruit and vegetables for sale and all manner of other goods, but on the whole, it was the scruffiest market I had ever seen. We tried to buy some fruit with our French money, but they did not want to know. Italian and Egyptian money were likewise turned down. Then they pointed to our cigarettes and we realised that we had something to barter with. A packet of 'V' cigarettes produced enough pressed dates and a bottle of cheap wine to satisfy the four of us.

Now, we retired to the shade of some date palms, bringing an audience of Arab children with us to watch us eat. We soon realised that there were as many pressed flies as there were pressed dates and this appeared to be the signal for the children to move in closer as the poor beggars were starving. They were obviously waiting eagerly for any scraps and it was not long before we began to throw them the odd date. It reminded me of feeding the hungry sparrows in the back garden at home because they hopped and jumped about diving and fighting amongst themselves, until it became too pitiful to watch, so we gave them all we had. Now, we had the opportunity to disappear round the corner and onto the beach, looking for a shady spot to drink the wine and smoke in peace and, finally, to sleep the hot afternoon away.

Later that evening, we found a nice French cafe and, after much bargaining, we finally got a good fish meal each with plenty of wine for more cigarettes. Soon, we were all very drunk on the unaccustomed wine and ready to take on the whole German Army. Yes, we were really plastered, not having had booze for months. Next minute, we were shown the door - the rear door, and now we found ourselves in a narrow dark alley with what looked like flitting shadows moving in the darker doorways. Immediately, the chap with the '45' whipped it out and sent a shot ricochetting down the alley. Actually, there was probably no one there, but we just felt as if we were going to be jumped on.

Now we ran staggering along, looking for the place to meet the truck, only to find the place deserted - we were in for a long walk. The road to our camp was just a dirt track and after a bit of arguing, we decided that we had found the right one and set off singing R.A.F. songs. After about four miles, one of my pals wanted to lie down right there and go to sleep as he was sure we were going the wrong way, but we insisted that we were on the right track. "Listen," someone said, we all stopped talking and listened, now we heard the sound of throbbing drums and women wailing. Yes! Down there, about half a mile away is the little Arab village that we came through this morning. So we set off once more and the drums and wailing got louder. "It sounds like a wedding party" I said! or a "Funeral Party," someone else said! As we got nearer to the village we saw a line of Arabs, perhaps, two dozen blocking off the road. We stopped at about twenty paces from the line of men, as we were now able to see that they all carried clubs or long staves indicating for us to go back. We also could see there was no way round because the track was lined with 6ft. high prickly pears.

We tried to talk to them in Egyptian Arabic, but their Tunisian Arabic was very different, or they did not want to know. One huge fellow in the centre moved towards us waving his club, he obviously did not know that we were armed. The situation was dangerous, but we did not want to walk back to Monastir. Now, our hands were on the guns which were still in our pockets, or down our shirts. The Arab got within four paces, his club raised to strike, then the 45 colt leaped into my pal's hand and I also drew the luger and as we closed ranks my other pal drew is '38'. The '45' was pointed right at the Arab's head and to my surprise my pal pulled the trigger! My God! Click, the safety catch was still on, but the effect on the Arabs was instantaneous; they fell back, opening up a way through, which we did not hesitate to take advantage of!

Now, we were running like hell down the track, looking over our shoulders as a shower of rocks came whistling past our heads. The cheeky sods! We stopped out of range of the stone-throwers and turned back to give them a volley over their heads. That did it! They all scattered in every direction, so we turned round and walked back to camp, reaching our tents just before dawn. I never found out why the village Arabs wanted us to turn back, it could have been any one of a dozen reasons. Perhaps, enemy troops, or our own had demanded food when the fighting swirled round the village; also the place could have been partly wrecked and some killed as the whole area changed hands. On the other hand, it may have been some religious ceremony and they did not want any drunken infidels to gate crash it. Never-the-less, we had had a very close shave; had we not been armed, I am sure we would have been stoned or clubbed to death!

When back in the scrap-yard the next day, one of my pals remarked that - "We had not been bombed or machine-gunned for about fourteen days." This was most unusual but never-the-less, a very good sign. Yes, we now had superior air power in Tunisia, and the enemy were fighting, running and squirming in a smaller and smaller area. Day by day, the fitters from many squadrons came clamouring for spare parts and as we worked with them we pumped them for news.

The R.A.F. had sunk three enemy destroyers which were bringing more troops across from Italy, and shot down dozens of transport aircraft along with their fighter escorts over the sea. Also, on May 7th, 1943, we got news that Berzerta and Tunis, were being attacked, heavy fighting was going on in the suburbs.

A few days later, we had a most unusual visitor, an old-fashioned biplane landed in a whirl of dust. None of us had seen the type before; it was a Westland Wapiti, which had been in service in India since 1929. The pilot had been hopping his way from India for days, flying over Persia, Iraq, Egypt, and the Western Desert, on his way back to England. The aircraft was going into a museum, if it ever made it, but now the pilot had to wait for a few days as it was not safe to go any further along the North African coast, just yet.

The following day, Tunis, fell to the 8th Army, and Berzerta, fell to the 1st Army, but it was not all over yet. For five more days, groups of fanatics entrenched in strong positions, fought on to the bitter end. Two hundred thousand prisoners were rounded up, but thousands more roamed about in armed mobs, looking for someone to surrender to. Until, eventually, the prisoners numbered two hundred and fifty thousand!

It was now safe for the Wapiti, to proceed on its way, but how do we start the engine? We had to asked the pilot who explained that three men had to form a human chain. Number one to take hold of the propeller tip, whilst the other two men had to make sure that they pulled the first man clear when the engine spluttered into life!

Everyone stopped work to watch this antiquated method of starting, but it worked first time and very soon the Wapiti appeared to float away at about ninety miles per hour!

Chapter 10

The Arab 'Mystic'

About two days later, after it was all over in Tunisia, we heard the good news that we would be allowed to visit Tunis. I was very lucky in the draw, finding myself in the first batch of about twenty men. We set off by truck the next morning, and soon we were passing the largest prison camp I had ever seen which the prisoners were enlarging and wiring themselves in. Later, we passed through a number of small villages and each one had huge queues of people waiting outside the banks. Eventually, we stopped to ask why the people were queuing? "Our money is O.K. thanks to the British Government" a delighted Frenchman told us. That was good news for us, also , it meant we had not sold our clothes for nothing after all!

After dinner we finally got to Tunis, and found it a very interesting place, at least, what was left of it! The centre was not badly knocked about, but, food, drink and anything else was in very short supply.

"Be at this spot after tea tomorrow, the driver said, I will be leaving at 6.30p.m." "O.K." we shouted, and then divided into small groups to explore the place.

A friend and I were going together. "Let's find somewhere to sleep before everywhere gets booked up." I said! My pal agreed. The place was swarming with troops of every nationality you could think of. Americans, British, French and New Zealanders, Indians, Gurkhas, and many more who I must apologise to because I could not recognise their uniforms.

Eventually, we found a small French Hotel who could fix us up with Bed and Breakfast. They showed us the room and we could not resist lying down on a proper bed for a few moments. The homely couple smiled at us, but they could not speak English and we spoke only a few words of French! Seconds later we got up to go out. Now the comic opera commenced with the four of us trying to communicate with hands waving, heads nodding, facial expressions changing as we blurted out half forgotten words in French and Arabic! Outside in the busy street we burst out laughing. "What the hell were they trying to say," my pal said. "I think they were telling us to be back for midnight and have a good time, but I am not certain what they said!"

At the end of the street we turned round to have a good look at the hotel and surrounding buildings, trying to memorize the place so that we would be able to find our way back. Later, we looked in vain for a place to buy some food or a drink of tea. It was a good thing that we had brought some rations with us, because there must have been a quarter of a million soldiers swamping the place and all wanting food and drink.

At last, we found a small cafe down a scruffy back street; here we could buy a coffee each at inflated prices. As we sat sipping the thick black coffee which tasted like burnt charcoal, we noticed an impressive looking Arab drifting from table to table. "He is probably flogging imitation 'Spanish fly' like they sold in Cairo," my pal remarked. "No! I don't think so, he looks like a 'mystic' to me, with his long white beard and piercing eyes." I said! I had developed some slight psychic powers in the last few months which had saved my life more than once, and I knew that this Arab was also psychic. I was watching him closely now, I knew that he was trying to persuade the different foreign soldiers to have their fortunes told. He had been talking in Arabic to some Algerian soldiers and in French to some Legionaries; now he suddenly looked up and ignoring the other tables came right across to ours.

I invited him to sit down and he thanked me in very good English, knowing he had found someone who was interested, and was probably even now reading my aura as I was trying to read his! He invited us both to come and hear what was written in the sand. My pal was not really interested as he did not believe in mumbo-jumbo, and neither did I, but this Arab was a born psychic. He had a little den just around the corner, so I asked my pal to have another coffee and wait for me.

Now I followed the Arab out of the cafe, down the street and into his den, which was cluttered with the usual occult riffraff. He invited me to sit at a small table, than he clapped his hands once and a young Arab boy appeared from behind a beaded curtain. The boy placed two small cups of coffee on the table and disappeared. For a moment I thought, this is it, my coffee contains a 'mickey finn', and I will wake up in the gutter, minus my money! The 'mystic' sat opposite to me, watching and reading my thoughts, than he invited me to choose any cup, which I already knew he would do. I offered my cigarettes and we smoked and drank together for a few minutes, whilst agreeing on a price. Then he got up and placed a tray of sand on the table and commenced to draw geometric symbols in the sand. Now, as he chanted in Arabic, I knew he was going into a light trance. Suddenly, he produced a leather bag of small pebbles and scattered them over the tray of sand, watching intently where each pebble fell. Then he began to speak and I realised his command of English was not as fluent as I first thought. He told me a hotchpotch jumble which is now mostly forgotten, but one thing made my heart beat faster, he correctly stated that I had been in Egypt, and had not landed in Algeria. Then he surprised me immensely by his last remark. "You will see your mother and father one day, but in a few weeks you will be back in Egypt." It was all over, we stood up and shook hands, each showering the blessing of Allah to be with us and to go with us.

I returned in a bit of a daze to my pal in the cafe, he was ready to go but also longing to hear what had happened. We strolled off down the street only to find that we could not get any farther because a huge burnt-out German tank was on its side, wedged between a wrecked bus and the buildings. So we about turned and eventually found a shady spot in a nearby park; here, we could sit and talk. When I told my pal about going back to Egypt, he laughed, "Impossible," he said, "we are already planning to invade Sicily and Italy." "Yes, I know, but that's what he said!"

We spent the rest of the day tramping around Tunis, and for every 5,000 soldiers and airmen we passed, we were lucky to see one girl, until suddenly to our delight, we heard loud female voices speaking English, with drawling American accents. Six well-fed American women in some kind of smart uniform, were arguing with an Arab street vendor who was pestering them to buy his trinkets. To the surprised Americans, we spoke to the Arab in his own tongue and he quickly disappeared, then we passed the time of day with the girls, and probably more perfect English than their own. They looked amazed, obviously we were English, but our skin was darker than the Arab's, also our uniforms were tattered and worn out as if we had been on a desert island, so they really did not want to know us!

Eventually, we traced our steps back to the small hotel, thankfully sliding between the crisp sheets of a proper bed, what luxury! Do some people really sleep like this every night? At breakfast the next morning, they even produced a small boiled egg each, but, the bread was like sweet sawdust. It was madam who served us with hands fluttering and head nodding as she tried to explain the food shortage. As we paid the bill, it was our turn to wave our hands, nod our heads and smile our goodbyes.

My God! These foreigners, why do they not speak English, forgetting for a moment that we were the actual foreigners! The rest of the day was spent searching for food and drink, but there was none. Tunis, had been under siege for months, so at six p.m. we were waiting anxiously for the truck to take us back to camp.

In the next few days I had about 150 of our fighters on their bellies in the scrap yard; parties of airmen were going out daily, scouring the countryside and bringing them back. Then the rumours of invading - Sicily or Southern France - increased, with more rumours that Italy was about to pack it in. "We may be home for Christmas," someone had to say again!

Now, it was June 1943 - and without warning, the mystic' prophecy began to come true! I could hardly believe it; four of us who had been the first ones to form the Salvage Unit in 1941, were being sent back to Egypt! The rest, who were mostly replacements over the years, would go on into Europe and Germany, through the back-door. We four, packed our kit, cleaned our rifles and sorted out our tool boxes; then we said our goodbyes as we climbed onto the ration truck. The first stop would be the Transit Camp at Tripoli, and three days later we were dumped there to await further orders. The journey back would take a month, but, we did not know it yet.

After about three days at Tripoli, listening to rumours that we may go by boat to Alexandria, we eventually arrived at Tobruk; here there was more waiting to be done.

Thousands of Army and R.A.F. were now waiting at the railhead, near Tobruk. The British engineers must have extended the line, because if I remember correctly, the railway did not reach Tobruk before. At last, we got on a very loaded train which puffed and wheezed for two more days on its way to the delta of Egypt. The train only moved at about 30mph and there were no facilities or room to make meals, so we had to stop for every meal at a 'tented encampment'; here, also, the train took on water and fuel. But we did not mind, nothing bothered us now, at least, not yet, and we were going to a place of civilization once more. On the second day, we suddenly stopped for the last time before we reached Alexandria, but, this was no meal stop, only water for the engine. Everyone crowded to the window spaces looking up and down the track, and there it was, a small shed and a signpost which said - 'El Alamein.'

We were the lucky ones, now puffing our way towards - Alexandria, except that the temperature had been increasing ever since we left Tripoli, and in

Ramleigh Square, Alexandria 1942. Photo given to me by Mr. K. G. Eslick of Truro.

Heliopolis, Main Street, 1942. Photo given to me by Mr. K. G. Eslick of Truro.

A Wellington Bomber at Heliopolis 1942. The photo was given to me by Mr. K. G. Eslick of Truro, he is on the left.

The Open-Air Cinema at Heliopolis 1942. Photo given to be my Mr. K. G. Eslick.

A captured Italian bomber in Egypt, and on the right is the nose of a Bristol Bombay of 216 Squadron. Photo lent by Mr. G. A. Jenks.

A 'Hawker Hart' at R.A.F. Cranwell, 1940, and next to it. I believe, is a 'Tiger Moth'. The 'Battle of Britain' was reaching a crescendo at this time, and rumours of an invasion flitted around the 'mess'. Later, in the Egyptian Desert, I was surprised to find 'Hawker Harts and Hinds' on the front line airfields. Many of them were used to pick up the fighter pilots who had crash-landed, often behind the 'enemy lines'.

A Kittyhawk being prepared for take off, Egypt. Photo was lent to me by Mr. G. A. Jenks.

Tripoli Cathedral taken by LAC Reid, June 1943.

I took this photograph after midnight with the help of a flash of lightening. Aboukir 1943.

Some of the ground staff at El Ballah, Egypt 1944.

The Great Pyramid and the Sphinx. An airman standing on the right-hand paw will give you some idea of the size.

One of the dancing baboons at Ismailia. The bridge in the rear is over the Suez Canal.

In the grounds of the Y.W.C.A. Cairo 1944. (the author)

Some R.A.F. pals at El Ballah, Egypt 1944 "TT Flight". Notice they are all wearing Army type battle dress.

The Italian monument on the road to Tripoli. We called it Marble Arch. Photo given to me by Mr. Thackery of Timperley. He was the pilot of a Wellington Bomber from 40 Squadron, 1943.

Hurricane's waiting for repair, somewhere in Egypt. Photo lent to me by Mr. G. A. Jenks.

A low flying "Suitcase" nickname for the Hampden Bomber which I serviced at Scampton, Lincolnshire.

British Service Men walking towards The Great Pyramid. The Mena House Hotel, where Mr. Churchill stopped is in the rear. Notice the abrupt dividing line of the Desert and the Delta. Another photo given to me by Mr. K. G. Eslick of Truro.

Eleven British fighters, almost in line abreast, presents a very good target for German aircraft.

Troopships at Gibraltar on our way home in 1945.

Near Gabes, Tunisia - June 1943. Some local girls, mostly French, and one of the Advance Salvage Unit's Spotter planes made of plywood.

Mr. Reid took this snap of the Forces Club at Tripoli 1943. Here, I had a proper cup of tea whilst sat on a proper chair after my ordeal in the Glass-house. (See Chapter 7).

I could not resist this snap of one of the many trains waiting at Glasgow, as the troopships unloaded on the Clyde in 1945.

Lillian (A.T.S.) at the Cairo Zoo 1944.

A snap taken on top of the Great Pyramid by the soldier who had been up there all night. (See Chapter 11).

On the beach with three Greek girls. Their chaperon gave me permission to place my hands on the shoulders of one. Aboukir 1943.

My friend, Mr. Reid, took this photograph of the amphitheatre at Sabratha, Nr. Tripoli, 1943. He was best man at my wedding later.

The second Pyramid at Giza, showing the outer casing stones which the vandals had to leave.

Part of the statue of Rameses II which had fallen over at Memphis, "The Good Place". Carved with copper chisels about 3,300 years ago. The weight was over 100 tons.

Part of the 51st Highland Division. Unfortunately, the light was fading when I took this snap. (See Chapter 3.)

American Harvard at R.A.F. Hednesford 1940.

A Hurricane fighter in the Sudan. It had forced landed on its way to Egypt, whilst flying across Africa from West to East. Photo lent to me by Mr. G. A. Jenks.

A Hawker Audex very similar to the Hawker Hart. (See Chapter 5.) Photo lent to me by Mr. G. A. Jenks.

The River Nile near Cairo 1942. The photo was given to me by Mr. K. G. Eslick.

A group of religious types doing the rounds of Jerusalem. I am sat next to my pal who is first on the left. "The Dome of the Rock" where Mohammed took off for heaven, is behind us.

The captured Junkers 87 Dive Bomber at El Ballah. (See Chapter 12). I am on the right. The other two men are Italian Prisoners

A Bristol Bombay of 216 Squadron comes down in the desert. Now they must all be glad that they carried an Engine and an Airframe fitter. Photograph lent to me by Mr. G. A. Jenks.

Just before the decisive battle of El Alamein. My friend LAC Reid from Stoke-on-Trent is acting the part of a German

Some of the 50-ton stones at Stonehenge, but don't ask me how the ancient Briton's managed to move them up and down hills for 30 miles.

I managed to get my Wings at 57, so my reason for joining the R.A.F. 40 years before had, at last, been fulfilled. The photo shows part of the Derbyshire and Lancashire Gliding Club.

The photo showing part of the British Cemetery at El Alamein was given to me by Mr. G. Ellis of Cirencester. It contains 7,500 graves. The German and Italian Cemeteries are near by. Then, less we forget, there are five more British Cemeteries in Egypt, and many others all the way to Tunis.

EIGHTH ARMY

Personal Message from the Army Commander

To be read out to All Troops

1. To-day, 23 January, exactly three months after we began the battle of Egypt, the Eighth Army has captured Tripoli and has driven the enemy away to the West towards Tunisia. By skilful withdrawal tactics the enemy has eluded us, though we have taken heavy toll of his army and air forces.

2. The defeat of the enemy in battle at Alamein, the pursuit of his beaten army, and the final capture of Tripoli—a distance of some fourteen hundred miles from Alamein—has all been accomplished in three months. This achievement is probably without parallel in history. It could not have been done unless every soldier in the Army had pulled his full weight all the time. I congratulate the whole Army, and send my personal thanks to each one of you for the wonderful support you have given me.

3. On your behalf I have sent a special message to the Allied Air Forces that have co-operated with us. I don't suppose that any Army has ever been supported by such a magnificent Air Striking Force. I have always maintained that the Eighth Army and the R.A.F., Western Desert, together constitute one fighting machine, and therein lies our great strength.

4. In the hour of success we must not forget the splendid work that has been done by those soldiers working day and night in back areas and on the lines of communication. There are many soldiers quietly doing their duty in rear areas who are unable to take part in the triumphal entry into captured cities; but they are a vital part of our fighting machine and we could gain no successes if they failed to pull their full weight. I refer especially to stevedores at our bases, to fitters in the workshops, to clerks in rear offices, and so on. I would like to make a special mention of our R.A.S.C. drivers; these men drive long distances by day and night for long periods; they always deliver the goods. The R.A.S.C. has risen to great heights during the operations we have undertaken, and as a Corps it deserves the grateful thanks of every soldier in the Army.

5. There is much work still in front of us. But I know that you are all ready for any task that you may be called on to carry out.

6. Once again I thank you all from the bottom of my heart.

B. L. Montgomery,

23rd January, 1943. General, G.O.C-in-C., Eighth Army.

Egypt, the roasting season was in full swing. We must have gone soft in the cooler climate of Tunisia, for now we felt suffocated as the hot winds swept out of the desert.

That evening we pulled into the last Transit Camp, just outside Alexandria, here, we would wait to be posted wherever someone thought fit. On the Friday, we went on Pay Parade, the second one in almost twelve months! Then, on to the town of Alexandria!

But, Egypt, was changing fast. We could feel a different atmosphere in the city, the threat of invasion had vanished, only to be replaced by hot-headed students, clamouring for the British to go home. But, something else had also changed - now, we met women from the R.A.F., Navy and Army; how nice to talk to girls who spoke the same language and who were not surrounded by chaperons.

Do not be too hasty though, thinking at last, you may be able to take a girl to the cinema once more, because, unless you were very lucky, you had no chance. Like the nurses who only appeared to go out with Medical Officers, so the W.R.N.S. etc. only wanted to know you if you were an officer; but there were a small number of service girls who chose to be different.

After a very enjoyable evening doing the rounds of - night clubs etc. we returned to the Transit Camp. It was now August, and I suddenly found myself posted back to the - M.U. at Aboukir. So I said my goodbyes to my three pals, whom, I would never meet again.

Now, it was parade for work and then sweat all day in the hangars or workshops repairing the fighters, once more. I thought about leave because my nerves were on edge and, I had had no leave for over a year except for an odd day in Tunis or Monistir. Yes, I was far too keyed up and jumpy, constantly weighing up the situation, noting the best cover just in case I needed to make a running dive into the nearest hole. Even though I knew that the war was far away now, I still unconsciously reacted to anything unusual, whether it was a sudden noise, or an unexpected quietness.

So I applied for fourteen days leave, intending to disappear up the Nile to Luxor, there, I would be able to quieten my jangling nerves amongst the old tombs and temples. Actually, it was the wrong time of the year to think of going to Thebes and Luxor, the heat would be unbearable but I had to get away and relax somehow. My application form was returned - they had knocked it down to seven days, so I had to be satisfied with Cairo.

The next day I applied for some of my 'back pay'. Three months would do very well for the moment, because I had already sold my luger along with a pair of German binoculars. Now, I only had to pack my kit and pick up my rail warrant and Cairo would be mine for a week, with plenty of money to pay the dancing girls for an many dances as I wished.

At last, the old steam train pulled into the station. Cairo was as hot and dusty as ever, but it was home, well, almost home. It was nice to be back. I never thought I would see it again or smell the familiar odours of camel dung, charcoal stoves, diesel oil, stale sweat and jasmine etc. But, the noise hit me like a hammer as a dozen Arabs surrounded me, each one clamouring for me to go to their particular hotel.

The trams screeched and clashed like symbols, almost drowning the sound of shouting street vendors, braying donkeys and grunting camels. My God! I thought, what have I let myself in for, as I jumped into the nearest horse-drawn carriage and let myself be taken to any hotel or hostel. Eventually, we stopped outside a small hotel which had an unpronounceable name; the owners were Egyptian, so cautiously, as always, I booked one night, bed and breakfast. It was quite a nice place in a good area, away from all the hostels full of soldiers and airmen sleeping ten to a room.

An Arab servant showed me to a tastefully decorated room, overlooking a peaceful garden. Yes, this would do nicely, I would be able to sleep in peace tonight, no drunks to wake me up at two or three a.m. asking me if I would like to buy a battleship. But now I must have a wash and brush-up, then put on my new tropical uniform which I had been given at Aboukir. On my way out I stopped to ask what time breakfast was and picked up a card which gave the name and address of the place in English, Arabic and French.

It was already sundown as I stepped out into the tree-lined road. I was free to do as I pleased and go where I wanted within reasonable limits. The heady perfume from the flowering trees delighted my nostrils as I headed for the city centre. But slow down, the night is young, there is even magic in the air tonight. I don't know what it was but I felt happy and relaxed, perhaps, my stars and planets were just in the right place, or Allah, was smiling on me!

The city centre was still quite a long way, when I came to a row of shops and a Greek cafe spilling chairs and tables onto the pavement. I stopped for a cup of tea and a piece of rich fruit cake which tasted almost like mother used to make. I was thinking of home and how lucky I had been so far because the war was close to starting its fifth year. It was then I noticed an Egyptian woman get off a tram and start to cross over the road towards me; her European dress told me she was probably not a Moslem. For a brief moment our eyes met and an enchanting smile flicked across her face. I could not believe it, an Egyptian lady out at night, without an escort and, that bewitching smile! Of course, I was in the mood to smile at anyone and had not delayed in this instance. Now she was making her way towards a chemist shop and I was glowing inside, and it was not because of the hot tea!

Moments later, she came out of the shop. My eyes were glued to her face because she was going to walk right past my table, but her eyes were now looking down until the last moment, when, with a flutter, she looked directly at me, and there was that bewitching smile, which spoke a thousand words. God! My luck is in tonight, if I am not mistaken. Let her get a few yards down the road, then pay my bill and pretend I am not in a hurry as I followed her.

She was now looking in a shop window, but actually she was watching me in the reflection, and as I got near, I said, "Good evening" in my best Arabic. This was the moment of truth, she would either ignore me or scream, but to my surprise she answered in broken English. In seconds we were in conversation and I was glad she knew quite a bit of English. I could see that she was about six years older than me, and her eyes now flashed with fire and 'eastern promise' as she said, "Follow me on the tram, get off when I do, but do not sit near me on the tram."

This was too good to be true; it must be a trap or a dream, but now a tram was already grinding to a stop. I let her get on first and move down the tram, just as if we were strangers. I knew the situation, she dare not be seen with me and I did not want a knife in my back. The ticket collector came and she had not told me what fair to pay, so I got a ten piaster ticket to start with; I could always buy another if it became necessary. I noticed we were going into a very nice residential area, with large detached villas standing in beautiful gardens.

It was like a dream unfolding, my blood was rushing through my veins in a frenzy of excited anticipation. Light a cigarette and calm down, but keep your eyes glued to the back of her head. Now I wished that I had my luger as I knew it could be a perfect baited trap, which we had all been warned about. Yet I had to go on, it was so intriguing, that enticing smile and flashing eyes had lit a fire within me.

The tram jerked to another stop, yes! She was getting up to alight. I slowly followed, making sure I was the last to get off, but watching closely which way she went and also checking that no one was loitering behind me. She moved quickly now down a side road, glancing back to check that I was following at a respectable distance, then she vanished into a side entrance of a large perfumed garden, in seconds I followed through a wooden gate, only to be confronted by a tall turbaned Arab, holding a thick walking stick. She glided to my side, reaching for my hand, as she whispered in my ear, "Give him twenty piasters." I was ready to give him the moon, but he settled for a handful of small change which was probably equivalent to a week's wages.

My God! Allah, was with me. Everything was going like clockwork as we ran hand-in-hand through a rose garden, then up a short flight of steps to a covered patio. Next minute, I watched breathlessly as she frantically searched in her handbag for a key. She was obviously as excited as I was, eyes flashing like her golden ear-rings peeping between her jet black curls. At last, she found the key and opened the door of a most fabulous house; as she switched on the lights, I found myself in one of the most beautiful rooms I had ever seen. She pressed another switch and all the curtains on three large windows gently swished into place. It was fascinating. The furniture was mostly oriental, inlaid with mother-of-pearl, and in the centre of a large room was a rock garden, complete with a fountain trickling into an inviting pool.

She led me by the hand to a pile of silken cushions on a raised platform near the pool; as I sank down on the cushions, surrounded with tropical plants, she poured out a drink of lemonade and sherbet into a crystal glass. I was halfway to paradise as she ran laughing up a marble stairway, calling to me that she would only be a moment. Now I could hear water splashing from a shower as she sang an Egyptian love song; I knew what some of the words meant and the fire within me grew to a crescendo!

The next minute the tinkling stopped. I held my breath in anticipation as she appeared at the top of the stairs, because I could see right through the flimsy dress that she wore, as she slowly walked down the stairs towards me. My God! She was beautiful, in moments we would be together in paradise!

Yes, there had been magic in the air last night, but destiny now turned the other cheek. She had told me that she was a nanny, working for a wealthy Egyptian family and they were holidaying on the coast near Alexandria. She had been sent back to collect some forgotten things and pick up some medicine for one of the children.

By some strange coincidence I had had my leave plans changed for me, and had returned once more to Cairo. Then, quite unlike my normal character, I had jumped into the first carriage outside the station and let myself be driven to any hotel, also at the precise moment I had left the hotel to walk to the centre of Cairo. I could have got a tram, but no! I had to walk slowly and see the tempting cake in the Greek cafe, and when I was halfway through the cake, the tram stopped almost opposite to me. From that moment on everything began to click together.

Now she had to catch an early train back to the coast. I was ready to change my leave plans and go to Alexandria, but she said it would be impossible for her to go out on her own. The trip back to the villa had been an emergency and she had grasped the few hours of unchaperoned freedom to fulfil her heart's desire!

We had both taken a tremendous risk, as anyone who was in Egypt, at that time, will confirm. Now we whispered our goodbyes in the rose garden, clinging together, knees trembling and eyes misting over. This was the end, as I forced myself to walk alone out through the gate of the perfumed garden.

I decided to walk back to my hotel for breakfast, forget the trams, I could not do with anyone interrupting my thoughts at the moment. Shall I look up the train times to Alexandria? I could give her a bunch of roses as she got on the train, but perhaps, I had better not, it could embarrass her and I may be set on by an angry mob for daring to talk to an unchaperoned Egyptian girl.

After breakfast, I took the tram to the city centre and was swallowed up in the stifling heat, dust and noise. Forget the Egyptian girls, it is no use going after them, I will try to find one of my own kind in the A.T.S. or W.A.A.F. I then made my way to the Y.M.C.A. as a plan was already forming in my mind and after a few discreet enquiries, I had the address of the Y.W.C.A. It was nearly lunch time by the time I had found it and obviously I was not the only one who had been searching!

Chapter 11

'Pandora's Box'

Yes, this was the place where all the - W.R.N.S., A.T.S. and W.A.A.F. girls who were on leave could be found. I had better stop a moment and think what strategy I am going to use to get in the place; you could not just walk into a Christian Womens hostel without a proper reason. So I lit a cigarette and lingered in the shade of a huge fig tree which was in the grounds of the Y.W.C.A., its branches spreading over the garden wall made a delightful shade on the footpath. I noticed that other servicemen lingered here and there in small groups, or, alone like me; whilst down a side street, I noticed a number of flashy cars parked, containing wealthy Egyptians, Greeks, Frenchmen, and more than likely, Italians from the large Italian quarters.

The competition was disconcerting, to say the least; now every man was watching the main gateway which led to a very large villa standing half hidden in beautiful gardens. Every few minutes a small or large group of service girls either came or went through the gates and, often they had soldiers or airmen with them. These lucky chaps were mostly officers or senior N.C.O.'s, what chance did I have, I was not even an N.C.O.!

Rank was going to be the biggest pull here, followed by money, but you could not just stand there and flash a wad of notes; in any case I had to get inside the hostel first. My mind raced ahead.

I lit another cigarette as a plan began to form in my mind. Yes, I would walk boldly in and ask if a particular W.A.A.F. girl was stopping there? Any fictitious name would do, and when they told me she was not there, I would ask if I could wait in the lounge for her because I had heard that she was coming. It would then be up to me to charm some girl before I got thrown out. As I approached the reception desk I could feel my heart thumping, the fictitious name was blurted out and the receptionist began to look through a list of names in a book. Meanwhile, I was busy looking for the door to the lounge and anything else of interest. The next moment, to my surprise, the receptionist said, "she is here, in the garden, I believe." I stared back, trying to conceal my amazement as I thanked her.

This was an unexpected situation. My mind raced ahead and juggled with new plans as I walked through an open rear door, down some steps and into the garden.

In front of me were groups of chairs and tables occupied with laughing men and girls, drinking tea or lemonade. My eyes swept round the garden, taking in the beautiful roses and vivid green lawns, whilst a new plan formulated in my mind. I was not going to walk from table-to-table of men and girls asking the girls names. Then I noticed one table was occupied by three A.T.S. girls on their own, which left one vacant chair. Here, was my chance. I walked up to the table and asked the nearest girl if the chair was being reserved for anyone. The girl said, "it was not, and invited me to sit down." I was in, my feet were under the table!

As if by magic, an Arab servant materialised from behind a clump of cactus plants. He was dressed in flowing white robes with a red sash round his middle and the usual red fez on his head. I was pleased to see him, my chance to break the ice could not have been better timed. "What did the girls wish to drink?" I asked. "We were just going to order lemonade," said one. I ordered a large jug of lemonade with plenty of ice, and the servant disappeared round the cactus plant.

I knew at once that the girl who had spoken came from London, so I asked her "How London was these days?", knowing by her half-tanned skin that she had not been in Egypt very long. At that moment the servant returned, dark eyes flashing and a gleaming smile played on his face because he knew from my face that he was going to receive a handsome tip.

Now I purposely but discreetly let the girls see that my wallet was loaded, even though I was not an - N.C.O.! After the servant had bowed himself away, one of the girls remarked - "that I must have waited along time for leave to have so much money!" At once I knew she was from Birmingham or Wolverhampton, whilst her friend spoke with a Welsh accent, tinkling in a sing-song manner. "Yes, I have waited twelve months for this leave, I have just got back form Tunis." Now, they were all ears, leaning forward to hear more. The questions flowed thick and fast - "What was it like in Tunis and the desert? Had I been to Tobruk etc.?"

Later, I explained how I had got into the hostel. They laughed at my cheek, but I had to be honest with them now that the ice was broken. All the time I was weighing them up wondering which one I could persuade to come with me later and, how could I do it without appearing desperate for the company of an English girl.

I mentioned that I could show them all the interesting places in Cairo, especially the night clubs, but we really need two more men, I ventured. I then drew my chair slightly nearer to the girl from London; she was quite a plain girl with glasses, but attractive in a sweet kind of way. I could see that she was bothered by the shaft of sunlight which had moved onto her head, so I asked her if she would care to change places. She readily agreed, our hands brushed together as we moved, and I knew she was mine, well, almost! Gradually, the other two girls realised we wanted to be alone. I was happy enough to sit and talk to all three for the rest of the afternoon, their tinkling voices fascinating me as it had been a long time without English female company. But now the heat was intense, it was not only mid-summer, but mid-day and only mad dogs and Englishmen are out in the noonday sun.

The girls wanted to go for a siesta which was understandable. The Welsh girl and the one from the Midlands, stood up to say goodbye. I noticed that most of the other tables were already deserted. At last, we were alone. "I will let you join your friends in a moment, but first I want to see you tonight, if that's O.K. with you?"

Her name was Lilian, and now she agreed to see me at seven that evening. I walked back to the reception with her, telling her to prepare to go to a dinner dance, so do not eat too much. We whispered our goodbyes till we meet again. I could not believe my luck, I had achieved something which my fellow airmen had said was impossible. The long walk back to my secluded hotel was nothing, provided I moved slowly from one patch of shade to the next.

Cairo slumbered in the stifling heat, even the trams appeared to have stopped and all the lame beggars and shoe-shine boys had sought the shady doorways to snooze in. The horse-drawn carriages were drawn up at the roadside, each one under a wilting palm tree. The drivers snored in the passenger compartment, whilst the moth-eaten horses slept where they stood, with their heads almost touching the baking roadway. Only small groups of British soldiers and airmen moved listlessly along the dusty roads; they had too much which they wanted to see and too little time to satisfy their curiosity.

Now I had reached the shade of the sweet smelling flowering trees where swarms of flies seemed to live forever. But stop and look closely at the low branches and gradually your eyes will pick out the silent chameleons, which cling like miniature prehistoric monsters to the branches. Only their eyes moved, swivelling back and forth, until a luckless fly settled within range of their long sticky tongues, then, almost faster than your eye could follow, the tongue shot out and the fly was on its way to eternity.

Back at my hotel, I decided to have a siesta in the garden; of course, I should have known better, but my mind was thinking of other things! I dragged a deck chair into the shade and eased off my shoes as I lay back. I had no sooner settled back and closed by eyes, when all the flies nearby pounced on me. It was impossible to stay, so upstairs to my room I went and under my mosquito net as quickly as I could. Just before I dropped off to sleep, I began to wonder 'how do all these Arabs sleep in shady nooks when the flies crawled all over their faces!'

I woke at 5.00p.m. exactly on the dot, like I had told myself to do before I went to sleep. But do not ask me who - 'I' and 'myself' are. I had pondered on that many times when I was alone in the desert. Now, it was wash, shave and change, then catch the tram to the Y.W.C.A. I was ten minutes early, but never mind, I could sit in the entrance hall and wait in comfort. A new receptionist was on duty but I had nothing to worry about this time. It was quite in order for men friends to wait in the entrance hall. Now I could see what a beautiful place this hostel was, I had been too keyed up last time to notice the intricate oriental decorations. This new receptionist was very charming, I told her whom I was waiting for so that her curiosity was satisfied. She must have been about forty, very well preserved and typically English, with a slight haughty-look, which was probably put on as she was obviously some officer's wife doing a little voluntary work. Now she was looking at me closely, with a merry twinkle in her eyes. Had she been told of my 'bluff to get in' at lunch time!

I was very curious to know how this beautiful building became a 'Y.W.C.A.' so turning to the lady with the twinkling eyes, I put the question to her.

"Yes, I can tell you, it belongs to . . . Pasha* a very nice Egyptian gentleman, a really good friend to the British, he is letting us use this place until the war is over."

I had taken a quick glance around the room whilst she was talking and now I realised why her eyes were twinkling, there must have been a dozen men sat around waiting for their lady friends - they were all officers! I turned to thank her for her interesting information and, at that moment, my new girl friend walked towards me.

*A titled Egyptian

She looked very attractive in her A.T.S. tropical uniform; we bade the receptionist good night and were off. I felt very happy, it had been so long since I had taken a girl out without a chaperon tagging along. Now we could walk side by side, even linking arms from time to time.

The hot streets of Cairo swallowed us up, the temperature had dropped to a pleasanter 100° or thereabouts. Lilian, had only been in Egypt about two months and this was her first leave in Cairo. She was fascinated with the place, as I had been and still was. I took her to a night-club later, after we had done a bit of window shopping. Unlike, at home, where all the shops are closed at 6.00p.m. these remained open till midnight and even later, so that the place was alive, vibrating with music and people of many nationalities.

The night-club was one I knew, I had been there many times when on leave, but never before had I been able to take a girl there. The food and Egyptian dancing girls I could recommend, and between the six courses of dinner we danced cheek to cheek. It was past midnight when I took her back to her hostel. The next day she had already booked with a party going to the bazaars, so I would not see her until 8.00p.m.

I was up early the following day after a very restless night. What shall I do today? How many days have I got left? Better go and see the pyramids again, I may not get another chance. So my mind was made up, or was it made up for me? I would set off right after breakfast, before it got too hot. I almost forgot my camera as I dashed out to grab a tram which was the wrong one, but never mind, it would get me halfway and then I would have to change trams. In moments the tram clashed and rattled past the secluded villa where I had spent my first nights' leave, which was now just another memory.

Almost before I realised, the next tram had reached the end of the line, and there it was - The Great Pyramid, beckoning me to go closer. Once more I could feel the power, but it seemed to be reversed now, whereas the last time I was here, the power was flowing outwards. I stood there mystified, perhaps, it ebbed and flowed, depending on the time, or what? It was beyond my knowledge, and I began to wonder how many more tourists had felt it!

Meanwhile, the tram had unloaded all the tourists who were mostly servicemen with a few service girls here and there. I watched them haggling with the camel drivers, then the grunting camels unfolded their legs, jerking backwards and forwards as they stood up with the burdens on their humps. Of course, if you wished to see all the Pyramids and the Sphinx, in one day, then you needed a camel, otherwise, you would be worn out on foot and still you would not see everything.

But it was The Great Pyramid which I had come to see and I felt it was going to be for the last time as I was drawn towards it. A few minutes later, I had reached the foot of the huge pile of cut stones which formed the base of this - the largest stone building in the world!

I stood with my hands touching one of the five-foot square-shaped stones at the foot of the pyramid, and as I leaned back to look upwards to the apex, 480ft. above me, a strong compelling feeling seemed to flow through me, urging me to climb to the top. Now I could feel my hair prickling at the back of my neck and my fingers were tingling on the hot stone, or, so it seemed. I took a few steps backward to look for the best way up, something was urging me to climb up there.

People did climb the Great Pyramid, I knew that already, but it was recommended that you have a guide to show you the way. Well, I had a guide, although, I had never seen him or her, but I had certainly felt their presence many times, and had they not saved my life more than once!

The north-west corner appeared to be the best way up. I stopped for a few minutes, studying the way to the top and then I was off.

Now I seemed to lose all track of time. The prickling at the back of my neck disappeared and the sweat rolled off me as I got higher. The first two hundred feet were very difficult, because each block of stone had to be climbed very carefully. Then there was a step about one foot wide where the outer casing stones had been stolen to build half of Cairo.

At three- hundred feet I wished I had never attempted it, as I began to get the shakes on one of the crumbling ledges, but how the hell was I going to get down again, I thought! Now I was clinging on to each block of stone for dear life as the wind blew shifting sand out of the crevices into my eyes. Stop for a minute and get my breath, I am past the half-way mark, but don't look down, for God's sake!

Where are my guides now, I need a real person to give me courage to go on, because I have got to get to the top now. I looked up again, there was still rows of huge blocks of stone to be surmounted, but at least the blocks were getting smaller, but the steps were smaller also and more worn by the weather. Finally, I got to the last row of stones, my hands had become like steel clamps which took all my will power to open and move to the next stone.

I carefully peered over the last row of stone blocks and there before me, was an almost flat top about twenty feet square and in the centre crouched the figure of a man. He looked up with disbelieving eyes as I walked towards him; there was fear in his face and his voice croaked - "Thank God, someone has come up". I replied - "Thank God, there is someone up here". He told me that he had climbed up the day before and was too afraid to approach the edge to climb down. He was a soldier on leave, and never did I see such a relief on a man's face. I said, "Give me a few minutes to have a cigarette and look around, and then I will help you down". I left him crouching in the centre of the square, he would not even stand up as he puffed madly on one of my cigarettes.

The view was breathtaking, due east was Cairo, and the desert rolling towards the Red Sea. To the south, Memphis and the desert - stretching to Khartoum, and the source of the Nile beyond. Whilst to the west, the Western Desert - the killing ground for the 8th Army and Rommel's men. But it was the view north, to the vivid green Delta which made the hairs tingle on my neck once more. Some kind of message was being given to me if I could only grasp it, for if I looked north-west, I could see a line of green on my right-hand side, whilst on my left, the desert abruptly started. Likewise if I looked north-east, there also, was the abrupt dividing line, whilst on my left - the green, and on my right - the desert, so that both lines formed the sides of a colossal inverted pyramid, whose apex was where I stood. I lit another cigarette, something strange was happening today, why had I been compelled to climb the pyramid on this day? Yes! The soldier was one reason, but was it the only reason?

Now, I could swear I felt lighter, not light-headed, but physically lighter in weight. I looked carefully over the edge and there, far below, like a doll's house, stood the 'Mena House Hotel'. I got the feeling that if I jumped off I would float down like a wisp of cobweb. Instinctively, I moved away from the edge as the overwhelming feeling tried to dominate my senses. A clammy sweat drenched my body, I could feel it flowing inside my shirt as I struggled mentally to overcome the sinister thoughts.

Now, I could understand the soldier's fear and I quickly joined him in the centre of the square, squatting down next to him to calm my whirling thoughts. We squatted there in silence, I dare not say anything to him about my own inner terror which was building up inside me. I dare not even show it. If this chap had been up there most of the day before, and then spent all night and this morning crouched on top of the Great Pyramid, in the scorching heat, he could be ready to crack. Perhaps, he may go crackers and either push or drag me over the edge! My God! We are in a fix; what the hell should I do? If I try to help him down, he could become panic stricken on the edge and grab me like a drowning man grabs at a straw.

I dished out two more cigarettes as I tried to think what to do. I dare not walk to the edge myself now, but I will have to do something fast; the longer this chap stops up here, the worse state he is going to be in and myself too. God! I wish someone else would come up. We crouched there in silence, puffing on our cigarettes, waiting, each one wrapped in his own thoughts, perhaps, even praying now. Suddenly, very gradually, I could feel the tension and inner panic slipping away, slowly, almost un-noticed, like the ebbing tide. I did not need to look up at the blinding sun, I knew it was, even now, above the apex of the Great Pyramid.

The moment had come, silently, like a fleeting shadow, now I could feel the power flowing outwards, it was as if the pyramid was a 'living thing' - breathing out to protect Egypt, as it had done so for thousands of years. I do believe that my friend could feel something also, for he now stood up and a glimmer of a smile flashed across his face. "Come on," he said! "I will buy you a pint at the 'Mena House Hotel' The change in the soldier was dramatic. I could also feel it as I stood up and we moved towards the edge of the 480 foot drop. But, I was still very uneasy. Was he really alright now, or had he cracked inside unknown to me and was he just waiting to see if I would float like a cobweb?

I kept my distance, just shouting to him to put his feet more to the left or right, until gradually and very slowly we got lower and lower and, at last, our feet sank into the sand at the base of the Great Pyramid. I got my free beer; normally, I only drink halves, but this time, I knocked back a pint in a very short time!

The soldier was eager to get back to his hotel, he said, "his pals would be wondering where he had got to and, he had already lost nearly two days of his leave" So we bid each other goodbye and I ordered another drink. I wanted to think about the queer experience of feeling lighter on top of the Great Pyramid. Had anyone else felt the same and, had any experiments been made with a spring balance at different times of the day?

I had heard that many people chose this place to commit suicide. It was said to be a very popular place, but had they really committed suicide, or just been convinced that they would float gently down, like a feather. Only one thing was certain in my mind, I would never attempt to climb up again!

I sipped at my beer, as the mystery went round and round in my head. How could I describe that peculiar feeling of power, 'ebbing and flowing' which I had felt on the apex of the pyramid. But what must the power be like on the few days of the year, when, because of the Pyramid's shape and because it was built at latitude 30° - it suddenly, at mid-day, swallowed up its own shadow? My mind was in a whirl, trying to grapple with one of Egypt's ancient mysteries. I felt that I had been given some kind of elusive clue as to why the great Pyramid was built on that particular spot and, why was it built at all?

Was the inverted pyramid shape of the Delta another clue? With its abrupt dividing lines marking out the fertile Delta from the barren desert on either side. But, then there was also the mysterious 'Sphinx' watching for the sunrise, but, not only watching, it was crouched, waiting in expectancy for the first rays of the sun to bathe its face in golden life-giving heat and power. Yes! I am certain that both objects are inter-related with each other in more ways than one!

The Sphinx, is not only silently waiting for each sunrise - it is on guard - the face of a man showing wisdom and infinite patience, made in His image, grafted onto the body of a lion - the king of the beasts. But, what has the Sphinx been guarding for thousands of years? And is mankind ready to open - 'Pandora's box', knowing or not knowing that the contents will turn the world upside down!!

I feel that the time is very close when a chosen person will stand in the appointed place, near the Sphinx, at the right time and say - 'dig here'. Then, let the people beware, for when the hidden wisdom emerges form the secret places, many will want to re-bury it in museum vaults or Vatican cellars. They will want to keep the secret knowledge to themselves, saying - 'the world is not ready yet!' But, they will be wrong, because 'pandora's box' will not be found until we are ready to receive it!!!

Chapter 12

An Unexpected Coincidence

I lingered over another drink in the shady garden, there was no hurry for me to get back to my own hotel, my date with Lilian was not till 8.00p.m. Yes, it was very pleasant and relaxing here, no shoe-shine boys were allowed to pester you, no peddlers of Spanish Fly or fortune tellers were allowed in to slink from table to table. It was a very high class place, even the Prime Minister, Mr. Churchill, had stopped here the year before on his way for talks with J. Stalin, who wanted to beg for more guns, but would not step outside the Iron Curtain to meet his benefactor half-way!

So. Mr. Churchill, who was a sick man of over seventy at that time, made the hazardous journey to see this Russian leader who was too afraid to come out of his own back yard. As my eyes swept round the peaceful garden again, I noticed that most of the tables were occupied by officers and I began to wonder if the Mena House Hotel had been made into an 'officers only' hotel, like the Sheppards Hotel in Cairo.

This train of thought lead me to reckoning up how long I had been in the R.A.F. I had joined in April 1938, for six years. My God! It will be six years next April, and I am still only a leading aircraft man. Many times in the Desert, I had had the feeling that I had been over-looked for promotion. Often I had met corporals and sergeants just out from Blighty, who had only half my length of service and they were not even regulars.

My mind was made up, I would see my C.O. when I got back to Aboukir, and put it to him. Meanwhile, I got the tram back to my hotel. Now my mind was busy planning where to take Lilian in the evening and, how to compose my application form to see the CO. when I finished my leave.

At the Y.W.C.A. Lilian was waiting for me in the lounge. I suggested going to one of the open-air cinemas; she was willing and curious to see what an open-air cinema was like. Of course, it was already dark and we soon found a cinema with a suitable film on.

The cinema was just an open space lined with trees and rows of wicker chairs on the sand, with the usual bar at the rear. Some American film was on blaring out into the night and probably upsetting the people in the blocks of flats nearby. The French language appeared at the bottom, with Arabic on the right of the screen and Greek on the left on separate small screens.

We had not been sat down more than ten minutes when the bugs came out of the chairs to devour the backs of our legs and arms, whilst mosquitoes dived behind our ears. So-much for the open-air cinema. We left in a hurry whilst I noticed the locals remained - were they determined to have their money's worth or did they have some secret weapon to ward off the bugs and mosquitoes?

We took a stroll along the banks of the Nile; it was a very romantic place in a sort of park but, danger lurked behind every clump of roses. There were very few couples and they were all Europeans, but, it was the small groups of Arab men lurking in the shadows that completely spoiled any romantic thoughts. I noticed them creeping up on us every time we stopped for a moment, it was hopeless; there they were peeping round the palm trees or through the bushes. It was far too risky to linger any longer, so we returned to the garden of the Y.W.C.A. Here, we could sit in peace drinking tea, as we smoked and talked whilst occasionally holding hands and later, kissing under the palm trees. It was all very nice as far as it went, Lilian, now wanted to talk about what to do tomorrow. She wanted to go to the Zoo and would I take her? I had never been there but I knew where it was, so we whispered our goodbyes till tomorrow and I set off to walk back to my hotel.

I walked at a reasonably quick pace with all my senses switched on because, not only was it very late, it was also quite risky to walk alone out of the centre of Cairo, in the early hours of the morning. Now, I was watching every shadow and especially the darker doorways, yet, although I felt ill at ease and wide awake for anything, I was still caught by surprise and ingenuity!

My hotel was still about two hundred yards away, when suddenly, a man limped out of a doorway in front of me. One foot was bandaged up and he appeared to be quite lame as he hobbled along, leaning heavily on a thick walking stick. I soon caught him up and passed in front of him but, a few seconds later I was fully alerted to the sound of bare feet running behind me. I turned quickly, just in time to dodge the walking stick which had now become a 'club' aimed at the back of my head. The blow caught me on the right shoulder as I stamped on his bare toes - now, I ran to my hotel leaving him hopping about on one foot!

Sleep was not easy for me that night, the bones in my shoulder were badly bruised. I tossed and turned all night, listening to the frustrated mosquitoes trying to find a way past the net draped over my bed.

Next day I stopped in bed till about 10.00a.m. My date with Lilian, was not till 3.00p.m. so there was no need to hurry. I would get myself a light lunch at the Greek cafe down the road and then walk to the Y.W.C.A.

I arrived in good time to take Lilian to the Zoo. We would have strawberries and cream beside the lake at the little cafe - like the brochures recommended. But, at the reception desk I got a shock, she had left a message to say that she had met an old friend and would not be seeing me any more. I thanked the receptionist and walked out of the door in stunned silence. So that was that, what shall I do now? Go and get drunk or go to the Zoo on my own?

I was just going out of the gateway of the Y.W.C.A. when Lilian came in with the Welsh girl. Now, she was full of apologies and said that she had met a soldier from her own camp but, she could still come to the Zoo with me if I wished because she was not meeting her soldier friend till 8.00p.m. I only hesitated a second, thinking it's better than being on my own, so I agreed to take her.

We had our strawberries and cream beside the lake, sitting under the palm trees in wicker chairs, but the magic had gone, my mind was already on other things. Eventually, I took her back to her hostel. We were later than we had expected to be and now the wheel of fate turned full circle, for coming out of the garden to meet Lilian, was the soldier whom I had met on top of the Great Pyramid! I could not believe my eyes, it was an unexpected coincidence. We stared at each other in amazement, then he offered to buy me another drink which I had to refuse, I was in no mood to linger. My mind was in a turmoil, so I said goodbye to them both and quickly disappeared into the centre of Cairo.

The last part of my leave flew by in a whirl of night clubs, booze and belly dancers. This surely is my last leave in Cairo.

Only the good news splashed across the front of the Egyptian Mail lifted me out of the depression into which I had fallen.

It appeared that whilst I was on the long road back from Tunisia to Alexandria, the British and Empire Forces, along with the Americans, had invaded Sicily. Now, Sicily had fallen and there were strong hints that the Italians were not only ready to pack it in, but to change sides also. On top of that, the British were also landing on the Greek Islands - and slowly winning them back. So now, the light at the end of the dark tunnel was, at last, beginning to grow brighter.

I had been back off leave about a week when I sent in my application form to see my Commanding Officer about promotion. Actually, I did not really expect anything to happen, never-the-less, I wanted him to know how I felt about being overlooked! A few days later, my request to see him became a reality as I was ushered into his office. He listened to all I had to say about how long I had been in the R.A.F. and also - how long I had been a leading aircraftman etc. Then he said - "Leave it with me, I will go into it." I returned to work feeling very pleased with the way he had understood my feelings.

The weeks dragged by as I continued to repair - Spitfires, Lysanders and Hurricanes, until one day, a buzz of excitement flew around the hangar. A Fiesla Storch had landed, not on the airfield runway, but between the hangars. I, and everyone else went outside to have a look at it. I could not tell if it was one of those I had worked on at Tripoli, because this one had been painted in R.A.F. colours. He had only come in for some petrol and very soon he took off again, hopping between the hangars like a dragon fly on a summer's day.

It must have been about one month after seeing my C.O., when I was promoted to - Corporal! I was very pleased to move up in the 'pecking' order, my only regret was that I had not done anything about it months or years before!

It was about this time, mid-September 1943, that we heard the good news - the 8th Army had landed in Southern Italy, some days before and had advanced over one hundred miles up the leg of Italy. Whilst more British and Americans had punched their way ashore at Salerno, just south of Naples. A savage German counter-attack, near Salerno, had nearly driven our forces back into the sea, but, they managed to hang on to a small beach head.

Italy had, at last, surrendered, and some of the Italians had turned on the Germans - a most unusual state of affairs! Italy was in a turmoil and slowly disintergrating as the Germans hurriedly dug-in from east to west across the country, near Naples, at first. So, Naples and other Italian towns were bombed by the Americans and R.A.F. and later, as we advanced, the Germans now bombed Naples and other towns to the south.

Poor Italy was being systematically smashed to pieces by both sides, but, as winter approached everyone became bogged down for a little while. In the meantime, we worked like maniacs, repairing hundreds of our smashed-up fighters which were still pouring back from the desert and, from as far away as Tunisia.

Another Christmas was approaching and there was still no signs of getting any more leave. I had only had seven days in the past twelve months, but, they would not let me nor anyone else have any more leave at the moment.

On the whole, we were lucky at Aboukir, even when the guard duties or fire pickets were chosen at Christmas and New Year, there were enough Jews on the Camp for them to take over these duties. Of course, when the Jews had their different religious festivals, we took over the unpleasant guard duties etc.

Another Christmas slipped by and we had a reasonably good time at Aboukir; we even had a camp dance! Bus loads of girls and, of course, their chaperons were brought in, mostly from the Greek quarters of Alexandria. As usual, the girls were out numbered by something like - ten to one, so even their overweight mamas were pressed into service on the dance floor; not a very satisfactory situation, although it was better than nothing.

After New Year 1944 - we heard that the British, Americans, Canadians, New Zealanders, Maoris, Indians, Poles and Free French, etc., had hammered their way for four hundred miles up the leg of Italy.

It was about this time that I was posted to an airfield on the west bank of the Suez Canal. The place was El Ballah, not far from Ismailia. Here, I was put to work servicing Harvard training aircraft. These dual-controlled Harvards, were the noisiest aircraft I had very worked on; the high-pitched whine, generated by the propeller, seared into my sensitive ears like a steel skewer. Even the sound of one Harvard taking-off, was enough, but when a number of them took-off together, the sound was most shattering and, it made me realise just how 'keyed up' my nerves had become.

Had I been normal, I suppose I could have stood it easier but, I had not really been normal since 13th June, 1942, see 'Nightmare Towards The Path' Each day I waited for sun-down and the peace which followed; now my head could stop singing for a few hours.

I had been at El Ballah, about three weeks when I got my first flight in a Harvard. My team of airmen and I had just completed a complicated repair after the aircraft had made a very heavy landing. Now, I asked the test pilot if he would take me up on test with him?

This was normal practice in the R.A.F. when the aircraft was a multi-seater, then afterwards, those who had repaired it were ordered to go 'on test' with it. It kept you on your toes and gave the 'test pilot' confidence. So, this time, I got a parachute and helmet with a built-in intercom: to enable me to ask the pilot if I could fly the aircraft. I had been planning for this chance as soon as I found myself working on dual-control aircraft.

So now I strapped myself into the front seat and plugged in the intercom. It was a pleasant surprise to find that the noise was not half as bad in the enclosed cockpit as it was outside on the airfield.

At 2,000ft. I asked if I could take the controls and the pilot said 'Yes'. I was delighted as I flew up and down the Suez Canal, turning left, then right, then diving down and up. Of course, as an airframe fitter we had to know how an aeroplane flew and what controls did what, etc. The pilot did have to correct me from time to time, but on the whole, he said "I was doing very well". After about thirty minutes he took over to make the landing. This had been one of the best flights I had ever had - from now on, I would be looking for more, not only to get away from the racket on the ground, but to get more flying instruction.

A few days later, after repairing another Harvard, I took advantage of my position in the 'pecking' order, to go up on test again. Remember, after my Court Martial for a 'silly' offence, I had told myself to get what I could out of the R.A.F. in future!

So, I had another half-hour instruction, keeping the nose at the right attitude and the wings straight and level; now the stick and rudder together as we turn left or right. The instructions came into my ears from the pilot behind me - "Don't let your nose drop when you turn, keep looking for other aircraft," and so on. "Now, follow me through as we make the approach and landing, i.e. keep your hands and feet lightly on the controls." This was wonderful, I was very happy and thoroughly satisfied with things, until one day tragedy struck one of my men!

I have already mentioned the 'ear piercing whine' which came from the Harvard, whether it was 'taking-off' or the engine being tested on the ground. The noise shattered your concentration, especially when three or four were testing their engines together in a row. Suddenly, in front of me and two more pals, an airman walked right into a whirling propeller. You can imagine the results, I do not need to go into the horrifying details. Whirling propellers were always an ever present danger on any airfield. How many airmen had been killed over the years by this method, I never knew, but to see it happening to a pal, was a paralysing shock, especially when you knew it could be anyone else, at any time and there was no second chance!

The weeks dragged by, I received more flying instruction in the Harvards, and then one day I was put in charge of a captured Junkers 87 - Dive-bomber.

Now, I had two Italian prisoners to look after as well. They had worked on German aircraft from time to time and, because they were now on our side, they were not really prisoners any more!

The Junkers was used for training our pilots in the best methods of shooting them down. It was not long before I went up in the dive-bomber for a flight. I was in the rear-gunner's position, but there were no guns now and, I hoped they were only camera guns on the Spitfires which came chasing after us when we reached about four thousand feet.

This was a real hair-raising experience and, I could see that the rear-gunner would have had no chance because the modern Spitfire carried four cannons and they could have blasted us out of the sky, whilst they were still out of range of any machine gun in the Stukas rear cockpit.

One after the other, the Spitfires came at us, first from the rear, then from the side or underneath us, as the Stuka turned and twisted in a very tight circle. Later, we went into a screaming dive from about six thousand feet. One Spitfire followed us down and, as we pulled out of the dive, I felt myself pinned to the seat like a 'wooden dummy', unable to move my hands or feet as the 'G' force built up. Then a mad whirl of sky, sand and more sky, as we twisted and turned in a dance of death, which fortunately, was not for real!

Chapter 13

Near the brink

Three or four months slid by and my nerves were getting more on edge, even though I had been away from the front line airfields for some time now, I could not unwind.

The damage had been done and, my subconscious mind was crammed with horrific sights and experiences of near certain death. But, not only that, a sinister apprehension was building up amongst many of the airmen who had completed three years, or more, of the recognised four year tour of duty in the Middle East. A dark cloud hung over us - were our names on the boat list for home and was it a 'fool proof' system, where your name automatically moved up the list? Or was it subject to some faceless persons drawing names out of a hat? If only some high-ranking official would re-assure us that we had no need to worry.

It only needed some responsible person to show a bit of wisdom and say, 'that the system is absolutely fair and square, you will be home when you have done four years, give or take a month or two. You will not be sent out to the jungles of Burma to see the Japs off until you have had a month's leave at home, unless of course, some unforeseen crisis flares up.'

I had now completed my six years service with the R.A.F. after signing on at 17, so I made out another application form to see my Commanding Officer. This was probably a subconscious wish to try to dispel the apprehension about the boat list but, I was curious to see what would happen. Would they discharge me and then call me up on the spot, or send me home with all the leave they owed me?

A few days later the C.O. sent for me and I told him that I should have been discharged the other week when my six years service were up; what happens now? He was a bit surprised, I could read it in his face but he had the answer in seconds. "You just carry on old boy, till the end of the war!" "Well, what about some leave, I said! I had only had seven days in the past eighteen months." This, really shook him - my application to see him had not mentioned a request for leave and, we were entitled to four weeks per year. "Leave it to me," he said! "I will see what I can do." Weeks slid by and nothing happened, except that now I began to experience horrible dreams two or three times a week.

In the 'mess' one night, we suddenly heard about the invasion of Europe from England. It certainly lifted up all of our spirits for a while. Then someone said "Don't forget the Japs, we still have to finish those bastards off and that could take years."

Of course, at that time, very few people knew that an Atomic Bomb had nearly been completed in Armerica. Thanks to the British scientists who had been studying how to make an Atomic Bomb since 1940, and probably before then! Remember, we had been'up to our ears' in the most devastating war which the world had ever seen and, after Dunkirk, we were on our own. At that time, it was suspected that the German scientists were also busy probing the secrets of the Atom. So, work went ahead in Britain, as fast as possible under the circumstances in which we found orselves.

But, because we were under seige with the enemy just over twenty miles away and bombing us almost every day and night, it was not easy to concentrate on such a huge complicated task. It would also be very dangerous to test an Atomic Bomb in our overcrowded islands So, plans were made to make the Bomb in Canada, out-of-the-way of our air-raids and threats of invasion. But, destiny stepped in, with the unprovoked attack on the American fleet by the Japs, who had not even declared war!

After their very rude awakening, the Americans became interested in how to make an Atomic Bomb. So, we invited their top scientists to come over and have a look at how we were progressing in solving the 'thousand and one' problems, which no one had ever heard of before!

With the dramatic change of world events, the British Government gave the Americans, all of our secrets of how an Atomic Bomb could be made. I should read that again if you have not grasped what I have just written.

In due course the British scientists went to America, to help them build the 'bomb'.. Here, they could all work together without being interrupted by air attacks but, it still took them till 1945 to solve all the problems.

Another two months passed by in a whirl of screeming propellers and ear piercing noise. The horrific accident to my pal played on my shattered nerves and now I could not sleep properly and when I did, the nightmares were waiting for me.

Often, I thought how lucky I had been to survive so far. Don't crack up now, you are still in one piece, you have only to hang on because next year you really could be 'home for Christmas'. But, now I was going worse, part of my face kept twitching uncontrollably and I was eating less and less.

Eventually, I had to go and see the Medical Officer. He listened to all I had to say, then the next day he sent me for a second opinion to the Medical Officer in Heliopolis. It was nice to see my old camp once more but, I did not stop long and was soon back at El Ballah, with a recommendation that I be given a job away from the aircraft in an office for a while.

This was, indeed, a nice change. I was away from most of the noise, sitting at a desk in the shade. What more could I ask for! But, my face still twitched and I was still the same, gradually going down hill, also the office staff must have been told to keep an eye on me, because now I saw the knowing looks passing from one to the other.

Some days or weeks later I was told that the doctor wished to see me again. So, the next day I reported to his surgery and was surprised to see an 'armed guard' hanging about in the waiting room!

The doctor spoke to me for a few minutes, saying, amongst other things, that I would be going to a hospital for a rest. "Go with these men to the ambulance outside!"

Another guard had appeared from nowhere and I walked between them to the ambulance. Then, I was even more surprised when they got in with me and sat on either side. I thought, "My God! they must think I am a raving lunatic," so I jokingly said "What are you two coming for?" "I am not going to go berserk, I have not gone 'round the bend' yet." Just a stony silence greeted my remark, so I shut-up also.

Now I was interested in the direction in which we were going and, I believe it was south, down the side of the Suez Canal. About two hours later, I noticed that we were approaching the gates of a huge Army Camp. But, this was no ordinary camp, the gates were twenty feef high made of barbed wire, strung on an open wooden frame-work. A similar twenty foot barbed wire fence enclosed a collection of wooden buildings. The whole lot looked like a typical Prisoner of War Camp, complete with armed guards at the gate. I thought, surely we are not going in there! But we did!Hell! If this is a hospital, my name is Napolean!

The ambulance stopped near a wooden hut, I got out with my bodyguards close to me on either side and we were ushered into the hut. I was told to stand in front of a long empty desk with three empty chairs at the other side of the desk. My R.A.F. guards now disappeared as one Army Red-cap took their place. I turned my head to look at him and observed that he was armed with a wooden club which looked like a pickaxe handle well blancoed. "Eyes front," he barked out, so I swung my eyes to the front and waited. Now apprehension swept through me, 'better watch this one, he will have me in a straight jacket or a padded cell if I am not careful.'

I waited for about twenty minutes with a a swarm of flies buzzing around my head. Then suddenly a rear door opened behind the desk and in walked three Army Medical Officers. I was glad to see that they were, in fact, Medical Officers! The Red-cap clicked his heels behind me, then I could hear his arm swishing in a salute so I did the same.

The officers sat down telling the guard to wait outside, whilst I remained standing infront of them in the centre of the room.

One of the officers was obviously a 'trick cyclist' and he fired questions at me as my right cheek continued to twitch and he rustled a sheaf of papers in his hands whilst the other two flicked their fly whisks around their heads every few seconds!

I had already answered a similar barrage of questions some days before, put to me by the R.A.F. Medical Officers, and now, even though it was all on paper in front of them, they still asked me the same questions.

"How long have you been having these nightmares? How long have you been unable to sleep or eat properly?" And many more questions. Now they started whispering together, the middle one turning left and right as they endeavoured to come to some conclusion of what may be wrong with me. But, I am sure that they did not realise my hearing had become hypersensitive through the experience in 1942. I could clearly hear all that was being suggested!

Now another question, which, so far, had been overlooked. "Are there any more symptoms which you have noticed happening to you lately?"

Yes, for the past few weeks, I have found myself having to perform a particular ritual, like some people find they must not step on a line on the pavement, or, others must touch every rail in a fence as they pass by, otherwise something dreadful will happen to them that same day or very soon.

I raised my hand to stop them intervening and they never batted an eyelid so I continued. My compulsion is slightly different but never-the-less, it is becoming annoying to me who should know better. I am not one of those who must cross themselves everytime they see a funeral, otherwise the bogey man will have them.

Now a flicker of a smile was on their faces. "Go on!" the middle one said. So I explained my little compulsion which had been growing more intricate daily. I know why I do it, I continued; I have been in the Middle East, three and a half years, so I have only another six months to do to complete my four years tour of duty. But now, I am full of apprehension; so many times I have been close to certain death, and yet, I have miraculously got away with it in the past. Therefore, I realise, that I have used up eight of my nine lives and will I get back home after four years, or will they send me to the Far East, instead of home? Which has already been done with men going home from India, who suddenly found themselves trapped in Egypt, for an unknown length of time!

I thought, I will 'rub it in' whilst I have their attention."Yes, I believe I know what is wrong with me and I also know the cure".

The fly whisks suddenly stopped and the man in the centre said, "and what is that?" "First", I said, "I have only had seven days leave in well over eighteen months. If I was sent home to the green fields of England for a months leave, I would be better before the month was up".

Only the buzzing of the flies broke the silence which followed. Had I gone too far? No! two of them were half smiling, whilst the third man put on a stony mask as he thought about the blunt truth. Seconds later, the guard was called into take me away and I knew by his searching look that he had overheard all I had said.

We walked off down a well swept footpath, past the regimented stones on either side which had all been carefully whitewashed. In vain, I looked for trim pretty nurses in well starched uniforms, but there was none, only groups of inmates, busy raking the sand over and whitewashing anything which did not move.

We came at length to a larger brick building, here, we waited at the door until it was unlocked from the inside. An Army Medical orderly who looked more like a prize fighter, told me to come inside. Now the Red-cap disappeared and the orderly locked the door behind me!

I found myself in a long corridor with grim looking steel cell doors spaced out on either side.The orderly produced his bunch of keys and unlocked one of the steel doors. Now with a sickly grin he indicated for me to go into the cell. Once inside, the door clanged shut behind me and I found myself in an almost bare room, a cage, with a small barred window, ten feet from the floor on the far wall.

I turned round to look at the door, a blood-shot eye was pressed to the glass peep hole staring at me, so I leaned forward and put my eye right up to the peep hole and stared back, eyeball to eyeball. This produced an animal-like snarl on the other side of the door, then a steel shutter was slid over the outside of the peephole.

What did they expect me to do - perform a somersault because I was happy, or crawl up the wall with my bare hands?

I realised I was under observation and that they were still trying to assess whether I had 'gone over the edge' or, whether they had caught me at the 'brink'.

Now I checked the rest of the room. I had already noticed an army-type bed in the corner, with a wooden locker and a chair by the bed. But, I was surprised to find that the bed was not only comfortable, it also had sheets and a pillow case on the pillow; this was real luxury!

The eye was back at the peep-hole again, but I ignored it, as I searched the walls for more peep-holes or a hidden microphone.

Now I lay on the bed searching in my pockets for a cigarette. I had been whisked away so unexpectedly that morning, that I had nothing with me, except five cigarettes and a few matches.

I had just settled down to have a quiet smoke, when suddenly, with a clatter, a steel trap door in the door was banged open and a man's hand came through with a tray of food. Leaping off the bed, I just had time to grab the tray before the hand was withdrawn and the trap door slammed shut as I said 'thanks'.

For the next five minutes the clattering and banging went on out of sight in the corridor. Occasionally, someone grunted or cursed as food trays clattered on the floor! But, the food was quite good. I had lived on much worse for years in the desert.

My toilet was a bucket in one corner of the room and later I was given a towel and soap, plus a tooth brush, but no razor, yet!

The days dragged on, no one ever came to see me, no thoughtful parsons or Medical Officers came to ask me how I was feeling, only the eyes watching through the peep-hole. My God! it's enough to send you up-the-wall, but I must stick it out until they are convinced that I am not Napoleon!

The nights were the worst part. The lights behind a grille in the ceiling, blazed all night so that I could be observed at all times. But, it was the noise from the other cages which kept me awake. Suddenly, a chair would be flung at a steel door, then a crazy scream, or gibberish shouting would quickly bring studded army boots along the concrete corridor. Then the shuffling and cursing as the man was over-powered by the heavy mob. I could see it all in my mind's eye, even the needles of the syringes going in as he was injected with - calming drugs.

Hell! it pays to keep quiet here, if you can, if that is the type of treatment they dish out.I lost count of time. Time, was just something which dragged on and on. Until one day my cell door opened and the prize fighter said "Come with me!" He followed behind me like a shadow, saying nothing except, left-turn, into a room at the end of the corridor.

A sergeant was sitting behind a desk and he motioned me to sit at a small table. Now, he actually asked me how I was. I said, "okay!" "But I could do with some cigarettes and a walk in the fresh air." He threw me a packet of cigarettes, watching me carefully all the time as he now slid a paper and pencil onto my table.

Right! I want you to tick what you think are the right answers to the list of puzzles on the paper. It was an Intelligence Test, the moment of truth had arrived. I thought what shall I do, as I glanced at the childish puzzles on the paper.

If I tick every correct answer they may think I have been swinging the lead, yet, on the other hand, if I appear too dim I will never get out of this damned cell! So, I decided I would give them a puzzle to sort out. I deliberately ticked some of the wrong answers to the easy puzzles and some of the right answers likewise. I did the same with the harder puzzles. That will give you something to think about, I thought, as I lit a cigarette.

The orderly took me back to my cell and the door slammed shut. I managed to get through a few more days and noisy nights, but I noticed the 'eye' was often missing from the peep-hole!

A few days later I was taken out of my cell and then the door at the end of the corridor was unlocked. The daylight and fresh air hit me as if I was a drunken man. The orderly told me to report to hut number so-and-so and I walked away on my own. This was unbelievable!

It was now that I realised how large the place was. I walked past a dozen or more numbered huts and passed groups of men still raking the sand or whitewashing lines of stones around the huts.

At last, I came to the hut which I had been told to go to. I reported to an orderly and he took me to a bed inside, saying "This is where you will sleep".

There must have been sixty beds in the hut and at one end was a veranda, full of deck chairs in the shade. I put my soap, towel and tooth-brush. In the locker and walked off to the veranda. Here, I sat with a group of gaunt-looking soldiers and lit a cigarette, eager to talk with anybody. "Have you just been processed?" One of the soldiers said. "You mean in solitary - under observation?" I said.

The soldier nodded, saying, "Hope you did not tick all the right answers in the Intelligence Test, otherwise you will be out soon; you want to act daft, it's cushy here! They will have you out in Burma, fighting the Japs, before you realise it and you want to keep away from those crafty swines. The Germans are civilised in comparison." He obviously had not recognised my shabby R.A.F. Working uniform, but now he carried on, saying, "He had been captured when Mandalay fell which resulted in him being a prisoner for a few weeks until he escaped.

"They treated us like animals, clubbing us with rifle buts and even bayoneting men who were tied up in the sun!" He had been five years in the Indian Army and thought he was going home when he boarded a Troopship at Bombay. Many had gone beserk when they were 'off loaded' in Egypt, to be re-trained as Infantry, on gruelling courses! "There are, at least, two camps like this in India", he said, "and have you met the nurses here?" He told me there were five nurses who had also cracked up coming from India, thinking they were going home, only to be 'dumped' in Egypt.

It made me wonder, how could the British Government treat the men and women like this and, obviously the British public had no idea of what was going on!

In this camp or hospital, there must have been something like a thousand inmates and that number was fluctuating all the time as the men recovered, or the scroungers were weeded out so that more could be rescued from the very brink of the abyss.

But, what was really happening at the top? The Whitehall warriors moving their little flags about on the world map; did they really understand that each flag represented tens of thousands of men, many of whom, had not been home to see their families for - four, five or more years!

These shattered men who I saw, had fought for years all over the world from - Tunis to Mandalay, re-writing history with their own blood. Even as I lost count of time in the cages, the rumours were filtering through that some British troops had mutinied in Italy. There must have been some good reason for this latest mutiny, if it was the latest mutiny! What red-tape or pigheadedness had roused the men to mutiny this time?

Come on! The soldier said, "grab your eating irons, it's dinner-time." I had no eating irons to grab but I followed him to a huge 'mess-hut' where a queue of assorted soldiers and airmen had already formed.

Everyone was dressed in any fashion, no hats, no socks, and no one gave a damn for anything or anyone - this was great, you felt the tensions slipping away. I had to wait until my new friend had finished with his irons and then I had a very good dinner

Everyone in the 'mess' appeared to be quite happy and now and then a group of them would start acting daft, pretending to be balmy. At least, I imagine they were only pretending.

Surprise followed surprise in quick succession, then round about three thirty p.m. back in my hut, I noticed a group of men getting ready to go swimming. "Where are you going to swim in this place? I said". "Follow us and you will see" the men said.

So I followed, bringing only my towel because I had no trunks. Soon we were approaching the twenty foot fence, but there at the foot someone had cut an opening. Once through the opening we were amongst the sand dunes on one of the Bitter Lakes, which link up the Suez Canal. I walked into the lake with my shorts and shirt still on - giving them a much needed wash. It was like walking into a hot bath, so hot that after a few minutes I had to come out to cool off in the shade of some date palms.

In the evening, my soldier friend said, "Come on, I will show you the N.A.A.F.I., and you may see the nurses, they are in there most nights since their processing. So off we went, I cannot remember if they sold beer, but we could get soft drinks, cigs. tea and rock cakes, if you had money.

By nine o'clock the place was packed with men all eagerly waiting for one thing, a chance to see someone of the opposite sex. Heads kept swivelling round every time someone came through the doors. At last, they arrived, everyone cheered and whistled as the crowd parted for them. The girls were celebrities and they knew it, if that did not help them to get better soon, nothing would.

Next morning I got another surprise, each hut had been rigged up with a loudspeaker and, at about 7.00a.m. beautiful soothing music drifted gently through the hut. What unexpected wisdom and no one chatted between the Strauss records. If only todays disc jockies could do likewise. But why did they not have the soothing music in the cages where it was more needed? Just think how much they could have saved in brute force and drugs!

I had been in the hut about ten days and was feeling much better. I no longer had to perform the stupid compulsive ritual and my right cheek only went into the uncontrollable flutter occasionally.

One day my friend from India, showed me the 'wired off' compound within the hospital grounds. "Come and see the Zoo" he had jokingly said one day, but it was no joke, only pity and compassion could flow from me to these poor fellows.

We stared through the inner barbed wire fence and I shall never forget the utter dejected blank faces which took no notice of us. They were zombies from the bottom of the pit. My God! How many mothers sons were there in that ghastly place? They walked aimlessly up and down or round and round in circles. Some pushed empty wheel barrows, whilst others swept the same path a thousand times a day! But, how many more were there out of sight, probably trussed up in straight jackets, or weeping like lost children in the padded cells?

I did not visit the zoo any more, the shock had been too much for me, poor beggars - were these the empty shells of men who had formed the human wedges hammered in at El Alamein?

How long have I been here now? Why don't the R.A.F. send on my mail? I had not had a letter from home for months but neither had I written home for a long time, it was impossible here. My money had run out long ago and in any case I did not want any army trick cyclist censoring my letters.

Now my only pleasure was creeping through the hole in the fence, I got immense satisfaction by doing that and then I would sit for hours watching the ships passing in the distance. One of these days I will be on one of those bloody ships going home, that will be the day.

I had got my weight back to normal and all the other queer symptoms had disappeared as if my magic. Now all I wanted was to get out and mix with normal people, especially some who were the opposite sex.

Then suddenly one day, I was told to prepare to be discharged from the hospital. "Be ready to see the Medical Officer at 9.00a.m. tomorrow." So the next day I said my goodbyes to my soldier friends and walked to the Medical Officer's hut. At last, he was ready to see me. I was expecting some kindly words of advice and a friendly cheerio but, wait for it, you will be as surprised as I was.

Now the usual Red-cap marched me into the room where the M.O. sat behind a desk, shuffling the inevitable sheaf of papers. At last, he looked up and I could see by his expression that he was not amused.

Then he spoke. "You have been wasting our time here, we can find nothing wrong with you". I was secretly elated by his outburst as he proceeded to give me a good 'ticking off'. His face became redder and redder and his fly whisk worked overtime until he finished with a curt 'dismiss'. But I was not going to be dismissed without a word, so I said, as calmly as I could, "I did not ask to come here!" Then I smartly turned on my heels and marched out with the Red-cap fuming behind me.

Chapter 14

More than Solomon's Wisdom

The Redcap marched me towards the huge barbed wire gates and I felt my heart beginning to speed up as the guard opened the gates and I half ran through them before they clanged shut behind me.

An R.A.F. jeep was waiting to take me back to - El Ballah, and a surge of excitement swept through my veins as I realised that I was free, well, free enough for the time being.

The driver was full of curiosity, he was bursting to ask me - "What was it like in there? It looks like a field punishment place!" I partly satisfied his inquisitiveness and then changed the subject as we sped down the side of the canal. "What day is it?" I asked. When he said it was Monday, I said, "but what is the date?" October 1944, he answered with a look of surprise on his face.

Back at El Ballah, the noise from the Harvard aircraft appeared to be ten times worse than before and someone had pinched half my kit whilst I had been in the hospital.

A few days later I applied for a week's leave as they still owed me about three weeks from 1943. My leave form eventually came back to me, but they had cut it down to three days. I was very upset, because it meant that I could not go further than Ismilia, about thirty miles away down the side of the canal. So, after pay parade on the Friday, I set off to hitch-hike to Ismilia, as there was no other way unless you swam down the Suez Canal.

Once in the town I searched for a nice quiet hotel, which I found away from the centre of the town; it was run by a Frenchman married to an Egyptian, and I was the only guest. This was just what I wanted, I had a nice room to myself where it was peaceful and had there been a girl also, I would have been halfway to paradise!

Later, I walked into the town centre looking for beer and females, but all the girls were, as usual, well protected by overweight mamma's. Hell! I am getting sick of this country and the damn chaperons, roll on the boat and let me get back to a more enlightened country.

Ismilia, was packed with troops and airmen on leave. I suddenly found myself standing outside a well stocked jeweller's shop. The owners were obviously Jewish by the name above the window. My attention was directed towards a tray of very beautiful dress rings, when suddenly I sensed someone creeping up behind me. An Arab in flowing robes had come within three feet of me, now, he acted strangely, but I had seen it all before in Cairo. He was inviting me to take a peep at something in his right hand which was thrust inside the folds of his robes. Very warily, with one hand on my wallet I leaned forward to take a look and there in his hand was a man's diamond ring.

The large solitaire diamond glittered mysteriously in the half-light caused by his robes. "How much?" I said, thinking that if this is stolen I may get a bargain. "Twenty pounds," he whispered out of the corner of his mouth.

"I will give you five but let me have a closer look first." My remarks were the signal for the Arab to go into the next routine of appearing hurt and insulted as he waived his arms about cursing and shouting to Allah, as he acted out a precise pattern of oriental salesmanship. But his next move startled me as I had not seen this one before. In desperation to make a sale he then scraped the diamond ring along the plate glass window of the jeweller's shop.

The screech was very loud and it had certainly cut the glass for a length of about twelve inches. In seconds the owner of the shop came flying out as the Arab melted away leaving me standing there to try and explain what had happened. I endeavoured to calm the Jew down before he had a heart attack as he was jumping up and down wringing his hands, when they were not waving frantically above his head.

The only way I could calm him down was for me to go into his shop and take a closer look at the tray of dress rings. Now I was more amazed at the transformation which came over the Jew, as he rubbed his hands together smiling in anticipation. His beautiful young daughter was gently eased closer to me with the tray of choice rings twinkling in her hands. A heavy exotic perfume transfixed me to the spot as the Queen of Sheba rustled and fluttered closer to my side. She knew exactly what she was doing to my pent-up emotions, but she had gone too far, for now my interest had been transferred from the flashing jewels to her twinkling eyes and entrancing figure. Even so,

I knew it was going to take the wisdom of Solomon to extract myself from the web without parting with my money or causing too much disappointment.

I praised the jewels, saying, they were even more beautiful than some of Tutankhamen's treasures as I edged my way towards the door. Once outside the shop I quickly lost myself in a crowd of soldiers who were watching an Arab manipulating two dancing baboons on the hot pavement. As I pushed my way towards the front of the crowd, I could also see there were two performing goats dancing like the baboons to a throbbing drum. The performance ended with the baboons riding like jockeys on the backs of the goats. Some of the soldiers tossed a few coins towards the Arab, and to everyone's surprise the baboons jumped down and ran about like children, picking up the coins and handing them to their master! I drifted away to explore the town which was situated on the edge of the Suez Canal.

Ismilia was only a small place and in less than two hours I was back near the jeweller's shop. Here, I found a form in the shade to sit on and have a cigarette as I watched the top superstructures of a convoy of British ships going south. They floated past the end of the street like massive buildings on the move as they made their way to the Far East.

Now that we commanded the Mediterranean sea routes, there was no need to go round the Cape. One of these days I would be going home up the canal and then turning left through the Mediterranean to England or Scotland, it did not matter which.

As the sun set behind me I made my way back to the secluded hotel for dinner or tea, call it what you like. I dined with the Egyptian lady and her husband, they had put on a good spread and very soon a lively conversation flowed in English, French and Arabic. I felt that they were watching my table manners so I carefully avoided drinking the water from the silver finger bowls, and all was well.

It was about 9.00 p.m when the meal ended and the conversation in three languages was becoming a little stilted, so I decided to go for another walk round; in any case I was longing for a cup of tea. The only place I could find to satisfy my longing for a cup of tea was the Forces Garden Club. Here, the tea was very good but the atmosphere was just as if I was back in camp.

After lunch on Sunday, I set off to hitch-hike back to El Ballah, arriving just before it went dark. Over the next few weeks our tents were being replaced by more solid buildings.

It was interesting to watch the Egyptian builders at work, here, were the descendants of the master race of builders. Their tools were still primitive, very similar to the ones you see in the Cairo Museum, but they knew all the easy methods of construction. The wedge, lever, roller, counter weight, screw and inclined plane, were all used effectively. Even the power of the sun was made to work for them and had the Suez Canal been a little closer, they would have utilized the water power to lift and carry for them.

What surprised me, although, it should not have done in Egypt was the method of making bricks on the spot and baking them in the sun! There were no wild-cat strikes, instigated by mindless agitators; no silly 'sit-ins' over who does what! They all worked harmoniously together, making light of lifting and pulling by singing 'happy-sounding' work songs. Was I witnessing some of the secret methods of their ancestors who had cut, shaped polished, lifted and moved into place - 'seventy ton granite blocks?'

On my many excursions to sites of Egyptian antiquities, I had seen things to make your mind boggle. Five thousand years ago when most of the rest of the world were running about in animal skins, the Egyptians were creating mysteries in stone which are still puzzling the experts today. Even after one hundred years of modern digging and probing in Egypt, the real key has not yet been found to answer the question - why, and how did they do it?

I was in the N.A.A.F.I. canteen one evening with a group of pals, we were relaxing and talking as we drank our beers. Eventually, as usual, the conversation got round to the boat home. Did anyone have any more news, were our names on the list or had they forgotten all about us? Then one chap spoke up, saying, "Let's try to get into that circle in hut four, they have some kind of seance nearly every night!"

This was an amazing bit of news and I, for one, was very interested, see my first book. So we finished our beers and four of us walked over to the hut. The light was on in the N.C.O.'s room at one end of the hut but the curtains were drawn over the windows. One window at the top was open wide to let the much needed air in and the breeze moved the curtains from time to time enabling us to peep through a chink. The room was crammed with airmen so there was no chance of getting in.

Two ragged circles of gaunt, deeply tanned emaciated airmen stood close together, leaning forward over a small square table in the centre of the circles. Four men sat at the table, one on either side; they each had one arm stretched forward so that they could lightly place one finger on an upturned wine glass which was standing on the polished table top.

At that moment I was squeezed out of my position so that someone else could peep through the gap in the curtains, but I knew that what I had seen was a Ouija-board. I told my pals, "it is a crude and often unreliable means of communicating with people in the spirit world." Through the open window we could hear what was going on in the room and from the whispered commentary from the man who had his eye glued to the chink in the curtains, we could follow the drama.

The glass is flying round the table spelling out words as it touches different letters of the alphabet, our commentator whispered, and one airman appears to be in charge asking the questions for the others. We were 'all ears' and also listening to the talking coming through the open window. No one bothered to ask "Will we win the war or when will it be over?" Time after time men wished to know only one thing - when would they be on the boat going home?

After a while we drifted back to our own quarters. I, for one was deep in thought. So it had come to this, such was the apprehension and uncertainty about our fate that some would do anything to find a glimmer of hope, anything to help them to hold on to their sanity!

I was comparatively new to Spiritualism in those days, my curiosity had been stimulated after my arrival in Egypt in 1941. It was only after numerous hair-raising adventures that finally brought me to the brink of the Spirit World and made me wonder just what awaited me if I had been forced by circumstances, to take one step beyond.

But, in the nineteen forties, especially in Egypt, very few people had heard about the Spiritualist religion and, even if they had, many were so ignorant that they called them 'Devil Worshippers' and threw stones at the windows of their little churches, even in England!

Likewise, in those far-off days, not many people knew that one of the top *R.A.F. Officers had been in touch with dozens of airmen and soldiers on the 'other side' who had passed on some remarkable wisdom from the Spirit World! So remarkable, in fact that the Officer wrote two books about it and urged Church men and scientists to remove their 'blinkers' and investigate for themselves.

Here, was a chance before they 'pass over' for all the bickering denominations and all other religions to put their heads together and become united in, perhaps, their last chance on 'this side.' How wonderfully progressive it would be for everyone to have such wisdom, instead, as yet, only a few can say - I know what Jesus meant when he said, "In my Father's House are many Mansions."

I cannot tell you too much about the Spirit Wisdom in this book, in any case, there are many people more advanced than me who can fill you with worth-

*Air Chief Marshal Sir Hugh Dowding. The man of destiny in the right place at the right time.

while knowledge. But, I do give you a tip in "Nightmare Towards The Path" - there you can find the 'key', if you are ready for it.

Chapter 15

British Go Home

Another Christmas Day slid by in the usual way. The 'mess' was decorated with a few wilting palm fronds and dried-up camel thorn branches. Someone with a dry sense of humour had lit a log fire, but it seemed a bit odd sitting well back from it with our shorts and tropical shirts on!

Meanwhile, the war in Europe was still being fought out to the bitter end.

The Germans were fighting stubbornly as they were remorselessly pushed back from the Eastern or Western front.

Hitler, flew into his many rages, calling for more of his now - non-existent panzers to be flung at the Russians, or at the British and Americans.

Unexpectedly, like a bolt from the blue, I was told to prepare myself for yet another posting. Where the hell are they going to send me now? Surely it cannot be to the Far East, I only have another few weeks left to complete my four years in the Middle East. The next day I was very relieved to find that I was only going to Fayid, further south, down the side of the Suez Canal.

R.A.F. Fayid - was quite a good place and I would be able to get to Port Suez at the southern end of the canal on my odd days off, that is, if I could get any time off!

The living quarters were huts with electric lights and showers. How lucky can you get!

Now, I found myself working on Hawker Typhoons, huge fighter bombers which dwarfed a Spitfire or a Hurricane. These aircraft were deadly killers in more ways than one because they carried four cannons and eight rockets at 400m.p.h. plus. Pilots came from all over the Middle East, on conversion courses to learn to master the Typhoons, and those who did not learn remained in Egypt for ever.

I had been at Fayid a few days, delighting in the luxury of the showers, instead of trying to bath in a canvas bucket! It was also heaven to get away from the 'ear shattering' noise of the American Harvard trainers. The British built Typhoons were a much quieter aircraft even though they had over three times more horsepower, and were twice as fast.

I decided to go to the Clothing Stores one day to try and replace some of my kit which had been stolen at El Ballah, whilst I was in the Army Hospital.

As soon as I entered the Stores, my heart missed a beat - in one corner, stacked from floor to ceiling was a pile of cheap box-like coffins. So I asked the storeman "What are all those for?" His reply shook me, he said, "We will probably use most of them up when the next conversion course starts". It was just a few days later when the next course started and we were kept busy keeping the Typhoons flying.

The weather, of course, was excellent for flying, there were no rainy or foggy days to give us a breather. We seemed to be constantly repairing undercarriages or replacing engines, propellers and wing tips.

I could not help noticing the apprehension on the faces of the pilots as the course proceeded and their numbers dwindled week by week! They were obviously very concerned as to how many would finish the course in one piece and where would they be posted to afterwards?

It was about the middle of April 1945, when everyone was talking about the end of the war in Europe, news bulletins were pinned up on the Notice Board every day and, groups of men milled around trying to read the latest news which meant so much to them.

Suddenly, one day there appeared another notice on the board, a list of mens names, rank and numbers. About two dozen men were being ordered to pack their kit as they would be moving to a transit camp near Suez, the next day. Wild rumours now flew round the camp as airmen pushed their way to the front of the crowd, frantically trying to see if their name was on the list

The transit camp near Suez, meant only one thing, you would be waiting for a troop ship either to go and finish off the Japs, or to go home. The unanswered question hung over us like a black cloud and every day the crowds swelled round the notice board, as each day a new list of names appeared. If you saw your name there you did not know whether to jump for joy or go beserk!

About the beginning of May 1945, I suddenly found myself reading my own name and number on the notice board. A clammy sweat began to trickle down my back as I walked away stunned with apprehension! I packed my kit in silence. Why do they not tell us the truth? Then we can be happy or crack up completely!

The next day I climbed off a truck in the transit camp near Suez. This was where it had all started over four years before. It was still a place of destiny where your future hung by a thread.

We remembered those first bewildered days when we had arrived as teenagers, wilting as the hot winds seared our flesh. We also remembered the tens of thousands who lay buried in lonely graves from Cairo to Tunis, who would not be going anywhere any more! Now, there were thousands of R.A.F. chaps in the transit camp and thousands of soldiers in a similar camp nearby.

Then on a wonderful day in May, the news flashed round the tents - 'Germany has packed it in'.

We celebrated with one bottle of beer between TEN of us, all watching closely as each man took a 'swig' in turn. Now keep your fingers crossed until you know where you are going to from here.

The following day we were all surprised to observe on the Notice board that - B.O.A.C. Airways (as it was then called) were asking for pilots and ground staff to transfer to them and be stationed in the Middle East.

We could have had our discharge on the spot and walked into a good job, but no one I met wished to go; we just wanted to get home.

For the next few days the Suez Canal, was full of ships going south. Four or five troop ships slid by followed by three aircraft carriers and many Royal Navy destroyers; they were all obviously, bound for the Far East.

One of the time-expired airmen remarked - "Now, the Japs are going to get what they deserve. Who did they think they were dealing with when they twisted the 'lion's tail' whilst we had one hand tied behind our backs in Europe.

Then another airman said, "Don't forget the Yanks, they are also after their blood." The Yanks will never forget or forgive their rude awakening at Pearl Harbour, when the American Eagle had a few of its' feathers plucked out!

Yes, the days of Japan are numbered; they have strutted about for long enough, bowing to their tin gods and forcing our captured soldiers to do likewise to avoid a bayonet in their backs! But, much sooner than anyone thought possible, the vanquished race were bowing to their victors as they handed over their swords like 'trashy souvenirs'. Now, no amount of bowing could save their face, they had paid the utmost farthing and, you all know how it ended, so I will not waste any more time on them.

A few days later we all climbed onto trucks with all our kit and were driven to the dockside at Suez. Now, we lined up by the thousands and the waiting began as we looked across the water at half a dozen rusty troop-ships. About two hours later, one troop-ship manoeuvred to the dockside - pointing north, and a wave of excitement rippled through the crowd of men. But, still we waited patiently, wondering how much longer it would be.

Then suddenly, two ambulances pulled up in front of us and to everyone's surprise, they were not full of wounded soldiers.

Both ambulances held about six service girls, each with a baby which was white, brown or black. The poor girls must have felt so embarrassed in front of all those men!

At last, round about tea time, we began to move up the gangplank; the moment we had all been waiting for - for years - had arrived! Quietly, at first, the men began to sing, 'Take me back to dear old Blighty'. Gradually, the volume of men singing rose to a crescendo and as the emotion generated, it brought tears to our eyes; many openly wept as they dragged themselves aboard.

About two days later, the first troop-ship moved north, up the Suez Canal - we were going in the right direction. We steamed past the Army hospital, the one with a hole in the twenty foot high barbed-wire fence. A lonely soldier sat where I used to sit dreaming of home; now, he stood up and waved his hand. I seemed to be the only one who waved back to him and I knew exactly how he felt, the desperation and the agony would be welling up inside him as he struggled to stop his eyes from misting over!

Soon, we slid past Ismalia, then the R.A.F. camp at El Ballah, and later we turned left at Port Said.

Many of us were dreading being sea-sick, like we had been for days on the voyage out. Eventually, we reached Gibraltar, and whilst the ships refuelled we put away our tropical kit and dressed in our normal R.A.F. or Army uniforms.

We left Gibraltar in a convoy of six troop-ships, heading northwards and very soon the sun lost its power, softening the harshness of the vivid colours, especially when huge white clouds appeared to grow out of the sea around us. Although it was July 1945, as we sailed past Portugal, going north, the drop in temperature from 130° in Egypt to about 80° was too drastic. We had become like hot-house plants over the years and needed time to adjust to a drop in temperature of 50°.

After tea, the decks were almost deserted as men sought the warmth below decks, except for small groups of gaunt-looking men with leathery faces, they were going to stick it out, muffled up in great coats and balaclava helmets. They stared northwards with far-away looks in their glassy eyes. They had waited too long, nothing was going to stop them seeing the first glimpse of the white cliffs!

In the lounge, out of the wind, a discussion group was in full swing, so I joined in and it became more interesting as soon as I found out what was being discussed!

A large group of soldiers and airmen were discussing their future as civilians and what jobs we may or may not get. Later, we talked about the future of the United Kingdom and the world in general.

Of course, in those days we still had 'freedom of speech' and could talk about any subject we wished, not knowing then, that in a few short years this 'freedom of speech' would suddenly be taken from us without a referendum of the people. Had we really been fighting for democracy?

It all sounds like an impossible pipe dream now. Tens of thousands from our homeland had paid the supreme sacrifice. What happened to the torch of freedom which we carried and held aloft on our own - until the Americans came to help us? You are fighting for freedom for you childrens' children, we were told, so we kept at it for nearly six years, not only for freedom and democracy, but for half the world also!

Then someone who had been fighting for years in India, to stop them being enslaved, stood up and said that he had been disgusted to read on the walls in Bombay "British get out of India".

Of course, the Indians, under British rule had this "'Freedom of Speech' had we not taught them democracy and shown them a more civilised way of life! But, we did not expect them to turn and bite the guiding hand as soon as the threat to their country had been removed!

Then someone else spoke up who had fought for years to save Egypt from the 'jackboot'. Yes! I saw the writing in Cairo, "British go home". It shouted from the sun-burnt walls now that the threat of the crooked cross had gone!

So, the Egyptians could also write and say what they wished, but who was behind it all, who was stirring up the 'hotheads' so that more could be 'brain-washed' to fill the vacuums later? I do not need to tell you that 'by their fruits you will know them'.

The British Isles had been one huge refugee camp before and during the war. Thousands had fled from the tyrants in Europe before the holocaust started, they had used their heads and got out whilst they still had them! They poured into our country and we welcomed them because they were Europeans, very similar to ourselves, who could, and did integrate quite easily into our way of life. But not only that, some were so advanced scientifically, that our progress in making the 'Atomic Bomb' was given an unexpected boost.

Much later, when we had given 'Home Rule' to India, and dozens more countries of our Empire, lo! and behold! These people did not want to stop in their own countries and be ruled by their own kind: how peculiar! Now, they clamoured for and demanded, British passports, then deserted their newly-freed countries by the millions.

Then suddenly over night came the clamp down on 'freedom of speech', the thin end of the wedge was hammered in, so that now, I and anyone else have to be damm careful what we say or write!

The time is fast approaching when, very soon, these crowded islands will not be able to accommodate any more. We will not need to be vaporised in the first wave of atomic rockets, all we will need to do is - stand together, shoulder to shoulder. There will be no room to do anything else, except wave little plastic flags, made in Hong Kong, and all sing 'Rule Britannia', as we sink beneath the waves.

There is only one hope left before we reach that stage as it is no use praying to our various gods for a so-called miracle, it just needs common sense and someone with the power and courage to say 'enough is enough'.

In the meantime, these millions of immigrants would be very wise to think about returning to their own countries, not only from a 'humanitarian point of view' to help to lift their own countries up in the world, but also in places like India, where there is plenty of room to run and hide when the rockets start to fall! But, more importantly, India, etc., may not even get an atomic holocaust, whereas, the U.K. would be a prime target! Then, there would be plenty of room for the few dozen who may survive just long enough to say 'I told you so, we should have listened to these gems of wisdom - that fellow was telling us the truth and trying to warn us'. I wonder how he knew?

At this point I would like to mention, especially, for those groups of 'brain-washed' people who are taught to grab the wrong end of the stick when anyone mentions coloured people. I have nothing personal against my fellow human beings who just happen to be more suntanned than myself. Would I go to so much trouble to warn them of things to come, if I did?

Try to get hold of my first book - 'Nightmare Towards The Path' it will help you to understand, because it has a message for you. When you get to chapter 14, I mention the Desert Rats coming into Cairo, on leave, they had lived and fought under the blistering desert sun for so long that they were darker than the Arabs! Of course, I meant darker than the city Arabs, who constantly, and at every opportunity, tried to get out of the sun to keep their complexions as pale as possible.

When thousands more British replacements arrived in Egypt, with their pale faces and white knees, they looked on the 'old sweats' of the desert with admiration, determined to get themselves well tanned or coloured, as soon as possible.

Naturally, you should not really analyse the sun tan situation like this, you may discover wisdom and truth which has not yet been fully eradicated.

That reminds me, I must buy a sunbed, these English summers are going worse, or should I have said, British summers, but I am English, am I not or am I Welsh! What does it matter, I can be a sun tanned Englishman with Welsh ancestors living in Britain, or should I have said England?

It must have been two or three days later when a surge of excitement swept around the troop-ship. Everyone was busy putting on their cardigans and great coats; it was freezing as we sought the sunny side of the deck, eagerly scanning the horizon for any sign of land. At dawn, the next morning, the excitement ran through us in waves, as suddenly, a misty land appeared on either side of us with vivid green hills bathed in watery sunlight.

In seconds, the Scotsmen amongst us recognised their homeland - we were sailing up the Clyde. Dozens of special trains were waiting to whisk us all away to different camps so that we could be sorted out and then be sent home on a month's leave.

The news must have spread like wild-fire that six troop-ships had arrived from Egypt. Crowds of Scottish relatives were pouring into the small town of Gourock, as the news spread down the Clyde to Glasgow, then over the misty hills to the Scottish highlands, and back south, over the border into England.

We were funnelled straight onto the trains as Scotsmen waved frantically to their relatives in the crowd. Train after train rattled away to the south, as something like fifteen thousand men came ashore. Hundreds of people were crammed onto every station we passed through, whilst hundreds more jostled on the railway embankments.

But, the trains never stopped and in desperation, notes were flung through the windows at every station - 'please tell Mrs. so-and-so, I am O.K. and will see you soon'. Now we were swaying and clattering past the vivid green hills on the edge of the lake district and still the notes were being flung through the windows, as crowds of people shouted and cheered at every station all the way to Blackpool.

At Blackpool, we filled hundreds of 'Bed and Breakfast' places, whilst we waited for our 'rail warrants' and 'leave passes' etc.

Although it was midsummer, dozens of us were suddenly struck down with influenza and, instead of going home on leave, we were shivering in make-shift hospitals. My home town was only fifty miles away, but I had to spend a week in hospital, along with many more pals, all willing themselves to get better as quickly as they could.

At last, the unforgettable day arrived - I could send off a telegram to my parents - 'I will be home tomorrow for tea'.

Chapter 16

Almost Democracy

Yes, I got my month's leave, at last, so now I could start and unwind or try to. My mother and younger brother met me at the station, but I found it hard to recognise either of them. My brother had grown about eight inches taller, whilst my mother had put on a lot of weight.

I was glad it was midsummer because when I put on a civilian suit, I felt frozen and had to put on my overcoat before venturing outside. Everyone appeared so pale and worn-out, of course, I knew that many civilians had been right in the thick of it during the air raids, even my old school which was about half a mile away, had been caught by a stick of bombs.

I enjoyed the local dances, it was such a nice change to choose a partner without having to ask her mother or uncle first, or buy her a glass of coloured water for each dance. It was also a pleasant change to walk round the shops without being constantly pestered by shoe-shine boys, deformed beggars, fortune tellers, pimps and pickpockets. But, of course, these were the early days when you could walk down the darkest streets on your own without your hand on your wallet and no fear in your mind! Yes, it really was nice to be back in England's green and pleasant land, everyone appeared much more friendly, trusting and helpful. Also, people still formed orderly queues for the trams or buses, no fighting to climb through the windows or ride on the roof. I was glad that I had got back home in time to see the old friendly ways before the pipe dream was over and the wind of change swept through the ugly tower blocks of the inner cities. But the lucky returning veterans of countless battles still had a dream - had we not been told that utopia was just around the corner. There would be plenty of jobs, houses to rent, pensions to look forward to, providing you paid your weekly contributions, of course.

Then there was the free medical treatment and sick-pay, providing you paid another lump out of your wages. It all looked very promising as long as we all worked together and paid our share, but these were still early days of peace and increasing plenty. The rot started later when we gave Home Rule and self-government to a quarter of the world. Dismembering of an Empire was, perhaps, a great leap forward for democracy, but did we really have to give them British passports also?

It was mid-September when I received a letter and rail warrant to remind me that I was still in the R.A.F. and was being ordered to be at R.A.F. Carluke, Lanarkshire, the following Monday.

To be posted to Scotland as winter approached, was the last thing I needed, it was the coldest six months I can ever remember. We worked in deep snow in a railway siding, six days per week, dismantling forlorn fighters and bombers. It was a heart-breaking job for us who had been trained to nurse them and keep them flying at any cost. Now we smashed them up, then flung them into rail waggons to be taken to the furnace.

We got a white Christmas alright, something I had dreamt of for years, but now I did not want it, because I could not get home to enjoy it.

At last, the shivering cold winter came to an end and I could discard the flask of brandy which had been my life saver for so many months. Now I knew and understood why so many Scotsmen were heavy drinkers.

Suddenly, the heart-rending task of smashing up so many beautiful aircraft came to an end. It had been like disposing of old friends, dumb, faithful steeds of the air, which had helped to save freedom and democracy for half the world.

Signs of Spring were in the air as we all paraded on the station platform in full marching order. All our worldly goods were pressed into one kit-bag plus the packs on our backs, as a special troop train hissed and squealed to a stop in front of us.

We were glad that the heat was on because we had quite a long journey in front of us. A surprising number of civilians had turned up to see us off who were mostly local girl friends, especially nurses from Carluke Hospital.

As the train slowly pulled out of the station, we settled down to the familiar clickety-click of the old steam trains. The first stop would be Manchester where it would be only six miles from home, but, of course, I could not go home because we were only changing trains and the next one would take us on our last posting to R.A.F. Sealand, Nr. Chester.

We were all very pleased to be moving south except, of course, the Scotsmen amongst us who I suppose would rather have been in Scotland.

Sealand was a nice camp especially now that Spring was here and we were only about six miles from the beautiful walled city of Chester. I was looking forward to exploring Chester properly, I had been once before on a day trip when I was about ten, but you need more than a day in Chester.

If only I had been posted to Sealand a few weeks Earlier, I would have met my elder brother whom I had not seen for about five years. He had joined the R.A.F. the week after me in 1938 and I believe the news shattered my mother for a while. She had known for weeks that I was going to sign on as soon as I was 17, but she did not expect my brother to follow me in a few days. He had just been posted to Rhodesia for a second tour of duty, having been there whilst I was in Egypt. So this unfortunate twist of fate meant that we would not see each other for another four years.

I had been at R.A.F. Sealand for about a week and, one night whilst I was sat in the N.A.A.F.I. canteen, drinking with some pals, when suddenly someone behind me was speaking to me in Arabic. I turned round in amazement because I had already recognised the Birmingham accent of a pal from the Salvage Unit.

We had last seen each other in Monastir, Tunisia, in 1943, when I said my goodbyes as I was posted back to Egypt. I got up to shake hands with my old friend, then I received another pleasant surprise as I saw two more pals from the Salvage Unit coming towards me with their hands full of brimming glasses of beer. What a night we had, drinking and talking of our experiences in the desert and how they had gone on into Sicily and Italy, chasing after our crashed fighters. But, the sad part was when I enquired about six more of my pals and was told that only two of them had made it back home. The other four never got beyond Naples.

A few days later as the camp filled up with more airmen who were on their last posting and waiting patiently for their discharge, my friend from Birmingham, bought a second-hand car; so on the Saturday night, the four of us piled in for a night out in Chester. We parked the car and went on foot from pub to pub on the look-out for female company. Eventually, round about 10.00p.m. we had only found two girls who were friendly, but it was obvious that we would not be able to fit the six of us in a small car, so two of us had to disappear and go for the last bus back to camp. A pal and I staggered off to the bus depot, only to find that we had just missed the last bus to Sealand. We were in no state to walk the six miles, but knowing that we had to get back by 23.59 hrs. or else, we had to try and hope for a lift.

After about two miles the road changed into a country lane with fields on either side and it was then that we saw a huge cart-horse watching us over a gate in the hedge. Both of us had the same thought, here, was the chance of a lift which may just about get us back in time!

Going up to the horse we began to talk to it as we stroked its mane, "But how are we going to steer it without reins, I said?" "I'll show you, said my pal". The next minute he had climbed the gate and got on to its back as he told me to open the gate. The horse never bothered at all, so I climbed up behind my pal who now dug his heels in and started clicking with his mouth until the horse moved out of the field. It started to turn left which was the wrong way, but to my surprise, my pal pulled on its mane and it moved to the right and up the road heading for the camp.

We found it rather awkward as we were nearly doing the splits because its back was as wide as a kitchen table. A few minutes later, after much clicking with his mouth and digging in with his heels, the horse started a slow jog, now we may just make it, providing we can stick on its back! But, I would not recommend this form of transport, especially if you are full of beer and have never been taught how to ride a cart-horse!

It must have been about half an hour later when we recognised where we were because the Guard House was just round the next bend and we must not be seen with the horse! I was hanging on to my pal's belt and shouting in his ear to stop the horse now - but it would not stop, it just went jogging on, so in desperation he pulled on its mane and managed to get it circling round in the road like a circus horse. Gradually it came to a stop and we slid off its back in a heap, whilst the horse just trotted away back to its field, I hope! We were both violently sick as we ran staggering to the Guard House at the main gate, booking ourselves in at 23.55 hrs.

The days drifted slowly by at Sealand, endless days of waiting for our number and name to appear on the notice board for discharge. We never worked on any of the aircraft on the airfield, our days were spent in make-shift class rooms re-learning how to be civilians again and brushing up our knowledge on half forgotten trades.

There was some kind of points system for discharge, your age and length of service earned good points but, if you had been a builder or a miner you jumped the queue. Everyone wished to get out as soon as possible to get the chance of a good job and start earning some proper wages.

I remember back in 1942 near Tobruk, the tattered remains of an English newspaper blew across the desert and I chased after it for something to read. The paper was already four months old, going yellow in the sun and falling to pieces but, one story caught my eye. There was a photograph of four or five English girls about the same age as myself and all dressed up because they were going to Blackpool for a holiday. The story said 'these lucky girls are off to the seaside for a well-earned holiday because they have been busy for months making bombers for the R.A.F. Now they have plenty of money saved up from the £17.00 per week jobs'.

I could not believe my eyes because I did not get 17 shillings per week and I had never had any wages for nine months because there was nowhere to spend it.

So you can understand our impatience to get out as quickly as possible but, we did not know that disillusion was waiting round the corner.

For instance, when I did become a civilian later and wished to work on aircraft, I tried - A.V.ROE's, but the aircraft industry had almost collapsed and hundreds of men had been sacked - the word 'redundant' was not used in those days. However, I was told that in any case I would not get a job until I had a union card. So off I went to the Engineers Union, local branch and was informed that I could not have a union card until I had a job. I pointed out that I could not get a job until I had a union card, so where do I go from here? "Sorry" they said, "but that's the rules".

Later, after much prodding, the Government stepped in and told the unions what they must do - give the ex-servicemen a card if they had been doing skilled work for so many years in the forces. So a bit of common sense over came pig-headedness!

I eventually got a job with an engineering firm making parts for civilian aircraft but, here again, disappointment hit me, the wages were not £17.00 per week, like the young girls received in 1942, but only £5.00 and - take it or leave it!

Some weeks later the final day arrived, a batch of about 200 of us had been told the night before, to pack our kit for the last time because we had to catch a very early train in the morning, first to Manchester and then to R.A.F. Kirkham, which was about ten miles outside Blackpool.

Yes, this was going to be a day to remember; the 7th of May, 1946, and it would stick in our minds for ever, like the day we joined, when we swore allegiance to King and country, ready to fight or fly anywhere and even pay the supreme sacrifice.

A small convoy of R.A.F. trucks met the train at Kirkham station and, about fifteen minutes later we jumped down off the trucks in front of a huge hangar which had been turned into a clothing store.

As we walked through the hangar doors, our names and numbers were ticked off on a list, there was no one missing on this parade. In front of us were rows of suits hanging on rails, then rows of raincoats and tables full of shoes etc., just like a huge shop.

Nearly everyone chose a suit which was not blue. I came away with a brown suit, brown shoes and a raincoat and finally, a brown trilby hat. No bowlers for the lower ranks. We then moved into the changing room to take off our uniforms and empty our pockets as we put on the civilian clothes but, to my surprise and many others, our uniforms were parcelled up in brown paper and handed back to us, just in case we were re-called we were told!

But, it was the last act which stuck in my throat as I was ushered into a room and sat in front of an officer. I cannot recall all what was said at that last interview. He did thank me for my service and then passed me a form to sign whilst he still held on to my final discharge papers. I had already checked the train times back to Manchester, whilst still at the station and I knew that I could just about make the next train home, providing that there was not too much of a delay. But, when I read the form before signing, I was shocked and amazed to read something to the effect that I had no complaints of my treatment whilst in the R.A.F.!

For a brief moment, the memory of the sick parade in Tripoli, flashed through my mind; I could feel the chains round my hands and feet as well as seeing the pistols waving round my head as the guards in the glass-house threatened to shoot us. The officer's voice broke into my thoughts, he was telling me what I already knew - that the next train to Manchester was in twenty minutes, as he waved my discharge papers almost under my nose.

The temptation was too much, I had waited eight years for this moment, so I signed the form and exchanged it for my papers. As I stood up to go I could feel my right arm automatically going up to salute, but I diverted it and picked up my brown paper parcel, saying cheerio as I flew through the door like a bird on the wing.

My mind was in a whirl, climbing up to cloud nine as I ran for the train home and feeling that if I flapped my hands, I would 'take-off' any moment.

Dashing past the guard room, I thought that no one is going to tell me - to get my hair cut any more - no more church parades on Sundays. You can stick your days confined to barracks, scrubbing floors and greasy tins in the kitchens. Also, to forget about the tears and sweat, salty tea, hard biscuits and weevils, or swimming in the Mediterranean.

No, you cannot forget the good or the bad times. The view of Jerusalem from the garden of Gethsemane - the pyramids and palm trees, also the sight of Table Mountain from the troopship at Cape Town. There would be no more flying in the open cockpit of a string-bag biplane and listening to the humming of the wind in the wires and struts.

A sudden gust of wind blew my trilby into the gutter as I rounded the bend to the station. My God! The train was approaching the platform as I snatched up my hat, stuffing it under my arm and then fumbling in my pocket for the rail warrant as I reached the ticket office. I could hear the doors banging shut, my heart thudding in unison and thinking does he have to scrutinize every word on the warrant. At last, the ticket was pushed slowly towards me; I grabbed it and ran the last few yards because a porter was holding a door open as I dived into the compartment.

Preston was the first stop and everyone had to change trains. I could already see groups of men on the platform trying to look like civilians but, their bearing and self assurance gave them away, even if their new suits and brown paper parcels did not. I just had time to get a cup of tea before an express from Glasgow squealed to a hissing stop and the next stop would be Manchester, where I would change trains and would be home for tea time!

So my career in the R.A.F. came to an end and, for all those people who have managed to read both of my books, I am grateful to you for doing so because so much has been missed out of the history books. But even though I have spent hours writing these books by hand, I regret to say that I have only written one quarter of what really happened in the Middle East to my pals and I during those desperate days.

Talking about pals, you will have noticed that I have very rarely mentioned another persons name. One reason for this is because all the friends or pals I made were constantly changing and often we only knew each other by nick names. Also, in view of the constant casualties, we never got too pally with each other, otherwise life would have become even more unbearable.

Some of the dates I have quoted may not be exact. I mentioned in my first book that during the retreat from Benghazi, in 1942, most of my kit was left behind, which included my diaries. After that, not only did I have no paper to write on, but I soon realised that life was too much of a chance to keep any records; never-the-less, the dates that I have mentioned in both books are very close and, after much research I found out later that many were correct.

I would like to add a few items of interest, some of it having come to my notice too late to include in the body of the book.

In Chapter 2 I mention my encounter with an Army field hospital and the weeks of agony which followed. I do believe that if I had reported sick to my own Medical Officer, when he turned up later, then I would most likely have been left behind and missed all the excitement of the greatest desert campaign of all.

Then in Chapter 3 - when a sergeant was instructing the Advanced Party to look out for mines and booby traps, actually, he had got the number wrong because it was not - five hundred thousand mines but five million, plus booby traps.

Many of these mines were our own which the enemy had dug up from all our fortified positions as we retreated to El Alamein. Likewise, they had captured huge bomb and shell dumps which should have been removed or destroyed by us but, at times of bedlam, many things got overlooked. So the bombs and shells were also used as mines by the enemy, creating a formidable barrier in front of themselves, which was miles in depth. However, it showed one thing, that they had a very healthy respect for the 8th Army.

I would also like to say more of the preparation carried out behind the El Alamein lines by the British Army and R.A.F. For instance, the Army worked very skilfully with wood and painted canvas camouflaging trucks to look like tanks and tanks to look like trucks. These were dispersed in groups over the desert and moved about at night time from place to place. Likewise, the R.A.F. created dummy airfields complete with dummy aircraft at the dispersal points. Then the Germans came over and dropped a shower of dummy bombs on them, but only after many raids with real bombs.

I would not like to end this book without mentioning the three Egyptians who came with us from the delta area to Tripoli. I did not see a great deal of them because they were always kept with the rear party, but at Castel Benito airfield near Tripoli, the rear party eventually caught up with us for a while.

I have often wondered how they went on. One day just before I was sent to the Glass House, the father and his two sons approached me; the elder was waving a piece of paper which he wished me to read and, hopefully translate into Arabic. It was signed by an officer and I was surprised to read something like the following - To whom it may concern - These three Egyptians have come with the R.A.F. Salvage Unit form the delta area. They have been very useful servants for many months and now wish to return to their family. Please help them to get back home.

I tried to explain that the piece of paper was very valuable and would help them to get back, Egypt was fifteen hundred miles away across two frontiers. Unfortunately, my Arabic was not fluent enough to tell them exactly what to do. I could only point them in the direction of Tripoli and endeavoured to explain that they may get a boat to Alexandria. That was the last I saw of them as they walked away, each with a bundle on his head, whilst the elder one was waving his piece of paper at another airman.

Yes, I felt sorry for these three Egyptians and quite disgusted at the treatment meted out to them. One would have thought that the R.A.F would have driven them into Tripoli - twenty miles away - then handed them over to a Transport Officer on the docks.

In Chapter 8 I mentioned counting the masts and funnels of about 36 sunken ships in the harbour at Tripoli. Since writing that, I have found out that the actual number found after the war was - 87 ships. How many there were on the bottom, in other places like Benghazi and Tobruk, I have been unable to find out.

In Chapter 11 I mentioned feeling lighter in weight as I stood on top of the Great Pyramid. This baffling mystery suddenly took on a new twist as I was completing this manuscript. I felt my hair trying to stand up as I read in a book that an Electro Magnetic Force Field has been detected on the apex of the Great Pyramid.

Chapter 17

The Storehouse of Knowledge

I cannot end this book without returning to Egypt, and as soon as anyone mentions that mystic place one immediately thinks about the pyramids. Of course, they are still there, seeped in mystery and they have been there longer than any other stone buildings which have been found on planet earth.

Hundreds of books have been written about them, but mainly referring to the Great Pyramid, the 'Bringer of Light' or a 'Bible in Stone', are other names given to it. But, stop for a moment and shut the book if you are one of those religious people who are easily offended by facts. It is better for you to remain where 'ignorance is bliss' rather than get upset, because I have no wish to offend anyone. Now the rest of you can carry on.

After reading a few dozen books about the 'Storehouse of Knowledge', I began to realize that a number of tantalizing questions still remains unanswered, such as - When was it built? Why was it built? and How was it built?

No one appears to have come up with a satisfactory answer to any of these questions, although, hundreds of people have tried over the past two thousand years and probably before then.

Now I am not an archaeologist like many writers of the hundreds of books mentioned, but there are other methods of finding out about the past without using a spade!

Apart from research into old scrolls or clay tablets, there is another method which may sound fantastic to many. But not to those of you who know anything about extra-sensory perception.

Some investigators have suggested that the Great Pyramid was built 25,000 years ago, whilst others say 6,000 or 9,000. Regarding why it was built, most say it was a tomb, whilst others, thinking about the air-shafts leading from the two chambers to the outer surface and known as the 'Kings and Queens Chambers' think it was a place of initiation.

Now we come to the third question. 'How was it built?' For instance, how on earth did the primitive Egyptians manage to cut, polish and manoeuvre many seventy ton granite blocks and place them in position, approximately three hundred feet up inside the pyramid?

They must have used a ramp, many say, but there is no trace of a ramp having been dismantled and scattered over the desert! You also have to consider that the base of the Great Pyramid is one hundred and twenty feet above the level of the Nile, making the apex six hundred feet above the Nile, so the ramp would have to reach that height!

I must mention that the nearest granite quarries are about 500 miles up the Nile, and the Egyptians did not have steel chains or dynamite. Plus the fact that they worked the granite blocks to a tolerance of less than one tenth of an inch, using copper saws and chisels by hand.

Of course, to have puzzles like these from the ancient Egyptians of thousands of years ago, can either be very irritating or stimulating, especially when you consider our present scientific age sending space probes to Mars and beyond. One thing it does drive home, no matter how much it hurts, the Egyptians were not as primitive as we first thought. In fact, to take this theme further, they do appear to have been more advanced in many ways than we are today. Either that, or they must have had the help of the Creator of Heaven and Earth.

This theory becomes less of a wild guess when you realize that they were later chosen to instruct the leader of the next chosen people, in all their wisdom and knowledge - and what happened to the next chosen ones? Very soon their leaders began to perform what the Bible terms as 'magic or miracles' or likewise, their God was helping them, the same God whom the Egyptians knew.

You can disregard the other sixty-odd pyramids at the moment, just concentrate your minds and computers on the Great Pyramid, because there is not a lot of time left to beat the clock! I just slipped that in almost unnoticed, but the other revelations to come, which will be made in and near the Great Pyramid and the Sphinx, will not go unnoticed!

Before your minds start to boggle too much, I would like to mention that the Bible was supposed to have been started by Moses writing the first five books. No one knows the exact date because for some peculiar reason he never mentions the name of the Egyptian Princess who saved his life and brought him up. Neither does he mention the name of the Pharaoh who saw to it that he learned all the wisdom of the Egyptians!

Can you imagine that - it does take a bit of swallowing, especially when he mentions the name and address of an Egyptian priest who lived some 400 years before he was born!

Joseph, the Hebrew interpreter of dreams, married the daughter of the priest called - Poti-Pherah - who lived in the city of 'ON' (now called Heliopolis). It is generally assumed that the date of the exodus was about 1,400 B.C. although, and this is strange also, no mention of the Hebrews being given a parcel of Pharaoh's best land to live in under the protection of Egypt, has yet been found in any of the writings so far discovered in Egypt, or anywhere else. Never-the-less, every word of the Bible is true, is it not? I will leave it to you to decide that point, but do not mis-understand me, we all know, or at least suspect that the scrolls gathered together to form the Bible, have been edited and tampered with. So let us return to the Bible in stone and how it may have been built.

A ramp of vast proportions may have been used, but have you worked it out how many men would be needed to pull a wooden sledge-like structure, loaded with a seventy ton block of stone up a long slope? But there could have been other methods, because if you refer to the Bible again, there does appear to have been a lot of magic and miracles around in those early days!

For instance, long before the time of Moses, a snake spoke to a woman who had grown to full size out of her man friend's rib and, she understood what it said to her. Later, they both spoke to God, and he talked with them many times until he cast them out of Eden. Two sons were born later, but one murdered his brother; the remaining son found a wife somewhere and they had one son whom they called Enoch. Now there were five people on planet earth, so Enoch built a city!

You can check yourself that I am quoting correctly if you do not believe what I write.

More magic follows in Exodus when Moses and Aaron stand before another un-named Pharaoh to ask him to let the Hebrews go out of Egypt. But before that, God talks to Moses and Aaron and tells them what to say and do to influence Pharaoh. "Cast your rod or walking stick on the ground in front of Pharaoh" God says. Aaron does so, and the rod turns into a snake but Pharaoh's magicians cast their rods down and 'lo and behold' they also turn into snakes. So, note this - God hardens Pharaoh's heart and he will not let them go.

The next day, at God's advice, Aaron turns the river Nile into blood, as well as all the water in stone jars, so it goes on through Exodus, with God deliberately hardening Pharaoh's heart a few more times.

Later on, we find Moses manipulating the Red Sea. Here, millions of gallons of water divide and rear up to form a dry pathway through the sea when he stretched out his arm. Looking at a map, I observed that the narrowest part of the Red Sea is approximately 50 miles wide, just south of Suez, so imagine how long the water would have to be kept in a reared-up condition whilst a tribe of thousands walked across dry-shod with their children, plus herds of sheep and goats. But check the map again and you will see that had Moses gone just one or two miles further north, they could have walked to Sinai, across the desert.

Don't say that Moses got lost, because he had already been on a reconnaissance trip to Sinai some time before; remember, he saw a burning bush and conversed with a voice which came out of the bush which was not consumed by the fire.

Now you begin to get a better picture from just the first two books of what could be accomplished in those days, providing you had been through the mystery schools of Egypt and been taught how to control infinite power, or if you had the ear of God. A few seventy ton blocks of stone would just be straws in the wind to an Egyptian mystic, unless, of course, someone has been pulling our legs for a few thousand years.

So now having checked the first two books of the Bible - and there are 64 more, one must admit to a bit of doubt or amazement creeping in! Especially, when you read that the Hebrews sojourned under Egypt's protection for about 400 years and yet they never once mentioned even one Pharaoh by name!

Let me return to the descendants of Abraham, for you to see the unfolding plan becoming more illuminated as step-by-step momentous happenings are slotted into place at the right time.

Of course, I know it would take a large volume to do this properly, but time is running out, so you will have to be content with a condensed summary of events.

I will start with famine which often blights the Middle East, even today. But, at the time of Jacob and his small tribe of approximately 300 it was just as devastating as they wandered through Canaan with their herds of sheep and goats scratching about amongst the camel thorn bushes.

In Egypt, of course, there was no famine because the Egyptians with their wisdom and foresight had stored up the granaries in the years of plenty.

Jacob hears that there is food in Egypt, so he sends ten of his sons across the Sinai Desert to buy food in Egypt before they all starve to death.

When the Pharaoh hears about their many days of travel on foot to buy food for their tribe in Canaan, he shows remarkable generosity, saying - "Return to your father and take enough of my carts with you and bring back your tribe to Egypt".

I will give you a parcel of my best land wherein you can dwell in safety and multiply under the protection of Egypt.

Four hundred years later, after many Kings of Egypt had come and gone and an Egyptian Princess had fished Moses out of the river Nile and brought him up as her own son, to be taught all the wisdom and knowledge in the Egyptian mystery schools'

Then the next part of the master plan was slotted into place, because Moses had far to go and much to do to safeguard some of the hidden wisdom as he passed it on in another tongue. By the time of the exodus of the Hebrews from Egypt, they had indeed prospered and multiplied into a tribe of over one million.

In their 400 years of safety they had learnt many things from the Egyptians, which would be of great value to them later. But now the new Pharaoh, not unnaturally, saw them as a threat in the midst of Egypt. Here, coming through the mists of time, written approximately, 3,500 years ago, is an unmistakable warning to kind-hearted rulers of nations.

Now the plan unfolds in a dramatic way, the unnamed Pharaoh decides to discomfort the Hebrews (see Exodus). He makes them work hard for Egypt, as a recompense for what Egypt, had done for them in the past.

Pharaoh's motives show clearly, but he is part of the plan also, and is being used, like Moses, who is suddenly told by a Hebrew that he is one of them, not really a prince of the House of Pharaoh!

So Moses leads the Hebrews out of Egypt, taking with him a large segment of wisdom and knowledge which he will incorporate in his writings later. This will be done in such a way that only those with the wisdom will understand that the master plan is being passed on to those who come later, as he effectively disguises his source material.

During their forty years wandering in Sinai, Moses would have plenty of time to choose and teach the next leader, as he organised the Hebrews into a force to be reckoned with in the years ahead.

Of course, Moses, after his initiation into the mystery schools of Egypt, would have been shown the master plan which had already been encoded in the Great Pyramid, some 2,000 years before, not in writing, but in the universal language of numbers, measurements and symbols.

Much later, came Solomon, and his part of the plan was to incorporate in his new Temple a selection of the old Egyptian wisdom of symbols and measurements into the structure, in such a manner that only those with the wisdom would understand that the plan was being passed on.

Suddenly, there came The Expected One - 'The Lynch Pin' whose name was Jesus. You will remember that his parents had to flee with him to the safety of Egypt, His life had to be saved at all costs. How long He remained in Egypt has not been disclosed, nor what He actually did there, 'at least, not yet'. But when He returned to Palestine, to fulfil His part of the plan, He then knew who He was and what He had to do, plus how long He had got left to spread the message. Years later, in the New Testament, the hidden wisdom was passed on, but only for those who had eyes to see and the wisdom to interpret the innocent looking parables which would effectively disguise it from the ignorant censors later.

Two more groups were activated to make sure that the hidden wisdom was not lost. The 'Knights Templars' and the 'Masons' would be the next to incorporate the symbolic wisdom in their organisations. Later, to be built into the Cathedrals of the West, under the noses of those who wished to destroy the hidden wisdom, but could not recognize nor understand the symbols with their closed minds, so that the symbols and sacred measurements remains intact today.

When you have got through the other 64 Books, plus the large group which the compilers of the Bible rejected because they deemed them to be false, then you are in a position to come to some kind of conclusion about the Hebrew and Christian religions. You will begin to realize why, right up till the Middle Ages, only the priests in Christianity were allowed to read certain selected passages to their flock!

The sheep were not allowed to read the Bible for themselves because they may ask awkward questions which the priests could not answer, or they may break away into hundreds of sects; each one claiming that they knew the truth because they had the wisdom to interpret the Bible.

So the Bible is full of magic, miracles and prophets, plus a lot of hidden wisdom, philosophy and bits of truth, but sorting the wheat from the chaff and deciding what is really meant by the words magic and miracles is another matter.

For instance, which word would you use if you saw someone walking on water, or turning water into wine; or if you were very lucky and saw a stone statue move, whilst on holiday in Ireland?

It is all very confusing, I think you will agree, so let us get down to facts and return to the Bible in stone.

The description is not mine, but it is becoming more apparent as our civilization advances in wisdom and knowledge that some group of people have sent us a message of real truth, to save mankind from their own folly.

It is also a very obvious fact that they went to a great deal of trouble to make sure that the message was not destroyed or altered. They did not want any despots altering scrolls or burning them, nor did they want any vandals chipping away at messages left on the walls. So how could they get a message across eons of time, which could not be twisted, distorted or misunderstood.

A message or series of messages which could not even be read by the majority in the dark ages, which the builders knew was to follow the completion of the Storehouse of Knowledge. But they also knew that the decline would not last and, later on, in the mists of time, a civilization would eventually reach the point of advancement when they could read the messages.

Now, the world or some people on it are in a position to de-code the mathematical symbols and reveal some startling facts. They have the knowledge and should have the wisdom to use the facts for the benefit of all, as it was intended!

I know that your ears must be itching for more, please be calm, because I would like to explain the build-up to this fantastic situation.

Most people have heard of a place called 'Atlantis', in the Atlantic, (not in the Mediterranean Sea) and like the Great Pyramid, hundreds of books have been written about it since it sank into the ocean.

The description of an advanced civilization which was destroyed 9,00 to 12,000 years ago, is naturally, a bit sketchy. But, from the accounts which have come down to us from the Greeks, via the Egyptians, it is obvious that the Atlanteans, were not only very advanced, but a colonizing nation of trading seafarers. No doubt, when they read the signs of destiny, they were already evacuating to their trading posts East and West.

Naturally, they would take all their records and knowledge with them and soon start interbreeding, if they had not even started long before.

Egypt and the Nile delta was one very good choice as the climate would be similar and, say 3,000 years later, the Egyptians would have accumulated a vast amount of Atlantean knowledge.

Of course, 3,000 years is a long time and, if you could go back that far now, you would have just missed Moses and all that magic or miracles. Or you could see Stonehenge in a pretty good condition.

You have all heard of Stonehenge, an intricate computer in stone, was one way an American described it after much study. A computer for predicting events before they happen and it still works.

I wonder who helped to build it with some stones of fifty tons and, many other similar structures to the east and west of the Atlantic?

But I must return to Egypt, the place where any up and coming civilizations sent their best men to learn from the Egyptians. Here, the seekers could sit at the feet of the masters and the Greeks realised this, perhaps, a bit late in the day for it was already about 500 B.C. and Egypt had been in a very gradual decline for centuries. Never-the-less, the seekers could still learn about - Astronomy, Medicine, Herbs, Architecture, Justice and Law, Mathematics, Geometry and many more sciences.

There was also something else, much more subtle, initiations into the secret doctrines and, you have all heard of initiations, many secret societies still practice it. Of course, they had to be very secretive in the dark ages, otherwise the misguided ones of other religions would have wiped them all out, after putting them on the rack first. So the ones sent to Egypt, who wished to advance further along the path, were made ready, but only after passing certain tests and possibly, the most important test was to be closely scrutinized by trained clairvoyants who could see and read the aura. (Reading the aura is like reading an open book of the person's character and motives).

Before any occult knowledge was allowed to be taught, the wise ones of Egypt had to make absolutely sure of the motives of their pupils, because knowledge is power and if you had wisdom also, you could become leaders of nations.

Perhaps, I should not have used the word 'occult' because I know that many people do not like it, especially if they belong to certain sects. You should have shut the book, but in case you have not, I will give you the full meaning of the word. Secret wisdom and knowledge passed on to those who are worthy and ready to receive it.

One such Greek who is well-known today by the English translation of his writings, which managed to survive the book burning era, returned to Greece with an unbelievable story. He had been told by an Egyptian tutor priest who was quoting from the Atlantean records, that when they evacuated their sinking island continent, they got away by sea and air.

This could be a dramatic clue as to what will be found very shorty, in or near the Great Pyramid!

Step by step, the seekers would also be taught the following subjects, providing they had passed the soul searching initiation tests. Colour healing and what we call Spiritual healing, not to be confused with faith healing. Hypnosis, but not called that. Astral travel and looking back into the past and forward into the future, so that they would know when to build a storehouse of knowledge. In what order these subjects would be taught, I do not know, but possibly one of the first things would be all about The King of Truth, The Maker of Heaven and Earth, The Compassionate One.

These are just some of the titles which the informed Egyptians gave to The One God, long before the Bible scrolls were written.

Now, the picture is becoming clearer, the people from Atlantis, passed on their wisdom and knowledge to the Egyptians, and they in turn, passed some of it on to the Hebrews, and later still, a portion onto the Greeks, and from them a portion of it moved westward through Europe, and thence via Great Britain, to those who are now called the 'Americans'.

When the Americans won their independence from the mother country, they soon realized that they needed to design a Great Seal in keeping with most European countries. For instance, we had a Great Seal for nearly 600 years, at that time!

Now on the reverse side of America's Great Seal is an unfinished Pyramid and, suspended or hovering above it, is the chief corner-stone, with the eye of The One God looking outwards.

Many of you will know why these symbols were chosen, it is almost as if they knew then that the wheel of destiny would soon turn full circle and eventually, the mantle of power would be placed on their shoulders. But note, that all these momentous happenings on planet earth have occurred inside a comparatively narrow band of latitude, namely 30° to 60° north. Perhaps, that is some kind of warning which I pass on to you, because it just happens to be the same narrow band where possibly, 95% of the vaporizing rockets are and also the target areas!

This narrow band just mentioned, appears to be a very unusual area of the planet. Notice how those nations in it, who have had the chance to study the occult or secret wisdom, have forged ahead. Especially, when they have got onto the right path and formed a democratic way of life which would include freedom of speech and just laws, based on the One God's laws!

Yes, there is something very unusual about the area mentioned. For instance, Atlantis sank there and many, if not all Great Empires have risen and fallen there, along with powerful religions who have fought each other.

But perhaps, even more amazing has been the scientific advances created there, such as the - steam train, motor car, aeroplanes, telephone, radio, television, printing press, jet engine, atomic power, computers and space probes, just to mention a tiny fraction. I know that some of these democratic nations are not perfect yet, but they are on the right lines, especially when you compare them with the rest! But they have to be very vigilant, constantly on guard against sliding into the pit by whittling away at free speech and the rights of man.

Once they sow these seeds, it is only a matter of time before the mantle is taken from them and given to another nation. But, of course, if you are in a real democratic nation which truly follows the laws of government by the peoples elected representatives then the downhill slide would be stopped, especially if the use of the referendum was implemented more.

So, back to the Egyptians of approximately 4,000 B.C. They had already learnt a great deal from the survivors of Atlantis, who must have taught them, amongst many other subjects mentioned earlier, how to see into the future. Notice, the Bible came later and is crammed with prophecy.

I am certain that they knew a gradual decline was on its way, so they began to look for a place where they could build a storehouse of knowledge. The building would have to be so large that it would discourage vandals and tomb robbers. It would also have to be such a design and near perfect workmanship that earthquakes would not destroy it. It also had to be in the right place like Stonehenge; too far north or south, would not do.

Since the launching of satellites, plus the persistent searching and measuring with modern optical and electronic instruments in and around the Great Pyramid, we have, at last, been able to confirm that the ancient Egyptians must have know that the earth was a sphere and even flattened slightly at the poles.

They also must have know the circumference of the earth at the equator, plus the surface distance from the selected site to the north pole and to the equator, not to mention the distance from planet earth to the sun.

These facts and many more are outstanding because they all relate to the dimensions, shape and position of the Great Pyramid. Ponder on this for a while, then try to figure out what were the Egyptians doing with knowledge like this, which we, 6,000 years later, have not so long been able to confirm!

So they found the right place to build the greatest and oldest masterpiece of engineering in stone. It was an outcrop of rock near a bend in the river Nile, just a few miles west of present day Cairo. This was and still is, a very special place.

I mentioned in my first book that the base of the Great Pyramid covered an area of over 13 acres. Now try to imagine an army of workers using copper chisels to cut the outcrop of rock perfectly level and square, over an area the size of, more than seven football pitches. When that was done and the sides of this mammoth square precisely orientated to the north, south, east and west, then the first blocks of stone for the first course were brought to the site.

These blocks were approximately five feet square, so if you have your calculators ready, you can work out how many blocks for the first course were required. How long it would take to cut them out of the quarry, then drag them across soft sand and the river Nile and up the first part of the ramp to the levelled platform 120ft. above the river.

Now you only have another 202 courses to complete, but the stone blocks get slightly smaller for each course and, the steps created also gets smaller as you build higher. This step has to be filled in later with an almost white polished limestone. Some say that these casing stones were built from the top down, but, of course, no one knows. What we do know, is that some of these stones weighing about 16 tons are still in position at the base.

Someone has worked it out that to build just the Great Pyramid, the Egyptians would have needed to have cut and transported two million, three hundred thousand blocks of stone. So imagine all this immense effort over many years, was it just to let us know that they, the Egyptians, of six thousand years ago, had surveyed planet earth before us, or are they trying to tell us something else much more important. Such as, keep on searching for more symbolic measurements whilst watching for the changing shadows and rays of light reflecting form the 'Bringer of Light'. Then read the hidden wisdom with great care, for it has been deposited for your benefit to save you from a destruction ten times greater than the sinking of Atlantis.

Not only are you about to receive the warning, but the true path will be revealed in a most dramatic way. The path which only a few have found after many life times.

Throughout the dark ages, many have tried to lead the masses the wrong way, carefully covering up the Path and closing their eyes and yours to it, whilst substituting ways of bondage and filling your minds with fear and hellfire, so that you could be more easily manipulated for money and power for those who could deceive the largest numbers.

Do not misunderstand my point and draw the wrong conclusion that all religious teachers were, or are determined on winning converts for their particular group, because that meant more money and larger palaces for them

No, that was not the case with them all. Many did and still sincerely believe that they are teaching the only true way of salvation for the sheep. Also, that they have the power to forgive your wrong doings and save you from hell-fire. Of course, had they themselves not been brain-washed as children, some of them may have found the true path and used their sincerity in a better way.

Fortunately, throughout the dark ages, there has, from time to time, been born a few men who have shone like beacons of light. At the risk of torture and threats of death, they have endeavoured to lift the masses out of the prolonged decline.

Such a man was GALILEO GALILEI, born in Italy 1564,. What a time and place to be born, whilst most of Europe slumbered under a cloak of fear and superstition, or fought endless religious wars between themselves.

Each fanatical religious group were convinced that they had the truth, whilst their opponents were of the devil, worthy only to be tortured to see if they could be forced to change sides, otherwise, put to the sword or burnt. No wonder it was called the dark ages.

Never-the-less, Galilei, the Inventor, Philosopher, Mathematician and an Astronomer, was reincarnated into the lions den. A wise one from the past had come to show them a glimpse of truth with his home-made telescope. But the ignorant members of the inquisition, who later accused him of heresy* would not even look through his telescope to see for themselves that he was right and, they and the holy church were wrong.

To simplify what Galilei was pointing out, you would have to check the chapter of Joshua, the leader of the Hebrews, who was chosen by Moses, before he passed on.

Start at Chapter 10, Verse 10 where, even God himself, is said to have slaughtered many of the innocent inhabitants of Palestine, so that the Hebrews could take over their land. Whilst Joshua, Verse 12, asked the sun

*HERESY: An opinion opposed to the usual holy church doctrine, punishable by torture and death, unless you recanted and said you were wrong. This is a tyrannical church law, dreamed up by holy fathers to stop the sheep from rocking the boat and undermining the foundations of the holy church.

to stand still and not go down until his army had slaughtered more of the inhabitants of Palestine. And the sun stood still for him or so the holy book says.

To the Inquisition, Galilei, is implying or saying in as many words, that whoever wrote the scroll of Joshua, could not have been divinely inspired. Likewise, the learned Bishops who gathered the scrolls together to form the Bible (rejecting those they deemed to be false) were not learned enough to point out Joshua's blunder in believing that the sun went round the earth, instead of the earth going round the sun, as it also turns on its axis.

So the holy church had been teaching an error for hundreds of years, which raises the question - how many more errors had they rammed down the sheeps throats purporting to be the truth?

Of course, Galilei's feet did not touch the ground after this bombshell, he was arrested and locked up to await the trial of heresy.

Later, the holy church threatened him with torture and death if he did not publicly confess that he was wrong in suggesting that because he had seen four of Jupiter's moons going round that planet, did not mean that the earth was not the centre of the universe, as all the sheep were taught to believe.

The real eye-opener came years after Galilei's forced confession and death. Without any fanfare, of course, the holy church had to quietly accept his findings as true, or become the laughing stock of the more civilized world.

Before I end this book, I would just like to return to Joshua, to make sure that I have clearly explained the remarkable astronomical phenomena which the Bible says happened.

The whole scroll of Joshua is worth reading, but I must warn you that you will be absolutely sickened by the slaughter of innocent men, women, children and animals.

Try not to get too upset about the Lord helping to slaughter some of his children, it could all be a very wild exaggeration on someone's part. But, would that mean the Bible is not truthful after all?

Anyway, it clearly states that Joshua asked the sun to stand still and not go down, whilst his army carried out the instructions of the Lord, and the sun stood still for about a day. Whether you would call that a miracle or magic or something else, I will leave if for you to decide.

These days most people know that the sun only appears to go round the earth, because of the earth' daily rotation on its axis. So, to make the sun appear to stand still, the earth would have to stop rotating, then start again hours later, just like that. Either that, or the sun would have to suddenly shoot off into space to keep its position over the rotating earth.

Both theories cannot be entertained in astronomy, which leaves only one more conclusion; some one writing the Joshua scroll has blundered. Then again, at Chapter 11, Verse 1 onwards, it says that a group of kings with all their armies banded together to defend their country against the invaders.

A multitude like the sands on the sea-shore, the Bible says.

But, notice, at Verse 6, the Lord said unto Joshua, "Be not afraid, for tomorrow will I deliver them up, all slain before you, then you can burn the chariots and cut the hamstrings of all the horses". (The poor horses would slowly starve or bleed to death in agony).

This was supposed to be the same Lord or God who gave Moses the Ten Commandments; remember, they say, Thou shalt not kill; Thou shalt not covet.*

To me, the Lord whom Joshua follows is past all understanding, unless, of curse, some one has got it all mixed up or mis-translated. If you wish to check that point, then you would have to study the book called "The Dead Sea Scrolls" published in 1956, before their full findings are hushed up.

The scrolls were found in 1947, and are one thousand years older than those used to compile our present day Bible. Some of you may remember reading about them forty years ago and, thinking like me, now we are going to find out something very interesting.

In 1956, after a large part of the scrolls had been translated into English and compared with the Bible, what did we get?

The whole of the Bible will have to be re-written when we have finished, said the writer of the book, because we are finding so many discrepancies between the old scrolls and the more modern ones.

So which ones are right and which are wrong? You may have to wait for ever for this hot potato to be sorted out and published.

In the pages of my two books, spirit friends have helped me to include scattered messages for the wise ones living now, those who have been reincarnated to fulfil the task. These messages are pointers to a treasure of such importance that any future life on earth may depend. Some of the clues are in cryptic form, so that only those with the wisdom will know where to look and when to dig!

*See Exodus for full list. Covet - (greedily desire) your neighbour's wife, house, servant, land or anything belonging to him.

SO SHALL IT BE
Wisdom from the past must find,
All is one, the greater mind.
Golden branch may make a start,
Sifting lines to help in part.

One for all and all is one,
Seek inside or you find none,
Isis and the black one same,
One from six then start again.

Pathways of the Gods must scry,
Two by two and one on high,
Forget the false, its end is near,
Spirit friends with wisdom steer.

In and out and round and round,
Old-time dance is most profound,
Anglo-Saxons near and far,
Hold a clue to Egypt's star.

Don't forget the Celtic lore,
Many times have been before.
Mystic pillars small and large,
Pathways to the Gods discharge.

It's too late now to stand and stare,
For one unfit is nearly there,
Must be guarded from profane,
Or all is lost, till start again.

H.A.O.

For those who are interested in seeking a treasure which will help all mankind, provided the right group of people find it, then it is necessary to read both of my books.

It is not just the gold which will astound the world, but the secret wisdom and knowledge which will be revealed for all living now.

Because I had to publish my first book before it was too late to help in the quest, I still have some copies left at the old price - £5.75 Postage free in the U.K.

Snow Harm, No Foul

HANNAH COWAN

Special Edition

ISBN: 978-1-990804-88-5

Cover illustration by: Sonia Garrigoux @artbysoniagx

Cover typography by: Melissa Doughty @mel_d.designs

Edited and proofed by: Sandra @oneloveediting

Interior Illustrations by: Jordan Burns @joburns.reads

Also By Hannah

Swift Hat Trick trilogy

Lucky Hit

Between Periods

Blissful Hook

Overtime

Vital Blindside

Greatest Love series

Her Greatest Mistake

Her Greatest Adventure

His Greatest Muse

His Greatest Treasure

Their Greatest Strength

Cherry Peak series

Strung Along

Catching Sparks

Chasing Home

Stealing Sunshine

Oak Point

Show Me How

Show Me You Remember

Harbour Of Hope

Power Shift

Amateurs In Love duet

Craving The Player

Taming The Player

Snowbell Ridge

Snow Harm, No Foul

Till Cupid Do Us Part

Fake A Chance On Me

For all of us who've fantasized about an older man spitting in our mouths and calling us angel.
Merry Ho-Ho-Ho.

1

Ivy

Dear Santa, I know I've asked you for this same thing for the last ten years, but PLEASE let this one be when you gift me smaller tits for Christmas.
I'm not even that picky. If you could just use your magic powers to shrink 'em from a DD to a C, that would be more than enough. My back hurts.
Sincerely, Ivy Bell.

I SCRIBBLE THE LETTER ON MY NOTEPAD AND THEN RIP IT OFF, crumpling it. With an arched throw, I watch it swoosh into the garbage can. I spin around in my desk chair with a quiet whoop.

The heat coming down from the vent above my desk makes my skin sticky beneath my heavy knitted sweater. It's the last week of November and minus thirty with the wind chill, so obviously, I dressed accordingly. I'm kicking myself in the ass for that now.

It's been a week since I've had to come into the office for work instead of doing it all from home, and I wasn't expecting it to be so damn hot. I usually keep my house cool in the winter to try to manage my heating bill.

Leaning back in my chair, I stretch out my back and wince at the tightness in my spine. I always blame my boobs for this—as seen by my crumpled Christmas wish—but really, it's my terrible posture. I'm going to have a massive hump in my spine by the time I'm forty at the rate I'm going. My tits will be making good friends with my knees then.

"I haven't seen you in forever!"

Turning my chair, I focus on the woman half inside my cubicle. Jill, one of my colleagues here at the Snowbell Ridge town office, flashes me a wide, honest smile.

Dressed in a red velvet skirt with a matching top, snowflake earrings, and red heels with white pompoms on the toes, she might as well be Mrs. Claus.

She's the one who helped me decorate the office last week. We spent hours together at the Christmas store racking up the bill before swiping our boss's card at the till and hauling bag after bag in from my car. It was quite the bonding experience.

"It's easier working at home," I tell her.

She fiddles with one of her earrings. "I prefer to be here. There's nobody for me to chat with at home."

"That's why I like it."

I'm not a grumpy person, but I do like my own space and privacy.

"Fair enough."

"Are you working all the way until Christmas?"

She pushes out her bottom lip. "Yes. I need the extra money too much to take any days off."

"Me too."

Not to mention that I've got a lot to do before then.

It's not only my first Christmas here in Snowbell Ridge but also my first as its marketing and events coordinator. I'm in charge of the preparations for the recurring Let's Get Blitzen'd event that's set to take place on Christmas Eve.

It's always held at the Frosty Mug bar downtown, and I'm supposed to have my first business meeting with the owner this Friday to start preparations.

That's the real reason I'm here today. All of the information from the previous events hasn't been moved onto the computers yet and is still in the archaic age of papers in a filing cabinet.

The woman I took over for is well into her seventies, and while she's lovely, I can tell her age solely from what she left behind for me.

I think that's why I was hired for this job in the first place. I'm only twenty-one, and I've got what it takes to bring some new life into an event that I've been told is slowly dying in popularity year by year.

Jill comes closer, taking a look at my desk and the red glitter pen I forgot to put the cap back on.

"Are you ready for your meeting Friday? The owner is a bit . . ."

I cock a brow. "A bit what?"

"Rude. He's kind of like the Scrooge."

I can't hold in my laugh. "I can handle rude. But isn't it a little redundant to be a Scrooge when you're hosting a Christmas event?"

"It brings in a lot of traffic," she says flippantly.

"Money talks, I guess."

"In this economy? You know it does."

Folding my arms beneath my chest, I tap a beat on my bicep. "I'm not above sucking up if it means my job will be easier. Even Scrooge has a weakness. Do you know his?"

"Most likely the hearts of virgins," she deadpans.

Dry humour with a bit of darkness is my favourite. Maybe that's why I get along so well with Jill.

"I'm out of the question, then. Know anyone who fits the bill? Any willing sacrifices?"

She laughs so hard she snorts and goes beet red. I grin and

add, "What about chocolate? Or booze? Does he seem like a whiskey or tequila guy?"

"He seems more like the moonshine type," she answers, stifling her laughter.

"Moonshine . . . alright. I'll see what I can do."

She winks. "Wrap it in a bow, too. Maybe that will soften him up."

"Think he'd wear a knitted sweater?"

"Like the one you have on? Don't tell me you made that!"

Diving toward me, Jill pinches the thick material of my sweater and rolls it between her fingers. Her deep brown eyes glow with interest.

I let her poke and prod at my work. "Yes. I've been knitting since I was a teenager."

"Really? What all do you do? Surely, not just sweaters."

"I'll do anything. I used to sell slippers and blankets at the farmer's market in the summer before I moved here."

"You have to do the Christmas market this year! It's inside the hockey rink on December twenty-third."

Interest zips up my spine. "I'd love to."

"Here, let me give you my aunt's number. She's the organizer, so if you really do want a table, she'll make sure you get one," Jill rambles, leaning back out of my space to grab my pen and start writing on my notepad. "It would be a great way to get your name moving around town. It's never easy being the new person, especially in a small place like Snowbell."

Snowbell Ridge wasn't my dream place to live, but when my relationship with my ex crashed and burned, I moved back in with my parents for five months and learned that I couldn't do it any longer. Nowhere close to Oak Point was hiring, so I had to expand my search.

I found the listing for the job I have now and, two weeks later, was moving into a cute little rental on the outskirts of Snowbell Ridge. It's a couple of hours' drive west of my hometown and is more than enough distance between my past life and the one I'm building now from the ground up.

"I know what it's like trying to find a place for yourself in a small town. Oak Point makes Snowbell look Calgary-sized. It's not even really a town because there aren't enough people there," I say.

"Where is Oak Point? I don't think I've actually heard of it before."

"It's south of Calgary, about a forty-minute drive from the Rocky Mountains. Close enough to Cherry Peak that I'd take drives up there just for a change of scenery."

"So, it's prettier than here?" she jokes.

I smile slightly. "It is. The mountains are the best thing about it."

"Well, I hope you don't hate flat land too much. I'd like if you stayed here for a while."

"I haven't minded it too much yet. The snowfall hasn't changed at all."

It's never-ending. Every morning, I wake up and don't understand how the piles keep getting higher.

"I have a snow blower you can borrow if you're tired of shovelling all the snow," she offers.

"I'd appreciate that, actually. I hate shovelling. It's a job I'm happy to hand off to a man."

She nods and exhales heavily. "I know! But ones nice enough to do that for you are hard to come by here."

"Maybe we need to put an ad out," I tease.

"ISO a strong man to help clear our sidewalks."

I laugh. "It sounds a bit dirty when you say it like that."

"I mean, I'm up for both types of sidewalk clearing, but I'll have to see how they do with my actual sidewalk first."

"Like a test run?"

"Exactly! If he can finish the job without complaining, then I'll consider him for something physically demanding."

"Sex with you is more work than shovelling heavy, packed-down piles of snow?"

She shrugs, the tips of her ears pinking up. "I like to be thrown around sometimes. Sue me."

"Hey, I'm not one to judge. I like that, too. Add some spanking and choking, and I'm not going anywhere."

A throat clears, the noise of it too deep to come from Jill. I press my lips together to keep quiet and slowly spin in my chair.

My co-worker's eyes flare wide as she takes in the man standing at the entrance to my cubicle, looking like a school principal ready to hand out detentions to naughty students.

Grayson Pierce, our boss, doesn't intimidate me as much as he does Jill. He's handsome—hot as fuck, really—and tall enough that he can probably change a lightbulb without needing a step stool to reach it.

But he's not my type. Too smooth around the edges.

I don't want a guy who would put me in detention when I misbehave. I want one that will bend me over a desk and spank me until he thinks I've been punished enough. Ideally, with a flaming red ass and a soaked pussy.

"Hi, Grayson," I say, shoving those thoughts from my head.

He crosses his left foot over the right and leans his shoulder against the wall in an attempt to look intimidating. "Ivy. Jill. I hope you weren't wasting the day away gossiping."

I stare up at him and blink innocently. "No, we weren't. Jill was just telling me how badly her sidewalks need to be cleared. Are you available to help anytime soon?"

Jill goes as red as her dress. Her poor ears don't have a chance now of returning to their normal pasty-white colour.

"I have a snow blower!" she blurts out.

I shouldn't be enjoying this as much as I am, but I can't help it. It's been a while since my chest has felt so light.

Keeping Jill beneath my gaze, I say, "You're letting me borrow it, remember?"

"I'll survive until you're done."

"Or . . . Grayson could help."

Clearly feeling pressured, our boss clears his throat again and stands as straight as a metal bar. "I can come by this weekend. There's supposed to be another five inches falling over the next two days."

Jill stops glaring at me long enough to offer him a grateful smile. "Thank you. If you're sure."

"I am. Now, get back to work. Both of you," he says before ducking out of the cubicle and most likely heading back to his office.

I'm not even sure what he does here, but I do know that he's the one who could fire me if I do something terrible enough.

Jill waits until he's out of earshot before glaring at me again and whisper-hissing, "You're not getting my snow blower now!"

I only laugh in response and roll back to my desk. She slips out of the cubicle but doesn't move a step further before pointing a finger at me.

"Text me before you meet the bar owner. I'll have to make sure to stop by and tell him to shovel *your* sidewalks."

2

Ivy

AFTER TWO LONG NIGHTS OF KNITTING WHILE BINGE WATCHING Christmas movies, I hold the new sweater in front of myself and inspect it for the final time. The deep green and red yarn doesn't really give Scrooge, but they're the colours I was drawn to. It was either green and red or my favourite purple and pink yarn I always keep balls of, which, from the descriptions I've gotten of the guy I'm meeting, don't seem like they'd really be his thing.

Or maybe I'm wrong and he's a guy who loves wearing pink and purple. Either way, I hope Niko still appreciates all the effort I put into making this gift for him and sees it as the olive branch I'm intending it to be.

The giant glass jug of moonshine on my kitchen counter is supposedly candy cane flavoured, but because I didn't want to risk alcohol poisoning after a single sip, I haven't tried it to check. Niko is a bar owner, so he has to be able to handle his liquor, right?

After folding the sweatshirt neatly, I tuck it into a Grinch-themed gift bag, add the moonshine on top, and stuff it full of glittery red tissue paper. My chin drops in a nod of approval before I'm taking the bag by the handles, grabbing my purse, and bringing everything out to my car, thankful for my remote start that's already warming it up for me.

The five inches of snow weren't supposed to have fallen until Sunday night, but it arrived early with the promise of more to come this weekend. Even bundled in my heavy winter jacket and thick boots, the chill is instant, burning my exposed cheeks.

I took Jill up on her offer and used her snow blower on my sidewalk yesterday. You'd never know looking at it today. Each step through the thick snow is grating, and by the time I make it to my car, I've broken into a sweat beneath my jacket.

Abandoning the gift in the passenger seat, I slip on my gloves and start clearing the snow from the roof of my car. It continues to fall as I brush away what's already accumulated, but at least the heater is melting the snowflakes hitting my windshield.

By the time I finish, I'm both sweating and freezing. I take my gloves off and yank my phone from my jacket pocket. It vibrates as I scroll for a song to play.

Shit For Brains: Are you sure you won't come back for Christmas? We could talk.

And another.

Shit For Brains: Come on. How many times do I have to say I'm sorry?

Talk about having the absolute fucking audacity.

I choose a song and then open the message, hating the way my stomach pinches at the sight of our last conversation and the memories it drags back up.

My reply is quick and blunt.

Eat shit, Travis.

It's been nine months since I learned my now ex-boyfriend had been writing the cruellest things about me in a group chat between him and his friends.

Every single one of my habits, both bad and those I thought were iffy but at least okay, had been sent to a group of men who made crude jokes and nasty comments about them. And it hadn't stopped there, either.

After one of them called me Mount Ivy during a Friday night football party we hosted and then looked like he was going to be sick afterward, I had this gut feeling that something wasn't right. I'd never been called that before, much less by one of Travis's friends.

I looked through his phone the next night and found all of my answers in messages where they'd been calling me that as a way to make fun of my heavy chest. It got worse after that somehow, with personal details of my body and what I enjoyed during sex being shared in a disgusting way that made me hate myself for a while. Every one of my insecurities was highlighted and shared as a way to get a few laughs.

The fact he has the nerve to still text me after I left and moved two hours away from him is beyond my comprehension.

I delete our conversation and slide my phone between my thighs as I drive. He's not going to get the better of me today. I've prepared for this business meeting with Niko for too many days now to show up distracted with this shit.

If I don't do well, I could be spending Christmas in a snow pile on the side of Main Street.

I keep my grip tight on the steering wheel the entire drive to the Frosty Mug. The roads aren't slick, but the snow is loose, and my winter tires are old—definitely not making it another year.

My nerves swell when I pull into the plowed parking lot and stare at the Open sign hung on the door. There are a few other vehicles here, but not many. Maybe that will change later.

"You've got this," I tell myself, inhaling a reassuring breath.

Fuck yeah, I do.

I don't give myself another second to doubt that before I'm grabbing my things and stepping out of the car. Locking it twice, I head for the bar.

Leather and popcorn are the smells I notice first when I get inside. I was expecting something like stale beer or oil, but this is much better.

I make quick work of wiping my boots off on the entry mat and shrugging my snow-coated jacket off. Then, I drape it over my arm and make my way through the tables at the front.

The majority of them are empty, but a few are occupied. An older couple flashes me quick smiles that I return before continuing my search for the bar. I find it past a few more tables, outlined with bar stools. Only a handful of them are occupied, leaving me plenty of choices. There doesn't appear to be anyone working the bar, so I take a seat at the end, well enough away from everyone else, and decide to wait.

I lay my jacket and purse over the stool beside me and set the gift bag on the bar top before pulling my blonde hair in front of my shoulders, hoping that the curls haven't fallen completely. My button-up pink blouse is professional and one of my favourites, but I notice the top button has come undone the way it always seems to. Doing it back up quickly, I worry my lip, realizing I forgot to safety pin it shut before I left.

It's okay. It'll hold now.

The sound of a door swinging open and shut comes before the scent of the fryer oil I was expecting to smell earlier. I focus on the short man who comes out from the back room with two baskets of fries in his hands and glides behind the bar to hand them out to the guys a few stools down from me.

He doesn't have a name tag on his plain black shirt, so I wait until he's coming back my way before waving him over.

"Hi!"

He pauses, his thick brows creasing as he looks at me. "Hey. Sorry, I didn't realize anyone else had come in. Do you have ID?"

"Oh! Yes, one second." I dig around in the zipped pocket of

my jacket for my small card holder before pulling my ID out. "Here you go."

The bartender takes it and looks between the picture of me and the version sitting at the bar before handing it back with a smile. "Thank you. Now, what can I get you, Ivy?"

I put the card back in my jacket before leaning over the bar and saying, "I'm here to see Niko, actually. Is he here? We have a business meeting."

Eyes growing wide, he stammers, "Uh—yeah. Yeah, he's here. Let me get him for you."

His obvious nerves are confusing. Is Niko really that terrible that the guy working the bar is scared just to get him for me? Surely not. But the only other reason for his weird behaviour is that I make him uncomfortable, and that would upset me too much to entertain.

I dressed nicely and spent extra time on my hair and makeup. My lips are glossy and a muted pink that matches my blouse. I put my tight jeans on for this because they're the only ones I own without rips in the knees. Sure, my breasts are stretching the blouse a bit, but for god's sake, does that really matter? I've done everything I can do to appear like I'm here for business and nothing else.

"Could I actually get a water first?" I ask, needing something for my dry mouth.

"Of course. Yeah. Coming right up."

"Thank you."

I chew on the inside of my lip and watch him pour me a glass of water and set it on a coaster in front of me. He adds a straw to the glass, and I flash a grateful smile before taking a sip.

"I'll go get the boss," he says after a moment of silence.

"I'd appreciate that."

With a rap of his knuckles to the bar, he takes off. I risk a look at the men eating fries and quickly turn forward when I notice they're already staring at me with obvious curiosity.

While I may have been in town for a few weeks now, this is

my first time in this bar. I'm wishing I'd have been here a few times before right about now.

I sit and wait long enough for me to have emptied my glass before the back door swings open again. Straightening my curved posture, I watch the bartender come out alone.

"He'll be right out," he tells me when I open my mouth to ask.

I settle on the stool with a nod. "Thank you again."

"No problem. Another water?"

"That would be great."

He takes my empty glass and refills it before setting it back on the damp coaster. I don't drink from it yet. When the back door opens this time, it's a large man who appears.

Focusing on not letting my eyes bulge as I stare at his massive chest, I swallow and bring my gaze to his shoes before cautiously sliding it upward.

God, he's so fucking tall. His legs seem to never have an end, and when I reach his waist, I still have a long way to go. He's even wide up top, with thick hips and bulky shoulders that are kept straight, his posture far better than mine. Biceps that I guarantee are wider than my head bunch and strain beneath a tight black henley.

Muscles like that . . . they're the ones that could have him lifting you up and manhandling you with little effort. My pulse spikes to the point I think I can hear it in my ears and feel it dropping lower and lower . . .

Even sitting on a bar stool, I have to crane my head back to find his face. There's a thick, dark beard around his jaw and up around his mouth that looks softer than it should, like maybe he spends a few minutes every day taking care of it.

My next breath gets caught in my throat when I lift my eyes past the wide bridge of his nose. I erupt with a cough that tears through the entire bar.

I know the hazelnut eyes that stare back at me. They're the same ones I remember seeing several times over the nine months that I was with Travis. The last time I saw them was during Travis's birthday in March when his dad showed up with pizza and beer.

He's Nicholas Shaw, Travis's father.

Niko.

My jaw flies open.

"Ivy?"

"Mr. Shaw?"

3

Niko

The Frosty Mug has been in my family since before my father was born. It was handed down to him at eighteen and then to me at the same age. I never wanted it.

At eighteen, I was a father to a two-year-old boy. Running a bar was not on my list of shit to do, but it was either take the responsibility or live with the guilt of knowing that I'd let my family's legacy go to a stranger.

What fucking legacy? That's the question I should have been asking myself.

I was in the back office trying to figure out how the hell this place was going to afford to host another Christmas celebration when Matty came to get me.

"There's a woman here for you, Niko. She's real pretty," he'd said.

A grunt was my reply. It wasn't until he came up and tugged my notebook away and pointed at my calendar on the wall in front of me that I remembered who she was. I'd been anticipating this meeting for days now. But when I work, I go narrow-minded, lost in stress and planning.

My blood begins roaring in my ears. I feel the pulse of every heartbeat in my groin. Matty leaves me, and I stand abruptly enough for my knees to smash into the edge of my desk, rattling the contents.

With sweaty hands, I leave the room and plow through the back door, coming face to face with my son's ex-girlfriend.

Gorgeous Ivy Bell with the heart-shaped face, kind emerald eyes that shine a bit brighter during Christmastime, and a rounded body that appears in my dreams far too often.

She's short with grippable hips and thick thighs, bright blonde hair that hangs over the swells of her large, heaving chest, and the same deep red lip gloss that I've scrubbed off wine glasses and coffee mugs.

I know too much about this woman. Twenty-one to my thirty-seven, she's a fantasy and nothing more. The kind that gets buried deep down and only comes out when my willpower grows paper-thin.

My body is completely still, every muscle I have strung tight as she drags her eyes up the length of my body with a bravery and fascination that makes my cock stiffen.

If she knows it's me, she's hiding it well. It's more realistic to assume she doesn't. Her email two weeks ago asking for today's meeting was too warm and gentle to be knowingly sent to her ex-boyfriend's father. I may not know the details of their breakup, but I know my son, and there's no doubt in my mind he was the cause of it.

Too fucking slowly, her eyes meet mine, and the interest in them is snuffed out, replaced with pain.

"Ivy?"

"Mr. Shaw?"

Our words overlap. She clears her throat and tips her chin back, blinking away the pain I saw in her stare.

"Niko," I grunt, correcting her.

"I didn't know you owned this place, Mr. Shaw."

It's less surprising than her sharp tongue.

With a glance around the bar, I signal for Matty to distract the gawkers at the bar and focus back on Ivy.

"We can talk somewhere more private. Follow me."

She hesitates. With a glance at the gift bag on the table, she freezes in place, only moving enough to chew on her bottom lip. I wait for her to work through whatever it is she's contemplating with my mouth shut.

Finally, she swipes the bag and purse from the bar, along with her coat, and strides to where I'm waiting. I feel like a fucking giant beside her, the same way I did when I met her, as she comes to stand beside me, the top of her head reaching my shoulder.

I palm my thighs and lead us through the swinging back door to the dim hallway. The kitchen is to the left and the bathrooms to the right, but I focus on the office door at the end of the hall. It's locked, so I jam the key in the doorknob and push inside.

The window beside my desk lets in natural light, but it's frosted up enough you can only make out the white cast of snow beyond it.

She reaches for the back of a chair at the small table beneath the window, but I snap my arm out and do it for her. I feel the weight of her narrowed eyes but don't stop.

Leaving the door open a crack, I take the chair across from her, my weight making it creak.

"I can pull out my own chair," she says before sitting.

Her things fall to the table, and my interest piques when she pulls the Christmas bag close to her, as if shielding it from me.

"I'm sure you can. Doesn't mean I won't do it for you."

She chuffs. "You should have taught your son how to do that."

I don't back down from the blow. It hits me right in the chest.

"Yeah, suppose you're right."

"I wasn't expecting you today," she reveals, staring everywhere but at me.

The crowded, messy desk, my single bed that I use when I can't be bothered to make it back home after work, and the empty glass on the table beside it with a thin layer of bourbon in the bottom.

For some reason, it pisses me off not having her attention. It's impossible not to give her mine.

The gloss on her lips shines beneath the natural light, and she rubs them together before peeling them apart with a soft smacking sound.

My chest constricts, and I sit a bit straighter, pressing back against the chair.

"Disappointed?"

"No. Surprised. Were you expecting me?"

"I only know one Ivy Bell."

Her eyebrows jump in understanding before she finally looks at me. The way my heart reacts to such a simple look is nothing but fucking trouble. I've been ignoring the way her closeness makes me feel since the first time I met her. The same day my son did.

Like someone's held an electric paddle to my chest and groin and keeps triggering the shocks, I spark and burn beneath my skin.

She's too young. Travis's ex-girlfriend.

Ex.

Maybe if they hadn't hit it off the way they did that day, or I had made more of an effort to speak with her before he swooped in and stole her—

Fuck. He didn't steal anything. Ivy was never mine to begin with. If I repeat those things to myself enough, maybe they'll start to get through my thick skull.

Ivy crosses her legs beneath the table. "You don't think it's unprofessional for us to work together, considering how we know one another?"

"No. We're adults."

Narrowing her eyes into a fierce glare, she asks, "Travis hasn't made you believe I'm an evil cunt? Or has he, and this is your way of getting back at me? By sabotaging my new job?"

I flinch, and her glare softens slightly around the edges.

"No. And don't call yourself a cunt."

She shifts in the chair, obviously uncomfortable. Her thick black lashes flutter as she stares out the frosted window, sighing heavily.

"Do you know why we broke up?"

"No."

"Are you sure? Because if you do, I . . . I don't think we can work together. I'll have to excuse myself from the project."

The pain in her voice has me on high alert, my protective instincts flaring. I hunch over the table and fix my gaze to her cheek, silently begging her to look at me again.

"What did he do to you?" I ask tightly, my jaw straining with the effort it's taking not to let my anger show.

She shakes her head once, still avoiding looking at me. "He's your son."

"That doesn't give him a free pass."

"To most parents, it would."

"I've never been most parents."

And maybe that's why my son turned out to be such an asshole. I let him get away with too much in an attempt to get him to choose me over his mother. Even after everything I gave, he still chose her. I raised a man who takes the world around him for granted because I was immature and reckless myself. The opposite of the kind of father I wanted to be.

Ivy turns her head, and our eyes catch. My head empties of everything but one simple word.

Mine.

The way it should have been all along.

She sniffles, and I zero in on the tear hanging from her lower lashes before it's wiped away with the pad of her thumb. Her tongue slips along her bottom lip, wetting it. I clench my hands beneath the table to keep from reaching for her.

"He—Travis, he would text his friends things about me."

"Like what?" I grit out.

Her cheeks turn so pink I can see it through her makeup.

"We don't have to talk about this. If you don't know, then we can still work together. I brought a folder of all of my ideas, and we can—"

She reaches for the purse on the table, but I move quicker. Flinging my hand out, I wrap it around hers, the warm weight of her fingers soothing something inside of me. Her lips part on a silent gasp as she focuses on where we connect.

I slide my thumb over the ridges of her knuckles, entranced by her smooth-as-silk skin. I'd never have dreamed of touching her this way months ago, but now . . . *fuck*. I'm horny for a simple hand holding with a woman sixteen years younger than me. What kind of man does that make me?

Regardless of the answer, I don't release her. I tighten my hold and lean as close to her as I can with the table between us.

"Tell me what he said so I can tell you he's wrong."

Her throat works with a swallow. "He wasn't wrong about everything."

"Explain it to me."

"Are you sure? We only have an hour."

I almost laugh, but I trap it beneath a few lowly spoken words. "We have as much time as we need."

She still doesn't believe me. I can see it in every twitch of her mouth and the tapping of her finger against my palm.

"Do you like beer?" I ask.

Blinking away her confusion, she shakes her head just once. "No."

I only asked to be polite, but I'm glad I did. I've seen her drink it on occasion with Travis, but I hide my confusion behind a blank stare.

"What do you like?"

"Daiquiris."

I give her hand a squeeze before releasing it. "I'll be back."

"Where are you going?" she asks quickly, her hand hanging suspended in the air for a moment before she brings it to her lap.

"To make you a drink, Ivy. You're welcome to watch."

"You know how to make a daiquiri?"

A laugh bangs at my chest but doesn't escape. "I'm a bartender."

"Right," she whispers, chest flushing above the struggling top button of her blouse.

I leave her there before I give in to my impulses and tug at the fabric to encourage it to open. A flash of her cleavage would bring me to my knees faster than a kick to the balls.

Matty is filling a glass with whiskey when I slide behind the bar and get to work on Ivy's drink.

"What are you making?" he asks once I've added ice to the blender.

"Don't you have work to do?" I grunt.

"Nah, not right now."

"Find some."

He chuckles. "But this is far more entertaining."

I crouch and open the small freezer beneath the bar to grab a bag of frozen strawberries. They go in with the ice.

"Make yourself useful, then, and get me the rum and syrup. The top-shelf shit."

"You got it."

When he sets them in front of me, I don't bother with measuring before pouring in the right amounts of each of the liquids. I add lime juice and then turn the blender on.

Matty stares at me with an annoying smile as I scowl and wait for the blender to finish. He doesn't look away the entire time, and the moment I flick off the blender and silence falls again, he's filling it with his voice.

"I've never seen you make a special drink for someone before."

"I'm a fuckin' bartender."

I search for a cup, wishing I had something better for her than a plain beer glass. Something more fitting for the woman in my office.

"Bartender, yeah. Romantic? I didn't know you had it in you."

"I'm not bein' romantic. I made her a drink 'cause she doesn't like beer," I argue, even if he is right.

Matty watches me pour the frozen drink into the cup and then hands me a straw still wrapped in paper. I nod in thanks and wrap my hand around it.

"You don't have to deny it, Niko. I'm happy for you. I've waited years to see you panting after a woman."

I open my mouth to deny it, but the words don't come out. Yeah, I'm more than aware that I'm panting over her.

It's not the first time, and I'm certain it won't be the last. I've just got to make her pant right back.

4

Ivy

Oh, my god.

What is happening right now?

Mr. Shaw—*Niko*—has always been cool, calm, and collected. He's the gruff, grumpy type of guy who only speaks when he's forced to, and even then, you'd usually be lucky to get two or three words from him. That's not been the case today at all.

Something is different this time around, and I'd bet it has to do with the lack of a certain face.

Not only has he been the one encouraging me to talk, but he's out there, what, making me a daiquiri just because I said I liked them? If I had known he was asking because he wanted to get me something, I'd have given him a blander answer. Or hell, even accepted the foamy piss water he offered to start with.

I've never been a beer drinker. It was one of my quirks that Travis hated with a passion. He thought my drink choices were dramatic and that I should learn how to handle a couple of beers without turning my nose up. I became okay with having a water or soda instead of a cocktail or mixed drink because there was no fighting then.

It wasn't until I left him that I realized how pathetic that made me. The first thing I did when I decided I was done with him was grab my backbone from wherever I'd hidden it over the nine months I'd spent with him and put it back into place.

It hasn't moved since.

I smooth my hands down my thighs and then touch the frosted window, needing the cold against my burning flesh. If I wasn't worried that I'd be caught with my front smooshed to the window, I'd try to cool the rest of myself off, too.

The office we're in is spacious, but with Niko inside of it, it may as well be the size of a supply closet. His blatant big dick energy fills the room and threatens to make the walls curve against the force of it.

It's not a loud confidence that he has but a quiet one that attacks when you're not paying attention. One second, you're trying not to cry, and the next, your heart is threatening to shoot through your chest at the feel of his hand around yours.

I rub the space between my breasts with my cooled hand and sigh. There are business matters to discuss, but I don't care about them at all right now. It's been months since I've felt this intense of a desire toward someone, and that's . . . I'm worried that there's something wrong with me because of it.

This is the man who raised the one I spent nine months of my life with. I thought I loved him, and we shared really intimate things.

Does it make me a bad person to be thinking about his father in a way that has me debating hopping onto the table and begging him to feast on me?

Maybe if Travis wasn't such a piece of shit, I would think that I absolutely am. But he doesn't deserve any kind of loyalty from me. Not anymore. So, aren't I just a normal warm-blooded female who finds Niko, a grown man, really dang attractive?

Yeah, I think I am.

With a rush of confidence, I pinch the straining top button of my blouse and let it fly open. The curves of my breasts appear, but it's nothing too revealing. A tease, really. Something to snag his attention.

Being devious like this is exciting. It makes me feel alive and sexy, and I don't want to put a premature ending to it, even if it doesn't lead to anything more than a few hours of good conversation.

Niko's footsteps are heavy as they approach the office. I mess with my hair and pull my shirt open a bit more before folding my hands on the table.

He comes into the room with a beer in one hand and a frosted glass filled with red slush in the other. My mouth spreads into a grin, and his steps falter slightly near the table.

"Thank you, Mr. Shaw," I coo, taking the drink and paper-covered straw that he offers to me.

"It's Niko."

"Niko," I repeat, letting my tongue curl around the word for longer than necessary, tasting it. "It's not very professional to call each other by nicknames."

He sits back in his chair and palms his beer with a large hand. The one he had holding mine only minutes ago. I'm fascinated by the clean, blunt nails at the end of each finger. They look better kept than mine do despite my bi-monthly manicure.

"I'm not professional," he says bluntly.

"Why not?"

"Don't need to be."

"Right now, or ever?" I ask, baiting him a bit.

He drinks from his beer. "Ever."

Hmm. "Well, I'm always professional."

I rip my straw out of its packaging and dip it into the red drink. Bending over the table, I bring the straw to my lips and flick my eyes up to watch him as I take the first sip.

The deep brown eyes staring back at me smoulder as they focus on my mouth. My blood heats below my goosebumped skin as I let loose a soft moan at the perfect blend of fruit and alcohol that hits my tongue.

"This is *so* good," I praise between sips. *So* professional-like.

Niko adjusts himself on the chair, his jaw clenched tight

enough that it looks painful. I flutter my lashes and close my eyes while taking another pull of the drink. When I unwrap my lips from the straw, a cold sensation hits my chest.

The chair across from me creaks loudly, and I slowly open my eyes to see Niko's attention no longer fixed on my mouth but lower. Following his gaze, I watch as a bead of red slush slides down between the crease of my cleavage and drips low enough to disappear completely.

Completely innocently, I bring my finger to the sticky red line left behind and swipe up the drying liquid. With a smirk, I open my mouth and slide my finger along my tongue, tasting the daiquiri.

Niko's knuckle blanches around the neck of his beer, and I wonder how much longer it'll take for him to grip it hard enough to shatter.

"Do you have a napkin by chance? I've spilled a bit," I say, continuing to stare at where my skin has stained red.

The poor chair whines this time, and I lift my gaze to Niko, offering a sweet, innocent smile. His expression makes my entire body tremble in anticipation. The open, blazing desire he's letting shine through is doing wonders for my confidence.

I've never had anyone look at me like that.

"Actually, I think I have one," I murmur before slipping a hand into my purse and searching for a pack of wet wipes.

The package crinkles when I pull it out and grab one before using it to clean my skin.

"What did he tell his friends?" His voice is a rumble I feel like a slap between my legs.

I blink, letting my hand go limp against my breast. "Whose friends?"

"Travis's friends." He lifts his beer to his mouth and gulps half of it down in one go. "What did he tell them about you?"

My temperature cools faster than it spiked. I remove my hand from my chest and ball the used wipe in my fist.

He won't let it go now that I stupidly brought it up. Once he learns the things his son was saying about me, my chances to get him to make a meal of me will disappear. If he's anything like his son, I'll be shamed for the things I like for a second time.

Steeling my spine, I square my shoulders and decide to let it all out. I'd rather know what type of man Nicholas Shaw is now before spending another minute in his company.

"He and his friends used to call me Mount Ivy while making fun of my tits. Apparently, Travis didn't like the way they shook while . . . you know. He thought it was distracting, and it was why he didn't like to do it face to face."

You could hear a pin drop in the silence. I'm pretty sure I hear my confidence disintegrating with each second that passes.

A beer bottle scrapes across the table, and then Niko asks, "He didn't like when they shook while what, Ivy?"

"You know," I push, feeling my cheeks burn with embarrassment.

"While you fucked, angel? Because that's when they move the most, right? When they're bare and exposed, your nipples hard little pebbles just begging to be sucked on," he says lowly, every word intensifying the empty feeling between my legs.

My nipples are exactly as he described, and they're forced to scrape against the cups of my bra with each of my trembled inhales and exhales.

Niko doesn't stop there or wait for me to reply before pushing forward, his fingers straining where they lie on the table.

"Did he force them into the mattress, Ivy? Were those big tits punished because he didn't know how to worship them properly the way that I would have?"

I roll my eyes up to the ceiling and grip the edge of the table when I feel like I could slide right off my chair. His words—they're like a tongue stroke along my slit.

"Mr. Shaw," I whisper on a breath, knowing he grows more uptight and frustrated with every use of that name.

When he kicks his chair back a foot from the table and

tightens those dark brown eyes on me, I know I've gotten exactly what I wanted.

A beat later, he's smacking his thigh. "Come here, angel."

"Angel?" I echo softly, wondering if I heard him wrong.

"Should I call you something else?"

I shake my head just once, warmth erupting in my chest. "I like it."

"Get on my lap, then, Ms. Bell," he demands, his voice hard as he teases me with the name.

"Can you say please?"

The laugh that rips out of him is cold, threatening in a way that makes my clit throb. "You're not innocent at all."

"What am I, then?"

"You're a sweet little slut, angel. Now, get on my fucking lap."

I slip out of my chair and, with a finger dragging along the edge of the table, sway toward him. I'm keeping my pace turtle slow on purpose, but when he snaps an arm out and grips me around the waist, I know I'm about to lose my power to this dominating mountain of a man.

He moves me to stand in front of him, his knees pressing against me before I'm yanked forward. I lose my balance and tumble onto his lap, gripping his bulky shoulders to try and gain some balance.

With a gasp, I find my breasts pressed to his chest and my jeans pulled tight across my ass as I straddle him. This close, I can smell the spicy cinnamon scent of his skin. Without thinking twice about it, I dig my fingers into his shoulders and pull myself closer, bringing my nose to his throat.

Two thick, beefy arms wind around me, holding me in place, and I moan, drifting my nose along his neck to the underside of his bearded jaw.

"You smell so good," I whine, pulling myself further up his lap until my thighs are braced around his waist.

The bulge that appears beneath my ass has my head snapping back and eyes falling to where we connect. I roll my hips forward and shudder at the pressure between my legs.

"Oh," I murmur, flicking my eyes between his. "Is that . . . ?"

He releases a rough breath and fills his hands with my hips, using the hold to keep me still. "My cock, Ivy. That's my cock."

"It's hard."

Slowly, he urges me to rock forward, dragging my pussy over that long, thick ridge between us. I slip my hand from his shoulder to the side of his neck, holding him there as I press down on his lap.

"I've been hard since I walked out of the back and saw you sittin' at my bar," he declares, a thumb creeping up beneath my blouse to rub the bare skin of my waist. "Nearly blew a load in my jeans when I got you back here and felt your hand in mine."

I swirl my hips and grind down on his erection. A fleeting thought has me darting my eyes in the direction of the office door, finding it slightly ajar. I'm not interested in interrupting the moment to have either one of us close it.

The thought of someone watching what I hope Niko's about to do to me only makes me wetter. I'll dive into the meaning behind that later.

"How have you lasted with me on your lap, then?" I ask on a breathy exhale.

He grunts, sweeping his other hand up my waist to hold me beneath the thick band of my bra. "By tellin' myself that there's a better place for my cum than in my briefs, Ivy."

"Where?"

Oh, god.

I'm so fucking hot I'm going to erupt into a living ball of flame in this man's wide, steady lap. Right and wrong are lost, meaningless in this moment because this is the best I've ever, ever felt. And if Niko was who I was waiting for to be able to experience something like this, then I refuse to believe it wasn't meant to be this way.

I've finally sorted through the basket full of rotten apples I'd been handed and found a glossy, juicy one. I'm ready to sink my teeth into it and take a bite.

"Where, Niko?" I ask again, the words nearly slurred with arousal.

Niko removes his hands from my body and inches them up between us. His knuckles stroke a hot path along the underside of my breasts and then my aching nipples, eliciting a whimper from deep in my chest. He keeps moving, even as I arch my back and push my tits against his hands, desperate for more. For him to spread his fingers and pinch my nipples between them hard enough to make me see stars.

I pout, wiggling in his lap when he ignores my need and toys with the top of my blouse instead, running the tip of his fingers across the silky fabric.

"You lack patience," he mutters, utterly focused on where my blouse has parted.

"Patience isn't my specialty."

Humming low in his throat, he shocks me by pinching both sides of my blouse and yanking them apart. The ripping of the fabric is instant, and the sound of buttons pinging all around the office comes next.

"Niko!" I gasp.

My breasts bounce as I shift back and stare down at them, now exposed beneath the lace cups of my nude bra. I grow tense, the messages I saw shared about me and my body popping into my mind and pulling me back to that dark place.

I lift my arm, intending to drape it across my chest, but Niko grunts his disapproval and takes my hand in his. He brings it behind my back and holds it there, eyes flashing with a warning.

"Don't hide your tits from me."

My chest burns bright red. "You don't have to pretend to like them."

Again with that dark, displeased chuckle. He leans forward, bringing his mouth close enough to mine that I can taste the beer on his breath. I inch toward him, seeking the feel of his lips. He uses our linked hands to yank me back. I bunch my brows together and narrow my eyes.

Keeping a grip on two of my fingers, he releases the rest and starts unhooking my bra. I keep my eyes on his as he works, and a beat later, I feel the band give, the tension around my chest releasing.

Habit has me reaching for the cups still hiding my breasts with my free hand, but there's no time to cover myself. In a blink, Niko has my bra on the table behind me and his palms on my tits.

A rough groan falls from his spread lips, and I think my eyes cross when he pushes my breasts together and squeezes. His thumbs find my nipples and rub them with soft, experimental pressure.

"Never seen a pair of tits like these," he reveals, awe thick in his tone.

I push into his touch, my eyes falling to half-mast. "Don't lie."

Calloused hands move my breasts side to side, making them sway and bounce before pushing them upward. Then . . . then, he's burying his face between them and cursing low and long. Turning his head to the side, he bites and sucks at the soft flesh before lapping at the sting with his hot tongue.

I go limp in his arms, my legs as open as they can be in my restricting jeans. My pussy is so wet I think I'm leaking through my panties. Shit, I'm so turned on that I'm shaking.

"Niko," I whimper, jerking my hips to try and find some sort of friction.

He pinches my nipples before beginning to roll them between his thumb and forefinger. I feel it all between my legs. He might as well be giving the same treatment to my clit.

"Do you still want to know where I ache to put my cum, angel?" he asks, dragging his face from between my breasts to hover his mouth over my aching nipple.

The scrape from his beard is a sensory overload, and I fucking love it. Want more of it. Specifically on my inner thighs.

"Yes," I coo.

The first swipe of his tongue over my swollen peak makes me moan, but it's the ghostly press of his teeth around it and the promise of delicious pain that has me crying out.

"Right here, Ivy," he spits, as if he's angry. "I want to coat these huge, soft tits in so much cum that you'll never be able to wash the scent of me from them. I've never seen ones like this, and I'm content never findin' another. I'm claimin' this rack tonight, and that's fuckin' that."

He bites down on my nipple, and I come.

5

Niko

Ivy's head falls back as she writhes on my thighs. She squeezes my fingers hard and cups my jaw, holding my face in place.

It's the first gentle touch she's given me. I wouldn't doubt her fingers have imbedded their prints in my skin from the blistering heat coming off them.

"Niko, Niko. *Ooh* . . ." she whimpers as I bite down harder and pull.

The door is still cracked open, and she's so loud that she'll draw attention to us unless I can quiet her up. But fuck, I don't want her to stop whining and moaning and letting me know how much I'm pleasing her. Every sound is a phantom hand around my cock, stroking it the way I like. Hard and real fucking fast.

I release her nipple and rub my beard against it before sucking it again just once. Wet with my spit and red from the stimulation, her tits may as well be begging me to fuck them.

Swatting her breast, I groan, watching it bounce. "Get on your knees, angel. I need my cock between these."

Her eyes are so innocent when they struggle to focus on me, and that shouldn't make me harder. But the thought of her still so naïve to pleasure . . . it turns me fucking wild. I want to show her just how incredible sex with me can be, one orgasm at a time.

Slowly, in an arousal-drunk haze, Ivy stands from my lap. Her smirk is wicked, devious as she bends to grab my knees and then falls to hers.

With dainty hands, she palms her breasts, smooshing them together before shaking them side to side. "Are you going to fuck my tits now, Mr. Shaw?"

I crush my molars. "Niko."

"You introduced yourself to me as Mr. Shaw the first time we met. Don't you remember?"

After releasing her breasts, Ivy leans over my knees and reaches for my waistband. I track her movements with narrowed eyes and scoot forward, parting my legs to give her more room. She bats her lashes up at me when she drags a finger up the length of my cock before beginning to undo my jeans. My briefs are sticky, moulded to the tip as I leak precum.

I wait until after she's begun bringing my jeans and briefs down my thighs before answering her question.

With my long fingers pinching her chin, I tilt it back in a silent demand for her to meet my gaze. "I remember the first time we met, Ivy."

"How well?" she whispers, keeping her eyes on mine even as my cock bobs free of my briefs and rests against my stomach, my jeans pooled at my ankles.

I palm my shaft and give it a single squeeze. Precum slips from the tip and drips onto my finger.

"Your hair was a caramel brown then, not blonde, and you had it braided down your back. The cardigan you wore was baggy and an exact match to the dark grey ring around the green in your eyes. Your lips were red and glossy, just like right now." I release her chin only to drag my thumb along her bottom lip, smearing the lip gloss across her cheek. "You wore black flats and a pair of jeans with holes in the knees. I only needed one look at you to know how special you were."

Her body quakes with a shudder, and then she's pulling my hand away from my cock only to replace it with hers.

"*Fuck,*" I hiss between my teeth. "Yeah, nice and tight, angel. Squeeze me hard."

She follows my instructions.

Staring down at her on her knees with her pupils blown and lip gloss smeared as she jacks me off, I'm already too close to coming. Her fingertips can't touch around my shaft, but she makes it work, twisting her wrist and squeezing with every downstroke.

I jackknife up, burying my fingers in the hair at her nape and *pulling.* A whimper escapes her, and I only have a second to question why I'd been so rough with her before she moans in pleasure and quickens her strokes.

"You like it when I'm rough with you, angel? When I pull your hair and bite down on your pretty nipples?" I ask tightly.

She wobbles over the barrier my jeans have created—

still pooled at my ankles—and folds herself over my thighs before leaning over my cock, the heat of her exhales rushing down the shaft.

"Look at you. So fucking horny for it, aren't you?"

"Yes. Yes, I'm horny for it. For you," she says on a breathy moan, her tongue darting out to lap at the pool of precum coating the tip.

"As beautiful as you are drinking up my cum like a desperate slut, that's not what I have planned. Now, push your tits together and slide my cock between them," I demand, my voice so rough it's nearly unrecognizable.

Spreading my legs as wide as they'll go, I wait and watch as she moves between my thighs. Crushing her tits together in her hands, she rubs them against my tight sack.

"If you're going to tease me, Ivy, it's going to cost you," I warn.

She purses her lips, continuing her torturous movements. "Cost me what?"

"Every minute it takes you to do as I say is another I make you wait to feel this cock buried in your fucking womb."

I've never heard her make such a wild, desperate noise. I don't think I've heard any woman I've been with in my entire life sound like that, and I need to hear it again. And fucking *again*.

Without another moment of hesitation, Ivy hovers her breasts over my cock. I hold my breath as she glides them down, enveloping my shaft between them.

Inch by inch, I watch as my dick is swallowed into the crease of her breasts. I pull at her hair, encouraging her to start a rhythm. Up, down, up, down, she jacks me with laser focus.

"You're so soft," I grunt, dragging a knuckle down her cheek. "Soft and beautiful but a fuckin' dirty girl, too."

She hums vacantly. "Yes."

"Look at me."

Sliding her gaze upward, she opens her mouth, her red lips parted wide, and I do something I've never done.

I grip her cheeks, tilt her head back, and spit in her mouth.

She doesn't flinch, even as surprise blows her eyes wide open. My hold on her cheeks tightens, and in a blink, her surprise slips away.

With a flutter of her lashes, she's smoothing the tip of her tongue along her top teeth and crushing my cock between her tits.

"Do it again," she mewls.

My brows jump. "Again?"

"Yes."

There's no stopping the roar of lust that floods my thoughts. My dick drips between her tits, making the glide of them along the shaft smoother. "Beg me for it."

I'm pushing it, yet I don't regret it enough to stop. My gut tells me that she likes what I'm doing. And when she leans further between my legs and pushes her tongue out in a silent demand for more, I know I was so fucking right.

"Beg me to spit in your mouth, angel. Then I'll give you what you need," I coo, stroking a hand over her hair and loosening the pressure on her cheeks.

She nuzzles into my palms and slowly pulls her tongue back into her mouth. "Please spit in my mouth, Niko."

"Tongue out. And don't swallow until I tell you to."

Before she has a chance to tell me she'll do what I've demanded, I have my mouth hovering a few inches above hers, and then I spit onto her still-moving tongue.

"Swallow."

She tries, but some slides off into the corners of her mouth. I bring my thumb to the mess spreading down her cheek and drag it into her mouth before finally, *finally* kissing her.

It's wet and warm and demanding, a year of pent-up desire and interest exploding into a single press of our mouths and clack of our teeth. Ivy's the gentle one at first. She's curious, and with every cautious flick of her tongue to the seam of my lips, excited, too. I let her in without a second thought and glide my tongue along hers, finding out how we taste together.

Fucking paradise.

I don't realize she's stopped moving her chest until my cock grows cold and I break away long enough to stare down between us. Her fingers dig into my thighs as she hovers off her knees, as if she's too afraid to do what she really wants and climb onto my lap.

With a hard kick of each foot, I've got my boots and jeans flying across the office and not a single fucking boundary left between her and where she wants to be.

"On my lap now, Ivy. Take off those fuckin' jeans. It's time to ride my cock," I grunt, dropping a hand to my groin and cupping my aching sack.

Her body shakes in one long motion that travels from her shoulders to her feet. "I thought you wanted to come on my chest."

"We've got all night, angel."

Eyes glazing over, she uses her hold on my thighs to stand. I hold my breath when she releases me only to peel the ripped blouse from her shoulders and let it fall to the floor.

Slowly but with an easy confidence, she palms the back of my head and runs nimble fingers through my hair before forcing it forward. I open my mouth automatically when her nipple brushes against it, demanding entrance.

"Yes," she moans, stroking my nape soothingly.

I suck at her nipple and wrap my arm around her back, pulling her right into me. She tastes like peppermint lotion and the greatest temptation I've ever had to live with, and I can't get enough.

I'm too impatient to wait for her to take care of her pants. I unsnap their button and shove them down her hips with no fucking finesse, only desperation.

"Enough playing. It's time I bust through your pussy, Ivy. I've waited an eternity already, and I refuse to wait one moment more," I say around her swollen, hard nipple.

She guides me from her right tit to the left and nods when I flick my gaze upward. "Beg me for it."

The smile I flash is a warning. "It's time to fuck, not beg. Now, sit on my cock before I bend you over my desk and have you ramming it against the wall for the next hour."

"Why do you always make your threats sound so interesting?"

I answer by pushing to my feet so quickly she gasps and grip both of her hips before spinning her and folding her over my desk.

She giggles and throws her head to the side to stare back at me behind a curtain of messy curls. "Are you going to spank me now, Mr. Shaw?"

Her jeans come the rest of the way down with one swift yank. They fall to her ankles as I glide a hand up her spine and back down, pressing her onto the tabletop by her hip.

"Keep count. Miss one and I restart."

"So, that's a yes, then?" she asks, feigning innocence with the lip she pulls into her mouth.

I swat her left cheek with the back of my hand and watch in awe as it jiggles from the impact. It's so fucking plump and round, more than a handful. I wait for the slap to register before roughly palming the curve of the warm, soft skin. I squeeze and pull at it before spanking her again, this time on the opposite side.

"Count," I demand gruffly.

"Two," she coos, pushing back into my thighs and wiggling her hips.

"You're dripping onto the floor, aren't you?"

I aim for the pink print I've left behind and hit her again. This time, she rocks forward against the desk, hips digging into the wood.

"Yes," she gasps. "Three."

She throws her arms out along the table, effectively sending my cup of pens clattering onto the floor when I ramp up the strength of my hits and spank her again.

"Mmm," she whimpers.

"That's four."

"Yes, Mr. Shaw."

Two more smacks as I grind my teeth.

"Five . . . *six*! Oh, shit."

I step up behind her and fit my cock against her flaming ass. Angry and wet, it slicks up her crack before slipping between her cheeks and gliding through.

"If you're aiming for my pussy, you're a little off," she says, her tone all breathless teasing.

"Keep mouthing off and I'll be taking your ass first."

She moans, flipping her hair over her shoulder and flashing me a half-lidded gaze. "Travis hated anal."

I take her hip in my hand and reach down to take my cock in the other. With a slight adjustment, the tip is sliding through her slick pussy lips. I growl at the heat that envelops every inch of my shaft but don't breach her just yet. It's too good like this, too intimate.

"Don't talk about him when I'm about to fuck you, Ivy," I warn, pulling back before thrusting along her slit.

She lets out a long, high-pitched noise and bucks against me. Her fingers move between her legs to ghost along where my tip has started parting her opening.

"Why not? Because it makes you feel guilty? Are you going to pull your pants up and leave me here like this, Niko?"

My laugh is low, darker than usual. Every fatherly instinct inside of me screams that I'm a selfish disgrace. I'm about to cross a line that I can't ever walk back over.

My son has never been my biggest fan, and I can't say I'm his, but he's still family. And I'm about to fuck his ex-girlfriend.

I'm about to fuck her, and I'm going to love it. It's going to change my entire life and, in turn, his. I should do exactly as she said and pull up my pants and get out of here. So why, instead of doing that, am I pressing forward and breaching her tight opening with the tip of my cock?

"No, angel. I don't want you to talk about him because all I want when I hear you speak his name is to fuck you so good you forget all about him and every fucking second you spent together. While that makes me a terrible father, right now, I don't fucking care."

With one hard thrust, I bury myself so deep inside of her that my balls slap against the skin she'd drenched with pussy juice.

"Niko!" she cries out, slapping her hands on the desk and clawing at it with red-tipped nails. "You're too big. It's too—I'm too full."

Pulling out to the tip, I hover there, petting the handprints I've left on her ass. My chest has shrunk in size as my heart spasms.

"No, angel. It's the perfect size for you," I muse before fucking back into her, gentler this time, as I guide her to lean back against my chest. "And for the record, I fucking love anal."

There's no time for her to reply. I reach for her thighs and settle them both on my forearms, lifting her off the ground. Once I have her weight in my arms, I haul her into the air, keeping my cock buried in the tight walls of her pussy.

Her head falls against my shoulder as I move us toward the door. She's on full display for all to see, but there's no one here, and with a rough kick of my leg, I shut the door to make sure it stays that way.

She's so small in my arms, so breakable, that I take extra care not to drop her as I bring us to the bed. Perching us on the edge, my grip on her loosens enough that she can spread her legs over my thighs, opening herself completely.

"Wish I had a mirror in here so I could see how perfect you look with my cock stretching your perfect cunt," I grouse, setting my chin on her shoulder to watch her fat tits heave.

"I can see a little," she breathes out, head tipped to watch when she twists her hips.

My shaft is squeezed, and more slick drips to my balls. "Describe it to me, angel."

I suck her shoulder and tease my teeth over the marks I leave while bringing a hand around her front to tweak a nipple. She contracts around me, squeezing me deeper inside. I thrust just once and revel in the pleasure that zips up my spine.

Ivy whines, rolling her neck and bringing her face to my throat. "I'm so wet you're shiny with it. I've never been spread so wide . . . I don't know how you're inside. You shouldn't fit. But you do, and I'm—I've never felt this good."

My balls tighten at her words, drawing up like I'm about to come before I force myself to settle.

"Of course we fit together. You're with the right Shaw now, Ivy. The one who's always been right for you. Do you get it now? Is feeling this snug little cunt taking me deep what you needed all along?"

"Yes. Yes, I needed this!"

She trembles in my arms, and her nipple grows harder

between my fingers. I tug at it and bring my mouth to her ear, sucking at the base.

"Then let me ride you hard. You can thank me by creaming all over my cock."

She nods repeatedly and grinds down on me before I plant my hands on her hips and start to guide her movements. Ivy doesn't need the help, though. With a confident hand, she's shoving me down on my back and using her knees as leverage on the bed before taking me for a ride.

Her ass rises in the air, cheeks spreading with the angle, and then my cock is moving even deeper inside of her. She squeezes my knees in a death grip, so I take her ass in my hands and give it the same treatment. Every glide of her pussy over my length brings me closer to the orgasm I've been fighting off since I first saw her here today.

I can do nothing but let my eyes cross from the bliss and hold on as she uses me like a toy. It's as close to a holy experience as I'll ever get, and I'm unsure how to repay her for letting me witness it.

"Feels so good," she slurs, rolling her hips on the downstroke and grinding her clit on my groin before rising again. "You hit me so deep."

"You take me so well, angel. You're made to take it. It's yours, and you're such a perfect girl. *Yeah,* that's it. Ride this cock nice and deep."

She preens beneath the praise, speeding up. I engage my abdomen and lean up while parting her ass cheeks. With a purse of my lips, I spit against the dark pink hole in front of me. Saliva drips down her crack, and I throb from the pretty sight.

My thumb circles the wet hole on her next downward grind. She moans at the touch, and it's all the confirmation I need before pushing it inside.

"Oh, fuck, Ivy. You're so perfect. Your ass is sucking my thumb right in."

"I'm close," she announces on a broken gasp.

I can feel the confirmation around my cock. She quivers fiercely, squeezing so tight it's like she's trying to keep me buried inside for the rest of forever. I don't stop moving my thumb inside of her, and because she's relaxed from the pleasure of riding me, there's no pressure keeping me from speeding up.

"Give it to me, baby. Give me your cum, and I'll feed this hungry pussy mine. You'd like that, right?"

She nods furiously and turns to look at me over her shoulder. The pink cheeks and swollen, parted lips are enough on their own to make me spill, but add the squeeze of her pussy walls and an asshole so tight only a thumb can fit inside—

"Yes! Yes! I'm coming, I'm coming, Niko. I'm . . . please!" she shouts, offering me her mouth.

I take it with hungry, frantic kisses. Promises of more than just tonight. Of everything.

My name, my house, this bar. Every fucking dollar in my bank account. And *me*. Every inch, inside and out, is hers. She just has to accept the offerings.

"Take it, Ivy. Take it all," I spit, unsure if I'm speaking of the cum now spurting from my cock or the man himself.

She milks every drop from my balls, and I stop hearing her moan when my ears pop with pleasure. I'm yanked from my body and then shoved back inside, all in the span of a single breath.

Once I've rewired my brain, I'm wrapping my arm around her middle and bringing us both onto the bed to finish the ride. She huffs her breaths at a pace that I know matches mine as we lie in silence.

It's . . . terrifying. The silence feels out of place in this moment. I don't know what to say now that we're finished. Words have never been my thing. I've spoken more to her tonight than I've ever spoken to anyone in only a few hours. I wish I knew what to say to her right now. Something soothing, maybe? An explanation?

My dick deflates inside of her, and a spark of disappointment hits me at the realization that I didn't get to do what I promised and come on her chest. It was the plan, but . . .

Slowly, I slip my dick from inside of her and grow still.

An apology for not using protection is what I should be saying. I fucked her bare and then came inside like a horny teenager before I remembered to pull out. Fuck, pulling out wasn't even a thought in my mind. I had more than enough time, but the thought of leaving her tight warmth was never there.

So, why can I still not say anything now?

"I need to go clean up," Ivy says, her tone more closed off than it was earlier.

I clear my throat and release her waist. "I've got stuff here. Some wipes and an extra shirt since . . ."

"Since you tore mine apart," she finishes.

"Yeah."

"I'd appreciate that," she says, her eyes darting around the room.

I all but jump off the bed and put my jeans back on. A minute later, I hand her a couple of wipes and a spare shirt. It's my favourite one, but I'm eager to part with it if it means she'll be wearing it.

"Thank you," she whispers.

I grunt in reply.

It would be polite to turn and give her privacy while she dresses, but I can't find it in me to do that right now. Not when it could be the last time I'll get to see her like this. Fucking hell, it sounds like a wicked brand of torture to only have a woman like Ivy Bell once in your life.

Maybe I deserve that.

No, I'm sure I do.

My marks cover her shoulder and chest, and I stare at them, trying to memorize each one before my shirt falls down her body. The black material is so old it's started fading, and the bleach stains are everywhere, but it's comfortable.

She's quick to wipe herself clean and drag her jeans up her thighs. When they reach her ass, she winces but doesn't make a peep.

"We should talk about the event now," I say.

It's the wrong thing to say. Even before she takes a physical step away from me and hurt slashes across her features, I know that I've fucked up.

Work doesn't fucking matter to me right now. Nothing does but her.

"We can discuss the event over email. I have other plans tonight," she replies evenly.

"With who?"

"Someone."

My shirt hangs off her shoulder and down to her knees. With quick, harsh movements, she collects the fabric and tucks it into the front band of her jeans before collecting her purse from the table. In her anger, she swings her purse too hard and sends it careening into the Christmas gift bag. It falls onto its side on the table, and whatever is inside of it clacks against the wood.

"Need that, too? A *gift* for the someone you have plans with?"

Her features tighten with anger as she fixes her purse onto her shoulder and stalks toward the office door. "Just a giant Scrooge I was warned about."

I ignore my instinct to go to her and lift the bag by its handle instead. The tissue paper has shifted in the fall, no longer keeping the contents inside hidden.

I'm overly cautious when reaching inside of it and discarding the paper. I touch the clear jar and tap the gold lid before pulling it out and holding it in front of me.

Peppermint-flavoured moonshine in a jar made into the shape of a stocking for a so-called *Scrooge*. Jealousy swirls inside of me when I think of her giving this or any other gift to a man who isn't me.

I set the jar down and reach back inside the bag to grab the second item. It's soft in my hand, but I don't recognize what it is until I pull it out and unfold it.

A Christmas sweater. The knitted kind.

My jealousy swells, and I abandon the gifts to ask Ivy who exactly they're for and why she made one for them if she knew she was coming to meet with me tonight. Only she's not here.

I'm alone, and the door's wide open.

6

THREE WEEKS LATER

Ivy

"WHERE ARE YOU WITH THE LET'S GET BLITZEN'D PREPARATIONS?"

Grayson's voice has me jerking up in my office chair and swiping the drool away from my chin. With my eyes heavy, I look to where he's watching me from the entrance to my cubicle. Today, he's shed the suit and opted for a stiff turtleneck colour matched to the bland paint in the office.

"What?" I ask.

"How are you doing with the event at the Frosty Mug? I haven't had an update in a week, and we're only one away."

It's an effort to keep a straight face. "It's going good."

His expression flattens. "Anything else? Maybe something more specific?"

"My folder is at home." Where I wish I was.

For the past three weeks, I've hidden in my home office and planned an entire Christmas event for the town without the help of the owner of the venue. Calls have been made, and orders have been placed without prior approval.

In all fairness, Niko's had the chance to tell me if he disagreed with something. He's *so* interested in the event, after all.

I've ensured that every contact I've spoken to has kept him in the loop, and I've yet to hear him complain about any of my decisions. I'm taking that as approval. If he thought I was doing something wrong or wasn't comfortable with a choice I've made, I'd have expected one of the several emails he's sent me since . . . *that night* . . . to include a gruff, demanded change.

God, that night.

Three weeks after he quite literally fucked the daylights out of me, and I haven't forgotten a single detail. Not the feel of his calloused, rough hands on my skin, the soft, testing pressure of our first kiss, or the ache between my legs that I had to soak away the next morning. The pain was a first for me, but with the size of his cock, it wasn't all that surprising.

Although, it was bad enough that I thought I was going to be stuck in the tub for days.

Then there was the mess he'd left on my skin. Not only was I covered in love bites and bright red handprints on my ass, but I had to scrub my skin raw just to get the dried cum off my thighs. I gave up trying to cover the hickeys with makeup the week after they appeared.

Good lord, I wish I hadn't left the way I did. After the sex we had, I was too emotional. The intimacy was giving me all the wrong ideas, and when he suggested work . . . it hurt me to the point I had to run.

His spicy cinnamon scent lingered on my clothes and neck for days. I couldn't bring myself to throw what was left of my blouse into the washing machine, so I draped it over my armchair and haven't touched it since.

The shirt he dressed me in before I left the bar is in my bed. It's pathetic, but I've kept it there because it makes me feel like he's with me. Just without all of the grunts and searing stares that led me into his arms.

I miss him.

One day together and I *miss* the man. It's crazy, maybe even a little naïve. The last few nights have been rougher than usual with my new stomach bug, but even before it hit out of nowhere,

I was having trouble sleeping. And when I'm asleep, he's there in my dreams.

It's easier not to sleep at all.

"Ivy? Are you still ill?"

I choke on nothing and wipe at my eyes, thankful I didn't have the energy to put makeup on this morning.

"Sorry, Grayson. What did you say?"

He takes a step into my cubicle and furrows his brows in suspicion. "I asked if you needed the folder to give me an update or if you were well enough up to date on your own to give me something to go off of."

"Oh, of course. Yes, I know about the project. It's mine, after all. It would be pretty pathetic if I didn't know everything off the top of my head, right?" I ask, attempting to make a joke but failing terribly.

Grayson doesn't laugh. "So? Tell me something."

"Yes, right. Okay. Well, I know we spoke last week about the fact that in the past, the event hasn't really drawn interest from the young adult crowd, so I actually reached out to a tattoo studio that's owned by one of my old classmates, and he's agreed to come run a pop-up. Tattoos would be discounted for a few hours, and he'll create a few custom designs that fit the whole Christmas vibe people can easily choose from."

"What's the name of the studio?"

"Into The Shade."

"I've heard of it. And you're right. It will draw the younger crowd. What about the kids?"

His praise makes me sit a bit straighter, proud of my work.

"I read in last year's plans that there were sleigh rides, and I think that's still a really great idea. It's not something that I think will ever really go out of style. So, we're going ahead with that again this year.

"I've also added a snowman-building competition, with the prizes being donated from a few of the businesses in town. There are some gift cards, a day pass for the rink, and I did reach out to a couple of places a bit further from us and found a contact for Steele Ranch. The owners have agreed to not only lend us a few of their horses for the sleigh rides, but they're offering a few certificates for free riding lessons," I tell him, stretching my legs out beneath my desk. "There will be hot chocolate stands and an area to make maple taffy, along with a few food trucks."

Grayson blinks at me, digesting all that I've said. When he recovers, he looks pleased, his features relaxing.

"What about the bar itself? I assume all of this will be taking place outside, but surely Niko hasn't allowed for there to be nothing bringing traffic into his territory."

I swallow my immediate response. If I told him that I'm pretty sure Niko would allow just about anything if I asked him to, he could pull me off the project, and I've put too many hours into this to have it stolen from me.

"I've tried to leave control up to him on that front, but I have given a few suggestions, like an eating challenge with an enticing prize or a raffle of some sort. Honestly, I think most people will go into the bar on their own without any sort of incentive."

"And he agrees with you?"

I sure hope so.

"As far as I know, yes."

"This is good work, Ivy," he says.

My cheeks heat. "Thank you, Grayson."

"I assume you have another meeting set up with Niko before the event? We're only a week away, and as great as this sounds, I need you to make sure things stay moving according to plan."

"Of course."

Shit.

He taps his hand to the wall and nods. "I'll leave you be, then. If you need anything, let me know."

"Will do—"

I cut myself off with a hand to my mouth. My skin turns cold to the touch as I shoot off my seat and shove past my boss into the hallway.

For the hundredth time this week, my stomach rolls, and my throat burns with vomit. The bathroom is unoccupied when I shove my way inside and immediately wretch into the toilet. Cool skin heats until I'm breaking out in a sweat.

It only goes on for a few minutes before my stomach settles, and I lean back on my heels. My hand trembles when I press the back of it to my forehead and take a deep breath.

Every time I think the flu has moved on from me, it comes back with a vengeance. It's frustrating, considering the majority of the day, I'm just fine. No nausea or exhaustion.

Oh.

Oh, no.

Surely not. There's no way. I'm on birth control. I have been since I was sixteen and my mom sat me down and gave me the sex talk. And Niko, well, *surely* he's too old to have that many sperm. Right? I know I let him screw me without a condom on, which, yeah, was super irresponsible, considering we didn't talk about STDs or anything, but . . .

I touch my cheeks and widen my eyes as the potential reality of this hits me upside the head with a brick.

There's a knock on the bathroom door that I know I left open, and then Grayson's voice slips through the crack.

"Are you ill, Ivy?"

"Yes," I squeak, rising on shaky knees to wash my hands.

"Do you need to go home?"

I let the water run cold and cup some to swish in my mouth and splash on my face. Spitting the water into the sink, I dry my hands on a paper towel.

"I'd appreciate if I could," I reply.

"Are you decent? Can I open the door?"

My stomach is unsettled for a completely different reason as I pull the door open on my own and dab my mouth with the damp paper towel.

"You can have the rest of this week off. Just send me an email with a recap of your meeting with Niko and if there's anything that you need my approval for. Other than that, you aren't needed here right now, Ivy. Stay home and rest," he says, and for the first time since I started at the office, his voice isn't bland and cool. There's a kind tinge to it that makes me smile slightly.

"You'll be at the event, right?" I ask.

"Yes."

"Will I see you at the tattoo pop-up?"

He snorts a laugh. "No. But I'll be around."

"Well, I guess it's time I wish you a Merry Christmas."

"Merry Christmas, Ivy," he returns before gesturing for me to exit the bathroom ahead of him.

It'll be a Christmas for sure. Only time will tell if it's merry.

Tipping the grocery bag upside down, I shake out the boxed pregnancy test and watch as it falls to the bathroom counter with a clunk.

It's like my brain has switched off to allow my limbs to move of their own accord. With every rip my nails create in the box, the knot in my stomach twists tighter and tighter. I'm doubtful that I'll be able to untangle it at this point.

The slim stick falls into my palm when I finally tear the box open. Once I pee on it, I set it on the counter with the cap back on and the little hourglass flashing on the screen.

I slam the toilet lid shut and set a timer on my phone before sitting atop it with my head in my hands and my feet tapping the floor. It said to wait two minutes, but why does that feel like the world's most impossible task? In this day and age, the results should be instant.

Maybe this would be easier if I wasn't doing it alone. Or if I had intended for this to happen. But a baby? I wasn't planning on one of those for a long time still. I'm only twenty-one, and I mean, come on! While I'm not exactly the most immature or reckless person, I doubt I'm mother material right now.

I don't even have a boyfriend! It was a one-night stand. A hookup. Even if it was the best I've ever had, and if he offered, I'd be happy to do it again.

I groan into my hands. What am I supposed to do? Niko's already lived through being a parent. His son is my age, for god's sake. I doubt he wants to start at the beginning again with someone who he slept with in the back office of a bar.

We haven't spoken in three weeks, not in a less professional setting than our business emails. How's this for an icebreaker?

The ring of my alarm sounds. I hold my breath and drop my hands from my face. It's like someone's tugging at my puppet strings as I stand and sway to the sink.

One look at the tiny screen and I'm gripping the edge of the counter for balance.

Positive.

7

Ivy

I've always loved Christmas.

My mother was a bit over-the-top with it when I was growing up, and I kept all of the same traditions living on my own that we had then.

There were years when the tree would go up before Halloween had even arrived, and I think those ones were my favourite. Mom would always order Dad to haul the bins up from the basement, and we'd spend the entire day figuring out where to put everything.

The theme for our living room tree alternated every year, from red and green to pink and silver and sometimes blue and white. Mom insisted we stick with one and work around it with the ornaments, tinsel, the tree skirt, and even the lights.

Then, we'd set up a second tree in the family room, where she'd give Dad and me free rein to decorate how we wanted with no rhyme or reason. I'd hold my box of sentimental ornaments to my chest and let Dad take his hockey ones, and then we'd get to work. Some years, it would take hours to get the tree how I wanted it, and I'd have Dad huffing and puffing from how many times I'd have him adjust something I was too tall to reach.

By the time we'd finish, Mom would already have Chinese takeout on the way, and we'd turn the fireplace on before making hot chocolate in our matching mugs.

It's those memories that I replay on the days when I'm feeling lonely. The holidays aren't the time to feel alone, but ever since I moved away from my parents, they've felt that way more than normal.

I always make the time to go back home for dinner and presents, but once you leave your childhood home and start a life on your own, it's just not the same as it was. They're growing pains, I know. Acknowledging that doesn't magically stop the gnawing in your gut and craving for something more.

Puffing out a long exhale, I continue down the road to the Frosty Mug. My tires sink into the heavy dump of fresh snow that has yet to be plowed, and I grip the steering wheel tighter, growing more nervous. Even with the quick swipe of my wipers, the snow is falling hard enough in front of me to make it hard to see where I'm going.

It's a December 22 white-out, according to the weatherman on the radio, and after exchanging a few emails with Niko, I was left with no other choice than to agree to see him today regardless of the weather.

Sure, he offered to come to my place, but if he'd done that . . . just *no*. First, I don't trust myself around him enough to welcome him into my home without pouncing like a horny animal, but second, I wanted to check on how the decorating at the bar has come along.

The last time I was there, it was bare and sad. But I've given him clear instructions on how everything should be decorated, and I'm ready to see if he followed them.

My stomach rolls as I come to a slick stop at a red light. Of course, there's more to my visit than just work.

I went to my doctor yesterday and had her confirm that yes, I am indeed pregnant. Three weeks along, to be exact. I'm nauseous from the morning sickness but also the nerves of telling him the news.

Will he be upset? Or tell me that he doesn't want it? God, I hope not. I don't know if I could do this on my own.

It was so reckless not using a condom. I've always known that birth control isn't ever one hundred percent effective, and surely, he knows that, too. We acted out of impulse, and now I don't know what to do.

The light turns green, and I softly press on the gas to avoid spinning my tires and ease through the intersection. It's too bright out to see the lights hung around town, but the wreaths on every shop door are visible. They're enough to make me smile a little before I pull into the bar parking lot.

A country rendition of "Jingle Bells" plays through the speakers as I put the car in park and settle a hand on my stomach through my thick jacket.

"I hope you like Christmas, baby. If not, you'll break your mom's heart. Not to mention your grandma's," I say softly.

Pulling the key from the ignition, I steel my spine and nod once to myself. When I step out, the snow attacks my face. Wind howls through the air, and I gasp at the force of it when it slashes my cheeks.

I pull my fur-lined hood up and jog through the piles of snow in the parking lot to the entrance. Even with my gloves on, the metal door handle is so cold it burns my fingers when I pull it open.

It's hot inside, and I drop my tense shoulders before patting my jacket clear of snow. I'm nowhere near showing yet, but I wore my baggiest jacket and dress as if that would make any difference at all today.

Footsteps approach when I start shrugging out of my jacket, and I tense automatically, waiting for whoever it is to reach me. The tables closest to me are empty, which isn't surprising, considering the empty parking lot and the weather outside. It's not exactly all that safe to be driving on the roads, and it won't be long before they're shut down altogether. I'll have to make sure I'm gone by then.

"I'll take that," Niko grunts, appearing from around the tables with his hand already reaching for me.

He grabs my jacket once I go to drape it over my arm and clutches it in a huge hand. When I lift my gaze, I'm immediately trapped beneath the weight and intensity of his hazelnut eyes.

"Hi," I mutter shyly.

"Hi."

With a blink, I'm able to free myself of his stare and finally take in the sight of him in front of me. My heart skips a few too many beats when I focus on the green-and-red sweater he's wearing with his jeans. I wheeze out a breath and pinch my shirt sleeve.

"What are you wearing?"

He has the nerve to stare down at himself as if he doesn't know why I'm asking him that question and shrugs a bulky shoulder. "A sweater."

"Why that one?"

"It was a gift, wasn't it?"

I snap my head back to stare into his eyes again, this time narrowing mine. "Maybe it wasn't for you."

"It's a bit snug, but I made it work."

"That could have been for Travis." It explodes out of my mouth before I can reel the words back in. I swallow an apology, even as his face thunders. "I mean, it wasn't, but it could have been."

The space between us disappears in a matter of a few seconds. Niko doesn't hesitate to take my face in his hands and crane my head back before swooping in to kiss me. I shouldn't let it happen after how we left things weeks ago, but as my eyes close and my stomach fills with flapping wings, I don't have it in me to pull away again.

It's a statement, but not for the public. Just for me. It's a reminder that while he stayed away, he didn't forget about me or what we'd done together. I smile into the kiss without thinking twice about it, and he deepens it, drawing me closer.

The yarn I used to make his sweater is soft beneath my fingers when I drag my hands around to rest flat on his back. He wasn't wrong about it being a bit too snug, but the fact he still wore it means more to me than I bet he expected it to.

He smooths his thumb along the edge of my jaw and then pulls out of the kiss to run it over my lip. "Come with me. I've already made you a drink."

The wings in my stomach vanish. "Oh, I'm okay with just water."

"I tweaked the daiquiri recipe. Thought I could put 'em on the drink menu for the event." He takes my hand and starts pulling me further into the bar. "Peppermints instead of strawberries."

"That's brilliant, actually," I muse, even if the thought of smelling anything scented makes me want to vomit.

I've cut using perfume at all after realizing that I hate the scent of my favourite one now that I'm pregnant. At least the smell of the bar hasn't upset my stomach much.

Niko glances down at me in surprise. "Yeah?"

"Absolutely. What else have you thought of putting on the menu?"

"Only came up with that one."

"You could have done anything, Niko. Obviously, you'll do a beer special, but you should do another once-a-year drink. Something with maybe whiskey?"

"Peppermint moonshine."

My cheeks flame. "Do you like peppermint moonshine?"

"I've taken a likin' to it the past couple'a weeks, yeah."

"Oh."

The conversation stalls as we make it to the bar, and I find it as empty as the front tables. Spinning on my heel, I confirm that we're the only people in the place unless there's someone hiding in the back.

There are also no decorations. Not even a single set of lights or a wreath.

"Where is everyone?" I ask, noticing the slush-filled, curvy pink cup on the bar.

Niko grabs the drink and offers it to me with something that looks a lot like hope shining in his dark eyes. My neck grows damp as I bite down on my lip and hesitate to take it from him.

"I can't drink that."

He blinks, and the hope is gone, replaced with cool indifference. Clearing his throat, he moves to set it back down when I reach for his wrist.

"It's not that I don't want it. I do. And it's incredibly sweet that you made it for me to try. If you want, I can have a co-worker come by before the event to taste it," I ramble, sounding as nervous as I feel.

He leaves it on the bar and crosses his arms. "I don't need anyone to taste it but you. Made it special for you, Ivy."

"Oh. Well, that's even sweeter, then."

"I shouldn't have expected you to want it. It's fuckin' cold out. I'm sorry."

"I do want it. I just can't *have* it. Can we please sit and talk? I'll explain."

Worry tightens his features as he nods toward the closest table. It's a booth, so I slide into the one side, expecting him to join me on the other. Instead, he moves around the bar and fills a glass with water. I breathe out a silent chuckle and wait for him to finish.

There isn't any Christmas music playing in the bar today, and now that I think about it, there wasn't the first time I was here, either. It's old rock instead.

"Why isn't there any Christmas music playing?" I ask once he's squished his large frame into the booth beside me and passed me the glass.

We're so close together, his thigh and bicep pressing into me. I subtly lean into his body, seeking the warmth he's exuding.

"I haven't changed the station in months."

"It's the holidays. Christmas music is kind of expected right now."

"Not here."

"Is there a reason for that?"

"Just don't like it much." He uses his knuckles to push my water closer to me. "Drink somethin'."

My chest warms at the blunt order. Despite his grumpiness, Niko is incredibly thoughtful, and it's nice being doted on.

I take a sip of the water and then ask, "Do you like the sweater?"

"Yes. I've never had one like it before."

"Even if it is a little snug?"

He flattens a palm over my thigh and squeezes. "Yeah, angel. I'd wear anythin' you made me, no matter the size."

"I can make you another one that fits right. What's your favourite colour?"

"Navy."

"Navy it is, then. I've got to finish up my collection for the Christmas market, so I'll add it to my list."

"You make a livin' off these things?" he asks, surprised but not in a doubtful way. Just genuinely curious.

"Not a living, no. But I love knitting, and it's nice to see others wearing the things I make, even if it's just a few sweaters or slippers," I explain.

"Would you make me slippers?"

I gawk up at him, a brow arched. "You want a pair of knitted slippers?"

"Why not? I've got feet just like everyone else."

"Massive ones, I'm sure."

He huffs. "Size thirteen."

"Yep. Just as I expected. Guys with big dicks always have big feet, and yours is massive."

"You think my cock's massive?"

"Don't let it get to your head."

His hand falls to the inside of my thigh and tries to pull it closer, even if it's not possible. "What did you want to talk about?"

The light mood between us shrivels up and dies as the reality of what I'm about to tell him sinks in. My palms grow slick with sweat, and I can't even wipe them on my thighs without risking touching his hand with one.

I grip my water and take a few long pulls before setting it down. My pulse throbs in my throat.

"I have something to tell you. And I don't know how you're going to take it."

Gosh, I can't even look at him. The booth across from us is old and wrinkled, but it's better than meeting his stare.

"Just tell me, Ivy. I'm a grown man."

"I'm more than aware of that," I mutter, tucking my hair behind my ear. "Look, I just want you to know that I don't expect anything from you. You don't have to stick around or offer me money. I might be young, but I was raised right, and while I'm not sure how I'll do it, I'm—"

Niko shuts me up when he hooks a finger beneath my chin and forces my head to turn. I'm met with clear and open brown eyes that somehow soothe some of my panic.

"You're pregnant."

Hearing it from his mouth makes it more real, somehow.

Holy fuck. I'm pregnant.

Emotion clogs my throat as I drop my hands to my lap and nod. "How did you know?"

"Can almost taste your fear and doubt in the air, angel. And we didn't use a condom. That and you refused my drink."

"Are you mad?" I whisper.

His brows scrunch together as he wets his lips. "Mad? No, Ivy. I'm not fuckin' mad about a baby."

"Why not? You're already a father, and I'm nobody to you, Niko. I'm not your wife or even a girlfriend. You didn't mean to knock me up," I argue, a large part of me still in disbelief that he's not telling me to hit the curb.

"Just 'cause I didn't mean to doesn't mean I'm upset that I did. And you're not my wife or girlfriend *yet*. Don't use that as a viable reason for me to walk out on you."

"What do you mean 'yet'?"

"Do you think I make a habit of sleepin' with all of my son's ex-girlfriends, Ivy?"

"No."

"That's right. So why would I have started now?"

"You're okay with what happened, then? And what happens next? Because I think I want to keep the baby, Niko. And that means that . . . *Oh my god.* Travis will have a brother. And I'll be its mother!"

In a rush, I start shoving Niko's arm and chest in an effort to get him to exit the booth. He frowns but stumbles out so that I can tumble out after him.

"Where's the bathroom?" I croak, reaching up to cover my mouth when vomit slithers up my esophagus.

Niko palms my back and guides me through the bar without another word. I gag behind my hand and wince at the burn that follows. All of my focus is on not throwing up all over him and the bar.

By the time he helps me into the bathroom, I'm barely making it to the toilet before expelling all of the water I drank at the table. I haven't been able to keep anything down all day, so there's no food to get rid of.

My stomach growls as I hunch over the toilet and squeeze my watering eyes shut. Embarrassment floods my system as Niko squats beside me and holds my hair and rubs my back.

"I'm sorry," I blubber, wiping at my eyes with the back of my hand. When I see clumps of black lashes in my vision, a sob escapes me.

He shooshes me gently. "How long has this been goin' on for?"

"About a week."

"Have you been eatin'?"

I shake my head, keeping it tilted down to hide my face.

"You've got to eat, angel."

"I can't. It comes up as soon as I do, and I'm just so damn hungry!" I wail.

"Okay. Do you need to throw up again?"

I sniffle. "No. I think I'm okay."

It comes and goes so fast that I've wondered if it's all just in my head. But it happens again so quickly that I know it has to be real.

Niko moves from my side to crouch behind me. He slips his hands beneath my arms and then helps me onto my feet, leaning me back against the solid wall of his chest.

"Let's get you somethin' to eat. We can talk about the baby while I cook."

I swallow thickly and touch my lips to make sure they're dry before turning around. The huge man towers over me but doesn't make me feel small in any way other than size. I've never felt like someone's equal more than I do with him.

"I might just throw it back up," I say in warning.

The corner of his mouth twitches like it wants to lift into a smile but can't quite get there. "Worth a shot. Come."

I hover a hand over my mouth when he brings his face closer to mine. "Are there breath mints somewhere by chance?"

"I'll get you one once we've made it to the kitchen."

"To the kitchen, then."

The place where we'll decide the next steps for the rest of our lives.

8

Niko

A *DAD*. AGAIN.

I'm going to be a dad for a second time.

I hadn't expected to have Travis. Young and stupid were the only two adjectives in my vocabulary back then. I didn't have a damn clue where life was taking me during those nine months with his mother, but the only destination was him. And as time moved forward and I grew up alongside him through the trials I faced as not only a father but as a man, I knew that if I got this chance again, I'd take it with open arms.

I am who I am today because of what I went through. Sure, I don't have a heavy savings or a big fancy house. My relationship with Travis's mother ceased to exist early on in his childhood, and I've never been father of the year. But I am proud of the way I grew and the battles I won. Of my small three-bedroom bungalow in a quiet cul-de-sac and this bar.

I made mistakes that I know how to avoid this time around. I'm calm when I was short-tempered and focused when I was distracted.

There were a fuck ton of things I thought Ivy and I would speak about today, but this? This wasn't even close to what I expected.

Our emails the past three weeks have been short and to the point, regardless of how many times I tried to hint at seeing her again. She never fell for my traps, and maybe I should have taken that as a sign, but I refused to because not having Ivy Bell as mine is simply not an option any longer.

And now, I'm only surer about my decision. It's the right one, without a doubt.

This woman was put into my life for a reason, and we've been granted a chance for a do-over. An opportunity for me not to let her slip into another man's arms and to take her into mine instead. I'm not letting her go again. Not going to torture myself with watching her with my son at every holiday and family event, knowing that if things had been just a little different, she'd be with me instead.

The fallout that could come with Travis learning of all this and hating me is always there in the back of my mind. The news of a baby may very well destroy our relationship.

A better man would heed the warning. That's not me.

We're all adults. And I know my son. If he wanted Ivy as badly as I do, we wouldn't be in this position right now. He didn't treat her right, and if he weren't my son, I'd have buried my knuckles in his teeth for what he did to her.

There's a discussion to be had soon, but today isn't the day for it. The only plan I have for the rest of my afternoon is to take care of the woman who's carrying my baby while trying to convince her that I'm worth a spot in her life.

"I didn't know there was a kitchen in here," Ivy says, now perched on the kitchen counter, legs dangling off the edge.

"Doesn't get used much."

The sizzle of the scrambled eggs I'm cooking on the skillet fills the space as I use a spatula to mix the chopped peppers around.

"Do you ever sell burgers here or anything like that?"

"Just fries."

"Why not more? You could bring in more customers if they could grab a bite to eat as well as a drink."

"I tried. There were no cooks to hire. Got lucky that Matty is handy with the fryer."

The few who applied for a serious position were better-qualified scrubbing floors. It was more hassle than it was worth. Now, the kitchen sits mostly empty until I find myself cooking something at the end of a late night.

At least it was stocked for today. There are plenty of other meals to cook if the eggs are no good for her stomach.

"You wouldn't want to be the one doing the cooking, then, I take it?"

I turn the burner off and spread out the cooked eggs before sprinkling some shredded cheese and pepper over them.

"No. I'm a cook out of necessity. Not out of passion," I answer.

"That's fair. I'm not bad in the kitchen, but I'm no chef."

"What do you like to cook the most?"

"What do I like to cook the most, or what do I like to eat?"

"Both."

She leans back on her hands, chest to the ceiling, and hums. "I love to bake. I'm not good enough to do it without a recipe or anything, but if I had the choice, I'd bake something before cooking a meal. And eating-wise . . . I really, really love mozzarella sticks. Or a thick piece of lasagne. *Ooh,* or maybe some tamales. I wouldn't mind a heaping bowl of buffalo chicken dip, either, though."

Her eyes nearly cross as she speaks, tongue swiping her lips like she can taste the food she's describing.

I grab a plate from the shelf along the wall and slide her eggs onto the centre of it. She watches my movements with interest, and when I pass the plate to her, she pounces on it. Her stomach growls loudly, so I move quickly to find her a fork and hand it over.

Stabbing the prongs of the fork into the fluffy eggs, she says, "Oh, my god, I'm so hungry."

"Eat, angel."

She shoves the bite into her mouth and moans before starting to chew, already spearing more onto the fork. I move between her legs and settle my hands on her knees as she devours the food. My chest tightens as I watch, my primal instincts pleased that I've taken care of her. She deserves it.

"These are the best eggs I've ever had," she says between bites.

"You're just really hungry."

"Can't I be hungry and honest at the same time?"

I trace the curves of her knees. "Yeah, you can."

She focuses back on her eggs, and I don't move from my spot, too content exactly where I am. I've always made sure to eat breakfast every morning, and apparently, I need to help Ivy get into the habit as well. Especially now that she's eating for two.

"What have you been doin' for the last three weeks?" I ask bluntly.

She slows her chewing and swallows. "Working, mostly."

"On the event?"

"You've been getting the emails, so you know the answer to that already."

"I've gotten plenty'a emails, Ivy. From everyone but you."

Her neck grows pink as she slides the fork along the plate to collect the small pieces of egg still left. "You were the one who was so concerned about the event. I thought you'd have been happy that I was keeping the focus there."

"You're what I wanted to talk about," I reveal.

She snares my eyes as her mouth tips at the corner. "Really?"

With a tight exhale, I grip the edge of the countertop on either side of her legs and lean into her space. The air shakes around us, but I only push closer, letting my connection to her draw me in.

Ivy tips her head back, keeping our eyes locked even as I bring my mouth to her cheek.

"I missed you, Ivy. You weren't supposed to run off that day. I had so many more plans for you that I had to let die. And now, you're back with my fuckin' baby in your stomach?"

I lift a cautious hand to rest against her lower belly. It's naturally rounded, but not with a baby yet. There won't be a bump there for a while. Still, the knowledge that there's something growing beneath my palm intensifies my possessiveness.

"I wanted you back here with me. But this is beyond my wildest dreams. You've given me the best Christmas gift, angel, and I'm goin' to be here for the both of you. Don't care that this is sudden or that we're still gettin' to know each other. I've got all the time in the world when it comes to you," I vow, offering my heart to her on a silver platter.

Ivy's eyes glisten while staring right into my soul. She discards the plate beside her and smooths her hands up my arms to hold my shoulders.

"Do you really mean that? All of it? Because there's a lot to me that you don't know. You might learn something that has you ready to run out the door."

"Won't happen. I'll prove myself to you."

Her smile is more stiff than usual. "If you say so."

"This is 'cause of Travis, yeah? The things he spewed about you to his friends? You're expectin' the worst of me because of it."

"Why is he the way that he is, Niko? Why didn't he respect me? I gave him everything I had, but I was too imperfect to please him. Too loud but not enthusiastic enough. High-maintenance but boring. Too fat for him to get hard without me putting in the work, and even when I did, I wasn't sexy enough for him to enjoy himself. I learned all those things when I went through his texts, and he never once had the balls to tell me to my face. I'm not trying to be hard to please, Niko. I'm just . . . I'm scared."

Anger burns my blood, turns it to lava in my veins.

I glide my hand from her belly to the curve of her waist, holding her firm. "I had Travis when me and his mother were fifteen. It was a reckless hookup that cost me everythin' at the time, and I'm still payin' the price of it. Did what I could to raise him right and show him how to treat those around him with kindness and respect, but clearly, I failed. The way he treated you, Ivy—fuck. I never saw it. Not once when you were together did I think he was acting like his old man did back in the day. Like the world and the people around him were steppin' stones. That's my fault. I should'a done a better job of showin' him how to treat a woman."

She shakes her head, brows knitting together. "You're not responsible for his actions. I'm not trying to put the blame on you for the person he became. I just, I don't understand why or how someone can be so cruel. For as long as I've known you, I've never seen you treat him poorly. You've been a good dad to him. I'm not usually an insecure person, but these past few months . . . yeah."

"I'm real fuckin' sorry, angel. You were always too good for him. Too good for the likes of me, too, but I'm not lettin' you get away the way he did. And this baby is a gift. I'm ready to love the both of you the way you deserve to be loved," I vow, dipping my head to brush my mouth across hers. "I've had a lifetime to prepare for you, Ivy. I'm not the same person I was when I had Travis. There isn't anythin' I'm not willin' to give up to keep you. No lines I wouldn't cross or deals I wouldn't make. You got that?"

"Yeah, Niko. I got that," she whispers before slanting her lips over mine in a kiss that hits like lightning.

I take her cheek in my palm and stroke her blush. It's impossible to get close enough to her. Every inch of my body wants to feel the press of her soft, warm skin. If I had it my way, I'd walk around every day with her glued to my front.

Pulling her lip into my mouth, I suck on it gently, teasingly. Ivy grips me tighter, her tiny hands clawing at my shoulders as she tugs me against her. Surprise has me leaning back enough to stare down at her.

Flushed cheeks and pupil-blown eyes greet me. I push her hair out of her face and try to hide a smirk.

"Are you needing more than a few kisses, angel?"

She wets her lips excitedly and tries to yank me against her again. "I've been so sensitive, Niko. I'm—I just need you to keep touching me."

I nip at her mouth and grip her thigh, using it to lift her leg onto the counter. "Where?"

She showed up here in a fucking blizzard with a baggy, ankle-length dress on and clunky winter boots. I was planning on scolding her for the lack of pants, but considering the ease of access I've been given to her pussy, I'll let it go this time.

With her leg up, I pull the laces on her boot and start easing her foot out of it. She watches me with drooping eyelids over the vibrant blue eyes that have visited me in my dreams every night these past few weeks.

I drop the boot to the floor before taking the opposite foot in my hands and bringing it to the countertop. She's splayed wide open for me now, but I keep my attention fixed to the boot I'm beginning to unlace.

"What a gentleman," she muses, the corners of her eyes crinkling.

I hum and slide the boot off. It falls to the floor beside the first, and then I'm pinching the edge of her dress, claiming her eyes.

"We'll need two pairs of slippers here from now on."

"Matching ones?"

I start lowering myself to my knees before her. "Whatever you want."

Ivy flutters her lashes, staring down at where I kneel. Her knees are bent, and the skirt of her dress is pulled tight over the V between them. It's a pretty sight, but not nearly as beautiful as the one I'll have in a minute.

Hooking my hands around her ankles, I tug her toward me, forcing her legs to spread to the point of discomfort. Her ass hovers over the edge of the counter, and I groan at the close-up view of her cotton-covered pussy.

I click my tongue. "You're wet, Ivy."

"I'm always wet around you."

Fuck. My jeans grow tight as I lean forward and run a knuckle over the seam of her slit.

"You've got such a needy cunt. I'll have to work overtime to keep it pleased, hmm?"

Her swallow is audible. "I guess so."

Pulling her panties to the side, I bare her to me. So slick and puffy, her pussy draws a groan from my chest. I spread her open and slide a hand beneath her ass to gain leverage.

"Let me start now."

I drag my tongue between her lips and suck at her clit for only a moment before releasing it. She snaps a hand down to grab my hair, and I repeat my motions once more.

"That's so good," she whines, jerking her hips up.

Finding her clit with my thumb, I start rubbing it softly before spitting on her hole and sinking my tongue inside. She cries out, and I remove my thumb, sinking it into her cunt instead.

"Have you been like this for three weeks, Ivy?"

She tightens her hold on my hair, and I wish her skirt was out of the way so I could see her eyes rolling backward. "Yes!"

I pull my thumb free and sink two fingers in instead, stretching her. Her arousal drips down my knuckles, and I lean back in to lick them clean.

"This is my pussy now, Ivy. I'm the one it gushes for and the only one who can kneel before it. I'll take good care of it and keep it real fuckin' satisfied. Best cunt I've ever tasted."

I lick at her clit, stroking it with a pressure that has her kicking her leg out and yanking on my scalp. My fingers brush the soft spot inside of her with every curl and thrust, drawing her pleasure out second by second.

She's already on the edge, and I keep her there until I hear the words I need.

"Tell me it's mine, angel. Not just this pretty pussy but the woman. You're mine from now till the sun dies," I demand.

A moan scrapes up her throat. "It's yours. I'm yours. We're yours."

I rock forward as the words blast through me. Throbbing in my jeans, my cock aches with the need to sink deep inside of the walls rippling around my fingers, but it's not the time.

Right now, this is what I need.

"Then come on my face, baby," I murmur before pressing into her pussy and speeding up my movements.

It only takes a few moments of my flicking tongue and pistoning fingers to get her there, and when she comes, I drop a hand to my crotch and squeeze, desperate for some sort of relief.

Pleasure coils and ripples through me so fiercely I'm forced to release myself. Wetness blooms through my briefs as I choke on a groan and turn my cheek to rest against her inner thigh, panting like I've just run a marathon.

Ivy lets loose a low, gentle sound and massages my scalp. With her skirt stretched above me, we can't see each other. I don't know if that's a good or bad thing, considering what's just happened.

"Is that something you like to do often?" she asks a beat later.

"Are you askin' about eatin' pussy, Ivy?"

"Yes."

Slowly pulling back from between her legs, I sit back on my heels and take a long look at her expression, reading it for any sign that she didn't enjoy herself. All I find is a blissed-out smile and a soft stare that punches through my chest.

I stroke her thigh, cautious of the burn my beard has left behind. "Could eat your pussy for every meal of the day. It tastes as good as it looks."

"Now you're just trying to embarrass me," she says, looking away from me.

"You don't believe me?"

"I've never been told that before," she admits.

My chest puffs up. "Good. I should be the only one sayin' that shit to you."

"Only if it's the truth, Niko."

"Angel, I just came in my fuckin' pants."

A long, tense pause. Ivy releases my hair and brings her hand to her mouth. "What?"

"I loved licking your cunt so much I came when I squeezed my dick. Never in my entire fuckin' life have I done that."

"That's . . . that's—wow. I'm flattered," she rambles, cheeks fire engine red.

I chuckle, unable to help myself, and her attention snaps back to me. Wonder lines her eyes, and I freeze.

"What's that look for?"

She smiles so wide she might as well be the only guiding light in a dark cave. "You laughed."

"I've laughed before."

"No, you haven't."

Then I'm an even bigger idiot than I thought. If chuckling makes her look at me like she is right now . . . then I'd be stupid not to do it again.

As many times as I can get away with.

9

Ivy

"SO, I COULDN'T HELP BUT NOTICE THE LACK OF CHRISTMAS decorations around here," I poke.

Niko carries on behind the bar, pouring a mixture of liquids into a blender. I hear crinkling wrappers before seeing him start to plop red and white candies on top of the ice.

We're still the only people in the bar, but he doesn't look concerned about the lack of business. I'm more curious than worried. I didn't know that a bit of snow and wind kept people locked up in their homes around here. Back home, short of a blackout snowstorm, everyone's up for a drink with a friend.

"I wanted you to help me with 'em," he answers bluntly.

My heart warms. "You have some hidden away somewhere, then?"

Darting his eyes up from his concoction, he snaps the lid on the blender. "Don't think I've forgotten about the Scrooge comments. Who told you I was a grumpy fucker who hates Christmas?"

"No one told me that, exactly. Just that you were a bit . . . *Scroogey*, per se. But I'm going to guess and say that you've been pretty closed off with everyone. Am I right?"

"Maybe."

"Exactly. So, you can't be grouchy about it."

Instead of replying, he keeps his eyes on me and starts the blender. I laugh at his obvious attempt to cut the conversation and lean my elbow on the bar, gazing at him with an ease that I feel deep in my chest.

Gosh, is it ever easy with him. Even with the heaviness of our earlier conversation and the daunting aspects of our future, I'm settled. More content than I've been in years.

I expected to be terrified of what's to come, but despite my lingering nerves, that's not the case. Maybe that's why we're always told to wait for the right person. From where I'm sitting right now, Niko looks like *the one*.

When the blender abruptly stops, he's pouring the red slush into an identical cup to the one he had for me earlier. I lean forward on the bar stool and try to remember if I saw him put any liquor in it this time.

"It's a mocktail, Ivy," he says, settling my curiosity. "Still need you to try the drink before the party."

"You didn't have to make me another drink. Gosh, I already know it tastes amazing."

He places the cup on the bar in front of me before adding a matching red straw. "Just try it."

"Fine, fine."

I pull it a bit closer and then take a sip. It's the same consistency as a normal daiquiri but is minty instead of fruity. The mild burn of peppermint grows when I take another drink and moan, immediately taking another.

It's not until I suck in through the straw and get nothing but air that I realize I've finished the entire thing. I lean back and dab the corner of my lips with my thumb, only slightly embarrassed.

"Good?" he asks, humour lining his tone.

"I told you it would be."

No longer behind the bar, he comes to my side and taps my chin, bringing my eyes up to meet his.

"Still need to hear you say it, angel."

I grin. "It's incredible. Maybe even the best drink I've ever had. It's like peppermint hot chocolate in slushy form."

He smooths his knuckles along my jaw, nodding. "I'll make it for you every day, then."

"Every day might be a bit excessive."

"The baby likes it."

"Let's give it a few minutes to settle before deciding that," I tease.

Niko leans a hand against the bar and ducks his head to bring us closer together with his height. "There are a couple of bins of decorations in the basement. I haven't gone through them in a while."

"I'd be honoured to go through them with you and then decorate this place. It's *really* not giving Christmas in here."

"We can't have that," he grunts.

"No, we can't. Especially not so close to the holidays. I want everyone to come in here and be smacked across the face with holiday cheer," I gush.

He offers me a hand, and I smile while taking it. Once I've slid off the stool, Niko surprises me by sweeping me off my feet in one strong lift.

"Niko!" I kick my sock-clad feet in the air and link my hands behind his neck. "I'm pregnant, not broken."

"Just let me carry you."

My exhale is dramatic. "Fine. If you insist."

"I do."

"Is this going to be a common occurrence? Or are you having a weird burst of chivalry right now?"

His chest vibrates against my side, but unlike in the kitchen, he doesn't laugh audibly.

"I'd carry you everywhere always if you let me. I don't see that happenin', though."

"Because I'm just so independent?"

"You are independent. But I was thinkin' more stubborn."

I gasp. "Stubborn? You don't know me well enough to make that conclusion."

"Don't I? You were around me quite often before. Just 'cause you weren't always talkin' to me doesn't mean that I wasn't payin' attention."

"Give me an example, then, Mr. Know It All."

"Okay, smartass. What about you hatin' beer but always sufferin' with it when you'd have me over for dinner? Why didn't you tell my son to get you somethin' else to drink?"

"I'm sure you're going to tell me," I say.

A smug smirk. "Because you're too stubborn to admit that you don't like somethin' that you've already gone along with lovin' for so long. And how about when you refused to do a gift exchange last Christmas because you wanted to buy gifts for everyone and not just one person? It would have been a helluva lot easier to shop for a gift without havin' to know the person I was buyin' for, but no, Ivy wanted to buy for everyone. I wasn't going to tell you no, so I spent weeks plannin' your gift."

I'm burning up from the inside out, both from embarrassment and the shock of learning just how much attention this man was paying to me and the things I did. It was a year ago that I was stress cooking a Christmas turkey for Travis's father in our cramped apartment, but I remember every moment of that evening.

The pride I felt when Niko took the first bite of dinner that I'd slaved all day over and told me how good of a job I had done. How relieved I was when he opened his gift and kept it clutched close all night. It was only a cheap lighter with his initials burned along the side, but after forcing Travis to tell me something about his father and learning that he loved cigars, I thought it was a safe enough gift.

Travis got me a pair of thick socks with sharks on them, and Niko . . . he got me a pair of fleece-lined leggings and heated gloves after hearing me complain once about being cold while brushing off my car in the mornings. I only noticed the tiny box he'd hidden in the left glove once he'd gone home that night.

There was a charm in the box for my bracelet. A ball of yarn with two hooks, one in each side.

Pulling my hand from Niko's neck, I jingle the bracelet around my wrist and blink past the burn in my eyes.

"I always thought that Travis had told you to get this," I whisper.

His jaw pulses. "He didn't tell me a fuckin' thing to get you. I wasn't sure if I was goin' to give it to you, but when you opened his gift, I knew you needed it. Fuckin' socks. Pathetic."

"The charm was my favourite gift last year."

"Shouldn't have been."

"I like that it was. Especially now," I admit, pinching the charm.

"What about your parents? They must have gotten you somethin' nice."

"They did. But nothing as thoughtful. Usually, they fill a giant basket with yarn and designs and magazines, along with a few gift cards for my favourite restaurants. I'm grateful for the gifts, but I just really appreciated yours. It was everything I needed at the time, you know?"

"Yeah, angel. I know."

"I feel bad that all I got you was a lighter."

He turns down the hallway and kicks open the door leading to a dark staircase. With a yank on the string hanging from the ceiling, light floods the space.

Even as we start down the stairs, he keeps me in his arms, no sign of setting me on my feet anytime soon.

"It's in my pocket right now," he says.

"The lighter? No way."

"I take it with me everywhere."

"You're crazy."

"Maybe. Doesn't mean I didn't love your gift."

I loop my arm back around his neck and rest my cheek

against his chest, inhaling his scent. My nausea hasn't returned since before I ate, meaning things are looking up. His cologne doesn't bother me, and neither have the eggs or the fancy drink he made me.

"I'll get you something better this year," I swear.

He palms my knee and shifts it as we turn a sharp corner and reach the open area beneath the stairs where stacks of bins rest against the wall.

"I've already got my gift from you," he declares, staring down at me with intense brown eyes.

"That's right! How could I forget about the sweater?"

I wiggle in his hold, and with a huff, he lets me down onto my feet. The small radio on the shelf beside a dusty bookcase catches my attention, and I start fiddling with the knobs before Niko can get to them.

Static screams before I find the local station that's playing Christmas music. "Santa Claus Is Coming to Town" floats through the mildew-infested basement, and I start rocking side to side with the beat.

"Do you dance, Niko?" I ask teasingly, offering him my hands.

The big man scowls, hands gripping his hips. "No. And be careful. It's dangerous down here."

"Will you dance with me anyway? Just for this one song."

Jutting my lip, I bat my lashes and wiggle my fingers. The song is already half-over, but as I swing my hips and grin up at him, I know I'd be content with only a few seconds of dancing with him.

I beam when he sets his large hands in mine and tugs me against his chest. With confident movements, he has a hand holding my waist and the other interlocking our fingers before leading us in a quick dance. My laugh is loud as I follow his steps and let him twirl me around the room. He's careful to keep me from the low dips in the ceiling and the stacks of bins, and I let my mind go empty as my trust in him grows.

I know he won't let anything happen to me.

The song comes to an end, but he doesn't release me. Another one starts, and he pulls me close. I don't have to look up to know that he's smiling at me again. There's a knowing feeling deep in my soul that tells me he's enjoying himself as much as I am.

The radio broadcaster interrupts the music. "That was 'Jingle Bell Rock.' We'll be back with more music in a few minutes, but for now, I hope everyone is bundled up with a fire roaring and those they love close by. The projected snowfall over the next twenty-four hours has risen to twenty inches with blizzard winds of fifty kilometres per hour. It's advised that everyone stay home until further notice. Road closures have started to take effect in the following counties . . ."

My mouth pops open as I lean away from Niko's chest and stare up at him. "You heard that, too, right?"

"Yes."

I blink once, and he's moving, on high alert. We abandon the bins of decorations, and I chase after him when he starts up the stairs. My pulse quickens the higher up the staircase we get until, finally, we're in front of the door.

Niko pulls the small red curtain from the window in the door. His inhale is sharp enough to cut.

The street is hidden behind a wall of white. The wind howls, and thick snowflakes blow in the air. It's cold enough that I can feel the nip of it sneaking through the crack below the door.

"We're not going anywhere anytime soon, are we?" I ask softly.

Niko lifts a hand to the back of my neck, holding it there. "No, angel. I'm afraid we're stuck here for a while."

10

Niko

If I was going to handpick who I'd want to be snowed in with, it would be Ivy Bell. Any day of the fucking week, I'd choose her.

That doesn't mean I'm not worried about what's happening, though. The weather here can be unpredictable on a good day, but during a Christmas snowstorm? Shit. I've got enough food for over a week, but with Ivy's sickness and our lack of other supplies, we won't need to last that long before things start going wrong.

They'll have the plows out as soon as the snow stops, but according to the radio station, nobody seems to know when exactly that's going to be. The power went out a half hour ago before the backup generator kicked in. If he were alive, I'd thank my grandfather for being so anal about keeping it in good shape.

"The heat's back on. It'll warm up soon," I mutter, draping a thick wool blanket over her shoulders.

Bent over one of the four bins I've hauled up the stairs, she stares at me with worried, tired eyes. Maybe I should be as concerned as she is about all of this, but I'm just real fucking happy that I get more time with her. Her undivided attention will be on me and us for however long it takes for the storm to stop.

That's a gift from the universe that I'm not deserving of.

"How are you so calm about this?" she asks.

"We've got a generator, food, somethin' to drink, and a bed. I'm ready to ride out the storm."

"You're not worried about anything back home? No pets? What about Travis? His mother? Won't they worry? I don't have any cell service last I checked. My parents are going to freak out when they don't hear from me," she rambles, clutching the corners of the blanket beneath her chin.

I cover her hand and stroke her knuckles. "I've got no pets. And Travis is spendin' Christmas with his mother, and she'd probably be grateful to see me trapped here forever. I've got nothin' to help with your parents, but they'll see what's goin' on and relax a bit. We'll get the cell signals fixed sooner than later."

"Why would your ex be grateful if you were trapped here forever?"

Her natural curiosity is one of my favourite things about her, but not when it comes to Tanya.

"Travis didn't tell you about us?"

"You weren't his favourite topic to talk about," she says with a wince.

I blow out a breath and dig into the second bin, grabbing a tangled mess of multicoloured string lights. Beginning to untangle them, I say, "Tanya was incredibly young when she got pregnant. Both of us were fifteen, but she got the brunt of the judgment in town. It's why she moved away and insisted on raisin' Travis in Oak Point instead of Snowbell."

"Why did you stay here?"

"Tanya and I didn't get along on a good day."

Ivy pulls a small light-up tree from her bin and starts fluffing its branches. "Because of what she went through?"

"Because I was an asshole. I was immature and angry with the world because I was exhausted and stressed. We weren't ready to be parents, and we didn't have a choice but to be. We loved our son but not each other. Every day we spent together made her resent me more.

"Our families were embarrassed by what we'd done and of the way everyone looked at us, so it was only us taking care of one another. I was hardly enough for Travis, let alone his mother, too. It was a fuckin' mess until we graduated and Travis started kindergarten. My father handed me the bar when I turned eighteen, and I put all of my focus into keeping a roof over our heads. Tanya got a remote job working for some computer programming company and moved out of town, so she decided she'd have Travis. He always preferred his time there, and I let go of hoping that would change."

I yank hard on the last tangle in the lights and fight to ignore the regret lancing through me.

"There are plenty of things I wish I had done differently in my life. Not spent so many late nights in the bar hiding from my fuckin' life, for starters," I spit, shaking my head.

Ivy sets the tree on a table and slips beneath my arms and into the space between them. With the scent of her sweet perfume flooding the air around us, she takes my hands and starts slowly guiding my fingers through where the lights are tangled. A calm in the storm.

"Everyone has things from the past they wish they could change. We're all human, and that means we have flaws. You're Travis's father, but he's not the perfect son, either. I was around to watch the way he spoke to not only you but those around him, and he didn't make your relationship easy, either. I've met Mrs. Grady a few times, but she was never really my biggest fan. She's very closed off and protective of Travis."

Mrs. Grady. It was never Mrs. Shaw.

We weren't dating when Travis was conceived, and even after he was born, we were together more out of necessity than want. I never contemplated marrying her, and I know how that makes me look. My mother loved to tell me.

Ivy releases my hands and reaches for my face instead. On her tiptoes, she rubs the tip of her nose against mine.

"You're a good man, Nicholas Shaw. And you're a good dad. I don't regret coming here three weeks ago or getting into bed with you. And I certainly don't regret winding up pregnant with your baby. You'll treasure him or her, I know it," she declares.

I don't know how to put my feelings to words, so I kiss her instead. She leans into it, accepting that this is my way of telling her thank you. That I'm happy she moved to this town and took the job that led her here to me.

I'll take care of you, I promise with every press of my lips. *Of both of you.*

Ivy stretches up onto her toes on the top step of the ladder and hooks the string of lights on a nail she's hammered in. I steady both her and the ladder, hovering at her back.

The blinds are closed on all of the windows now that the sun's set, but she's flicked on every light in the bar, complaining about how dim and yellow all of the bulbs are. I'll have to pick up white ones once the storm has passed.

"I can do this, angel," I offer for the millionth time.

"And so can I," she insists for the millionth and one.

My hold on the ladder tightens when she leans to the right and reaches across the window to hook the opposite side of the lights on another nail.

"You're not balanced at all."

"That's fine. I have to move windows now anyway."

"Ivy," I mutter.

She pushes at my chest, and I inch back once she starts down the ladder. "Yes, Niko?"

"You're pregnant. There are plenty of other things for you to do to decorate."

"See, there's one thing you're going to learn quick about me." Her lips tip up into a smug smile as her finger pokes my chest. "I love being commanded in the bedroom, but outside of it, I'm pretty content taking care of myself."

I dip my head and speak against her temple. "See? Fuckin' stubborn."

Her white teeth gleam when she grins and sidesteps me, heading for the near empty bin of decorations. We're already on the third one, and the bar is starting to look brighter. Cheery, almost.

The final string of lights is gripped in her hand as I haul the ladder over to the next window and wave a hand at it.

"Up you go, then."

She blows me a kiss while climbing the steps. "Thank you, kind sir."

"I thought I was Scrooge."

"More like Scrooge's twin brother. The one who can be kind from time to time," she teases.

The skirt of her dress is pulled tight across her ass as she lunges up the final step and balances herself there. I've never hated a dress more than I do this one. It's so fucking long that it hides everything from her ankles up.

My heart jolts as I bring a hand to an exposed ankle and start dragging it up her calf, my fingers tapping softly the entire way. The smooth skin grows bumpy when she shivers and huffs a breath.

"Concentrate, angel," I coo, climbing higher to the curve of her knee and inner thigh.

She whips her head back to glare at me and hisses, "I'm trying."

"Try harder."

The heat from between her legs basks my fingers as they ghost over her bare slit. Her panties are in my pocket, stolen after my meal in the kitchen. I'm real damn thankful I chose to remove them when I did.

Her moan escapes at the same time my finger glides between her lips and sinks inside the tight hole that I've grown obsessed with.

"Hang the lights, Ivy," I grunt, stroking her walls.

She lifts her arms, shaking while hooking the first side. Her pussy ripples around my finger, and I'm already done with not being able to see her properly.

"Take your arms out of the dress," I demand with a curl of my finger.

The lights clatter against the wall when she releases the string and quickly works her arms out of her sleeves. Pale skin splattered with dark freckles appears, and then the dress is falling down her body and pooling at my elbow.

"Flawless," I whisper.

Even from behind, with only a view of her elegant back, round, grippable hips, and plump ass, she's a masterpiece. A photograph wouldn't do her justice.

"Be honest, Niko. Be real," she pleads.

I can tell that she's got her arms folded over her front like the last time I had her naked in this bar. With her face hidden from me, I can't see the pink tint to her cheeks or neck that I'd bet money on being there.

"You want me to be real, baby? Fine." Gripping her hand, I pull her down the ladder and then force her to spin to face me, her dress forgotten on the floor. "One look at you and I knew I'd never seen anything so perfect. You're gorgeous in looks, in figure, but also brains. There's no part of you that I'd change. You were created with my every fantasy in mind."

With a softer touch, I move her arm from her chest to rest at her side. Large, soft breasts with rosy nipples, a round belly, hip dips, and thick thighs I've grown to love pressing against my ears. Staring at her is enough to have my cock hard and aching.

Her eyes glisten with unshed tears. "I'm going to look different in a few months."

"You mean when you're round with my baby?"

I cup her belly, rubbing the centre of it. She nods, lip quivering.

"I can't wait to love you through every change. The good and bad."

She blinks, and a tear drips down her cheek. "Promise?"

"I fuckin' promise, angel."

11

Ivy

Niko hasn't stopped staring at my ass since he forced his Christmas sweater over my head and gave it a smack, telling me to finish up the lights.

I'm beyond horny, my hormones all out of whack. It sure doesn't help that we went from him having his finger inside of me to tears dripping down my cheeks in a moment of insecurity. It all happened so quickly, but even as he keeps me busy with fluffing the branches of the artificial Christmas tree, I can't ignore the ache in my core.

Each shift of my thighs and brush of my nipples beneath his shirt ignites another blaze of desire that has me growing wetter. My lack of panties means I've made my thighs slick, another reminder of how badly I want Niko to just fuck me already.

"Multicoloured or white lights?" I ask in an attempt to distract myself.

The tree is taller than me, but he can easily touch the top. I'm like a small child in comparison to him, and I'm not all that happy about him being the only one to decorate the top part of the tree. Especially not since he loves to stick the ornaments in bunches instead of spreading them out. But it's his bar, not mine, so if he wants a cluttered tree . . .

"You know what? Can you actually take those three red ornaments and spread them out a bit?" I blurt out, pointing at the cluttered section.

Niko blinks down at me in confusion, his hands drifting up to where the hooks of the ornaments are hung.

"These?"

"Yes. The biggest rule when it comes to decorating the tree is that you spread out the ornaments. It makes it look fuller. Did you not do that with your tree at home, either?"

"I didn't set up a tree at home."

Pain slashes through my chest. "What? Why not?"

He simply shrugs and shifts the first ornament over to another branch. "Didn't feel the need to."

"Niko," I whisper, palming his wide chest.

"I'm more like Scrooge than I thought," he grunts.

My frown is so intense the muscles above my brows start to burn. "No. You're not. Because I'm going to change all of that. From this year on, we're going to put up a massive tree in your living room and spend hours decorating it with all sorts of ornaments and tinsel. Multicoloured lights, too. My first question was redundant. I've always thought plain white lights were lame."

My exhales rip out of me as I huff. Niko watches me but doesn't speak. I splay my fingers out from where they're pressed to his chest, and his heartbeat thrashes against my palm. He's so calm on the outside, but I know that if I got the chance to slip inside his head, I'd learn that he's anything but.

"Is that okay with you?" I ask, pushing and refusing to let this go without something more from him. "If you don't say anything, I'm going to assume that you don't want me to do that—"

"Anythin' you want or need is okay with me, angel. I'll set up thirty trees if it'll make you happy."

I squeal as he wraps me in his arms and lifts me off my feet. My eyes are already closing in preparation for his kiss when I feel the first puff of warm breath on my mouth and beat him to it.

Rough, strong, yet somehow gentle, his lips lead mine into a slow embrace. I've never felt so protected and cared for with only a kiss before. But with Niko, even a single look from him is able to incite those feelings. He's so solid, somehow creating a solid foundation of love and care no one has been able to provide me before.

Maybe that's why I make my next move. I'm blasted with an incredible sense of thankfulness that drives me to want to give him something in return for his affection. That and my inability to keep my hands off him.

It's easy to slip from his arms when he isn't expecting me to. The fall to my knees is quick, and I'm so turned on that the pain from the slam doesn't register. With a coy smile, I pull his shirt over my head and drop it beside me.

"What are you doin', Ivy?" he asks, his tone rougher than normal.

"What does it look like I'm doing? I'm going to suck your cock."

I hold his stare while unbuttoning his jeans and stroking the length of him through them. He's huge, even without being fully hard, and that's more than enough to make me drip down my thigh.

"You don't have to do that."

"I want to."

His eyes smoulder, the warm brown heating to a liquid. "Then get to it, angel."

The pet name has quickly become one of my favourite things in the entire world. There's something about the way he says it . . . almost like a prayer, that just does me in.

He guides strong fingers through my hair to hold the back of my head. I lower his zipper before beginning to tug his jeans down his thick thighs.

I've only seen his dick once during our first time, and having it in front of me right now with nothing between us? My mouth waters as I take it in my hand and stroke the silky length, exploring the different veins and ridges.

"You make me so fuckin' hard," he groans, tightening his hold on me. "Looks so good in your hand. Those pretty nails wrapped around it."

"Do you like the colour of them?" I ask, wiggling my fingers.

"I'd like any colour."

"Do you have a favourite?"

"Need to try them all. Test them all just like this," he grits out.

I scoot forward an inch and pump him harder, twisting my wrist the way I remember him liking. When his thighs clench tight, I bring him to my lips, rubbing the wet tip across them.

Precum coats my lips while my other hand finds his balls, massaging them. He grunts a breath and throbs in my hold.

"Gonna coat those big tits this time," he promises, thrusting into my hand.

I grin, letting him inside my mouth. My tongue swipes along his slit, drawing out another groan from his chest as I suck. Power swells inside of me with every noise he makes, until I'm vibrating between my legs.

He's so thick it's hard to fit the entire width inside, but I flatten my tongue and force myself to relax enough to let him in. A gag tears through me when he bumps the back of my throat, and my eyes burn before tears slip down my cheeks.

Crying this time is different. This is purely sexual. My insecurities have been cast away, and now, the only thing I want is to make my man come.

"Relax your throat, angel," he orders on a tight exhale. "Gonna slide all the way in."

My eyes grow wide, nerves tumbling through my stomach. I've never taken anyone down my throat before and certainly never tried with anyone as big as him. Travis was at least three inches shorter and not as thick, but he never bothered trying to teach me.

Niko strokes my cheek and angles my head further back. He grabs my throat and tightens his hold just enough that my next swallow is strained.

"Breathe through your nose for me," he instructs calmly.

I jerk my chin in a quick nod.

He presses on my pulse. "Good girl."

Fuck, he might as well have licked my pussy. His praise is as good as a stroke of his cock inside of me, and I immediately need more of it.

Breathing with my nose like he said, I watch him through teary lashes and wait for him to move. The first glide of his shaft along my tongue has me gripping at his thighs for stability.

"Don't close up on me," he coos, continuing to pet my skin. "I'm goin' to slide inside now."

Just now? What was he doing before then?

With a jerk of his hips, his cock moves deeper, and I gag around him. Drool collects at the corners of my mouth and slides down my chin, but I don't care. I hold on to him and blink through the tears.

"Oh, fuck, angel. Such a tight fuckin' throat. I'm goin' to . . . *shit*. Swallow again."

I do, and he somehow slides deeper, no longer bumping my throat but slipping down it. My nails dig into his bare thighs so hard I wouldn't be surprised if they've broken skin. I don't dare look away to see.

The complete rapture in his stare keeps my attention as I ache to see just how insane I can drive him. How much I can pleasure him.

I'm dripping down my thighs, so sensitive that a spring breeze over my clit could make me come. My eyelids start to flutter shut, but then the hand around my throat tightens.

I try to focus on him through the wall of tears and swallow again.

"Eyes on me, Ivy. Don't look away while I'm fucking your throat. I want your attention as I claim you here," he spits, sounding more beast than man.

I nearly purr in response and keep my eyes pried open.

His grip on my throat relaxes slightly as he moans in approval and palms the top of my head. With a sharp thrust of his hips, he starts fucking my throat. In and out, in and out, I rock with the force of his movements and tighten my hold on his thighs.

"Push your tits together, baby. I'm gonna come," he warns through clenched teeth.

I release his legs to grab at my breasts. A strangled moan escapes when a knuckle bumps my nipple, and sharp pleasure ripples down my spine.

"Fuck yes, angel. Just a little longer . . . *Christ*. Here it comes."

Niko pulls out of my mouth and wraps a hand around his cock, stroking hard and fast. I'm covered in drool and precum, but apparently, I'm too far gone in my horned-up state to give a shit.

I push my tongue out and lift my breasts high, rubbing them together as I stare at the rough treatment he's giving his shaft. I'd be more loving, tender, and maybe that's why he's the one in control right now.

"Keep that tongue out."

His eyes narrow as the strong lines of his throat strain around a growl. The first rope of cum hits my collarbone; the next drips over my right breast.

I'm about to close my mouth when a third splashes over my extended tongue, making me pulse between my legs. Unable to help myself, I run a finger through the cum on my breast and bring it to my aching nipple before squeezing it softly, needing . . . needing *anything*.

"Fuckin' beautiful," Niko rasps.

I nod, dazed, and intensify my pinch. "Please."

"Please what, angel?"

Shuddering, I rub along my collarbone and then down to my pussy. The heel of my hand feels perfect as I push hard on my clit, my hips rocking.

"I need to come," I whisper brokenly, so unlike myself.

Fingers wrap around my wrist, and then I'm pulled to my feet. Even while I moan in protest, I let him manhandle me. He moves us to a booth and presses my stomach against the table, my ass in the air.

"I'll give you what you need. Always," he swears from behind me.

I press my cheek to the table, smelling the scent of lemon cleaner. "Fuck me, Niko. I don't care how, just—"

I'm so wet he slides in with only a bit of struggle. Without being stretched first, it's a tight fit, but I'm ready for him.

"*Oh,*" I whine, reaching back to touch his stomach.

It's not as muscled as his son's, but it's still hard, strong. Niko is fit in the *built like a brick shithouse* way. In the *don't fuck with me unless you want to deal with missing teeth* kind of way. And I've never been as attracted to a man who looks like that as I am now.

He's the exception to everything.

"How are you still hard?" I ask on a gasp.

"Always hard 'round you."

With two hands on my hips, he drills into me, neither of us having the desire to go slow. I'm on a hair trigger, and with his next thrust, I'm putting the entirety of my weight on the table, too weak-kneed to hold myself up.

He rubs against my G-spot, maybe even my goddamn cervix, because I can't breathe. Pleasure strangles me, the blast so intense that I slam my hand on the table over and over, gasping for air.

"Shouldn't be able to come again already, but you're milkin' it out of me, baby. You're such a slut for it, aren't you?" he asks gruffly.

"Don't stop!" I nearly scream. "Don't stop. Don't . . . stop."

"Can't."

His movements grow fiercer and quicker, and that pressure inside of me blooms and shifts into something I've never felt before. I'm on my tiptoes, leaning back into his every thrust when whatever it is bursts.

Wetness floods down my legs and onto the floor, but I'm too lost in an ocean of pleasure to care that I must have wet myself. My nipples scrape against the table, intensifying the bliss turning me inside out.

"Holy fuck. Coatin' me," Niko grunts, his fingers now stroking between my legs, touching the mess I've made. "I'm comin' again."

I feel it shoot deep inside of me, coating my walls in warmth. My lips tip up in a lazy grin, and I stroke his flexing stomach as his groans fill the bar.

"I think I'm losing my mind," I murmur.

He leans over my body and takes my hand, interlocking our hands. "Why?"

"I'm already falling in love with you."

There's no chance to grow nervous about the declaration. He doesn't make me wait for a reply.

"Losin' my mind with you, then."

12

Niko

The bed is so fucking small.

Don't know why I thought my six-foot-four ass would be comfortable in a single bed to begin with. Over the past few years, I've spent more nights in this office than at my home and have woken with kinks in my neck that I'd complain about for days.

I nearly bought a new bed a hundred times but never pulled the trigger. And now, I'm glad I didn't.

Ivy lies sprawled over my body, her chin propped up on my chest and our legs tangled. I draw my nails up and down her naked back beneath the heavy quilt covering us.

"Did you ever reconcile with your parents?" she asks, her tired eyes focused on me.

It's late into the night, and my generator is still kicking. We ate ice cream and frozen strawberries for dinner, and I didn't have it in me to insist we have something with a bit more protein once she grew excited.

"No. I haven't spoken to them in nearly a decade."

"I'm sorry."

"Don't be. They weren't worth knowin'."

"Then I'm even more sorry. I'm close to my parents, and I

know if they chose to back out of my life that I'd really miss them."

I continue scratching her back, letting the contact soothe me. "Sometimes, it's easier to cut contact with someone than it is to fight to fix a broken relationship. Doesn't matter if they're blood or not."

"How does it feel knowing that you're so much wiser than me?" she teases with a kiss to my sternum.

"It'd be fuckin' embarrasin' if I wasn't. I'm nearly double your age."

I wince at the reminder. Yeah, I might not care enough to let her go, but I've done a great job of pretending that she's not so much younger than me. It won't affect my life, but it could damage hers.

She taps at the corner of my mouth. "Don't scowl. I don't care how old you are."

"You should. There are assholes everywhere outside this bar."

"Scared people will think I'm only with you for your money and fame?" she pokes.

"Is that what you'll be, Ivy? With me once we get out of here?"

Fuck, it sounds as desperate out loud as it feels.

"Well, I would certainly hope that we'd be *together* after everything that's happened. I don't particularly want to raise this baby in a broken home."

"We have a lot to learn about each other still."

"And we have the time to learn it." She adjusts her position until she's further up my body, her face directly in front of mine. "We skipped about a thousand steps, but we can go back down them and take them together. The only difference now is that we're having a baby. I'm up for the challenge of getting to know you properly. Are you up to get to know me, too?"

I curl a finger beneath her chin and pull her in for a soft, short kiss. She smiles against my mouth.

"Your place," I start, diving in like a needy fuck. "Is it big enough for a baby?"

"Babies are pretty small."

I scowl at her teasing. "Babies are. But I'm not."

"Oh, you're really asking about you. I had no clue that's what you meant." Her devious smirk says otherwise.

"You're talkin' like you're not too exhausted to be bent over my knee. I'll have you countin' how many times I smack your smart ass."

"I'm never too tired for that."

I drag the tip of my thumb along the blue ring beneath her eyes. "Not tonight."

"In that case, I'll let you know in advance that I wouldn't be opposed to being woken with sex."

My chest shakes with a silent laugh. She rests her cheek on my pec, eyes drooping.

"I'll keep that in mind."

"My place isn't big. It's just somewhere to sleep. My own space. What about yours?"

Despite having come twice in the span of a few hours, I harden beneath her at the prospect of her coming to my place. Seeing her in my bedroom unpacking her things in my closet might send me to an early grave.

"It's big enough for us. Three bedrooms, a finished basement, and a big backyard," I say.

Despite her dreamy smile, she tuts her tongue. "For us? You haven't even taken me out on a date yet, Niko."

I set my hand flat on her back and hold her against me, my eyes growing heavier and heavier. "What does a perfect date look like for Ivy Bell?"

"Honestly?"

"Mmm."

Her eyes scroll over my face as she thinks, her mouth twisting in an adorable way. "I've always wanted to be taken out somewhere I can be shown off. Not in an over-the-top way, but I want to be on someone's arm and have them be proud to have me there. It doesn't even have to be anywhere fancy. We could go to a movie theatre to watch a cheesy film in the middle of the day or take a stroll through the park. I just want to feel wanted. Desired, I guess. Especially on a date."

"I usually save the movie theatre for the second date, but I can make that work."

Her eyes crinkle at the corners as she giggles. "You mentioned being older than me, but when you let loose enough to joke around, you seem younger. Like you don't have so much on your mind."

"You bring that out of me."

"So, I should be thanking myself, then?"

I hum, burying a hand in her hair and massaging her scalp. "Other than knittin', what do you do outside of work?"

"Hey, not so fast. You didn't tell me what *your* perfect date looks like."

"You want to know what I like to do on a date?"

She rolls her eyes. "Obviously."

"I could crack a beer and sit in an empty room with you and be content. I've never put thought into that, considerin' how little I've dated."

"Not even casually?"

"I've been so focused on this bar that I haven't put effort into it. Even casually."

"You've slept with women, though. Like, one-night stands. Surely, I haven't been your only one."

"Spent a lot of time with my dick in my hand, angel. Never cared much for a quick fuck. Not before you. And even then, I wanted far more than somethin' quick."

I gave that shit up a long time ago. It's usually more effort than it's worth. The risk of an awkward encounter in this town, especially in this bar after sleeping with the wrong woman, has kept me pretty damn celibate over the past decade.

Ivy blinks at me, disbelief burning in her eyes. "You're being straight with me? Completely?"

"I give you my word. Before you, I hadn't slept with anyone in a real long time," I confirm.

"Wow."

"I'm not a fuckin' Casanova."

"Maybe not. But you're incredibly good-looking and successful. That has to draw plenty of women in your direction."

"I've never cared much for attention."

She blows a raspberry. "I wasn't expecting that."

"Should I be offended?"

"What? No!" She balks, scrunching her nose. "I just, I mean, I've slept with a few guys after Travis. Rebounds, you know? Especially after everything that led to the breakup, I wanted to know I wasn't some hideous monster and could feel attractive. Even to a stranger. It didn't ever mean anything more than sex, but . . ."

"What you did before you came into this bar three weeks doesn't matter. You're not goin' to be sleepin' with anyone but me from now on, so at least they got a taste before I took you as mine," I grunt.

"You know when we were having sex and I . . ." She trails off nervously, ducking her head.

"When you squirted all over my cock, angel?" I guess.

"Oh, my god. Is that what that was? I've never done that before."

"Mm. Damn right it was. Sexiest thing I've ever seen. Took everythin' in me not to work for more."

Her eyes soften, some of her shyness fading. "You're just a bit too good to be true."

"Been thinkin' that about you for months."

"For months," she echoes, nuzzling her cheek against me. "That's still hard for me to believe."

"Which part? That I was wantin' my son's girl or that I finally got you in the end?"

"All of it."

"Wouldn't change a thing now that we're here," I declare.

"I would. Even just coming back sooner after the last time could have made a big difference. Three weeks is a lot of wasted time."

"Not compared to the next few decades."

"Your confidence in us is admirable."

"Maybe."

"I like it. It's comforting. A reminder that I'm not in this all by myself."

"You'll never feel like that again, angel. Not with me."

"I know," she whispers, blue eyes disappearing behind heavy lids. "Do you want a boy or a girl?"

I pause, considering the options. "A girl would be different. Not sure I'd be any good raisin' a daughter, though."

"I think you'd be a great girl dad. You're burly and grumbly enough for it. She'd never dare bring any boys home to meet you."

"So, I'd be a scary dad? Not sure that's the best thing."

She flutters her eyes open, snagging mine. "You wouldn't be scary to her. I have a feeling you'd put her up on a pedestal and treat her like a princess. Kinda like how you treat me."

Something unsettled grows peaceful in my chest. "Yeah, I think you might be right."

"I'm always right."

I huff a laugh. "Sure."

Ivy slips a hand down to rest at my side before digging a nail into it. I jerk to the side and tug gently at the roots of her hair.

Her giggle twinkles through the room before she shuts her eyes again, growing quiet. "Travis's mom . . . is she going to be upset about this? About us?"

"She'll have somethin' to say, but I don't care enough about her opinion to listen."

My answer seems to settle her. She holds me tight and snuggles impossibly closer, as if seeking more of my warmth. It's blazing beneath the blanket and her soft body, but I'd rather sweat to death than release her.

The heat is doing wonders for my exhaustion, anyway. I've never been one to fall asleep easily or dream deeply. I'm restless and can be woken by the lightest footstep or breath that doesn't belong to me.

When Travis was a baby, I'd sleep in the hallway outside of his room with the door cracked open to listen to his breathing. I'd never slept worth a shit before he was born, and once he came along, it only got worse. Twenty-one years later and I'm still not fixed.

Maybe Ivy can be the cure. She is for every other fucking thing wrong with me.

"Do you think the power will be back on tomorrow?" she asks, her voice soft with sleep.

"Not sure, angel."

"I wanted to do the Christmas market tomorrow. I have a whole bin full of blankets and slippers that I've made to sell."

"If the snow doesn't stop, you can sell them during the event. We can have a pop-up market."

"You think so?"

"I'm the boss, aren't I?"

The corner of her mouth twitches with a smile. "In a way."

"You'll have a spot to sell your things, Ivy, and you'll sell out. I'll make sure of it."

Even if I have to haul every single person in town down to buy from her until there's not one fucking piece of yarn left.

13

Ivy

I wake to pressure between my legs and a firm body beneath mine. A moan slips free when that pressure shifts and pleasure spears through me. Blinking quickly, everything around me starts to come into view.

The dim light slipping through the open window signalling early morning, an array of clothing strewn over the table and chairs and on the wood floor. A filmy water glass from the night before is on the desk beside a crumb-coated plate from the toast Niko encouraged me to eat in the middle of the night when I woke us both with my growling stomach.

There are little bits of us all over the office, but my favourite part of it is us. The way we fell asleep together and didn't dare separate even in our unconscious states.

"Mm," I hum, rolling my hips as Niko rubs the pad of a thick finger over my clit, jolting me further awake. "Good morning."

His beard is thicker today than it was yesterday, and his eyes are so wild it's like he's more awake than he's ever been. I flash a goofy grin and press myself up to peck his lips with two hands on his chest.

I've straddled him in my sleep, and he's snaked a hand behind my ass to play with my pussy while I slept. When I shift, he's forced to pull his hand back, leaving my naked core rubbing along his also *very* bare erection.

He glides between my slickness, the ridges brushing against sensitive skin still a little sore from last night. Bliss parts the clouds of sleep in my mind, but I remain in a loose, sleepy state.

Fingers slipping into his mouth, Niko makes a show of sucking my taste from each one of them. I'm holding my breath in anticipation when he brings them to my chest and pinches both of my nipples, using the hold to guide me back down to his chest.

"The power's back on," he grunts.

I turn my head and glance out the window, realizing no snow is falling. At first, all I can see is a cloudy sky, but after another few moments of staring—

"There's snow up to the windowsill," I say, mouth gaping.

Niko runs his thumb along my lips before pressing down on my tongue. "Windy as fuck last night. The snowdrift's gotta be four feet high."

I wrap my lips around his finger and swipe my tongue over the blunt nail before releasing it. He tightens his gaze on my mouth.

"You'll have to shovel us out of here today," I murmur.

"As long as you're tucked up warm in bed while I do it."

Every grind of my pussy has me tightening up, this ever-lasting need for him making itself known again and forcing all other thoughts and topics somewhere out of sight. It's like we're under some sort of spell, and the only way to end it is to keep fucking until we no longer want to jump each other's bones.

I'm beginning to think that will never happen, and I can't think of anything better.

"I can do that. Be a little cheerleader."

"Prettiest cheerleader I've ever seen," he rasps, releasing a nipple to move his hand beneath me once again.

He plays with me from behind, toying with my clit before

sinking two thick fingers inside my pussy. I toss my head back and cry out at the fullness.

"I've taken you everywhere but right here."

"Where?" I croak, already knowing the answer.

His slick fingers retreat from my pussy to my ass, rimming the tight hole. "Will you let me fuck your ass, angel? Can I slide my cock inside?"

I whimper at the first gentle breach of his finger. "Right now?"

"Right now," he confirms.

The hard cock between my legs is distracting, but it becomes even more so when he reaches between us to guide it inside. I bear down on him, the stretch not as bad after last night.

"This isn't my ass," I whisper, planting my hands on his chest and swirling my hips.

"Gotta stretch you first, baby girl. You're too tight here to take me yet."

He strokes my asshole with confident pressure. The sensation is similar to the first time he pushed his thumb into me, but it's more intense this time. I'm so relaxed that he's able to add a second finger and work me harder.

"I'll be so empty without you inside my pussy, Niko," I mewl, swivelling my hips with every backstroke as I ride him slowly.

I know what I'm doing with my dirty words. He's the most fun when he's not holding back, and considering what we're about to do, I want him feral.

"Fuck, you've got such a needy cunt," he curses, spreading his fingers wide inside of me in a scissoring motion. "Got no lube, but you're so wet I don't think I'll need it."

Our panted breathing fills the small office, and the bed squeaks beneath us. My knee is nearly off the edge of it, but I don't let that stop me from pushing onto my heels on either side of his body. The adjustment changes the angle, and I gasp when his cock jabs against that spot from last night, my vision darkening around the edges.

With me now sitting properly on his lap, Niko adds a third finger into my ass, thrusting them into me at a quick pace. I use his chest for leverage and lift my lower half, dragging my pussy up his shaft before dropping back down.

"Christ. *Fuck*, Ivy. You're goin' to kill me."

I grin, my eyes crossing with pleasure. "This would be a good way to go though, wouldn't it?"

The column of his throat stretches around a deep, wild laugh. I stare at his mouth with laser focus, shock rippling in my chest.

"Do that again," I demand, repeating my lift and drop motion, chasing the beginning of an orgasm. "Laugh again."

This time, it's not joy in the sound of his laugh but disbelief. I don't blame him for it, either. He gets another one of my firsts as the sound of his full, gruff laugh brings me to a mind-obliterating orgasm.

I lose sight of his face when I come so hard I collapse onto his chest. He drives his cock inside of me, forcing me to ride it out around him.

"You're a fantasy," he chokes out, pistoning his fingers into my ass at the same punishing pace as his thrusts. "My fuckin' fantasy. My only one."

I moan into his sweaty chest and press an open-mouthed kiss to his sternum, searching for his heartbeat. "Do it, Niko. Take my ass."

With a feral noise, he slips from my pussy and rolls me off his body. My back presses to the mattress, and then he's hovering above me, his brown eyes nearly black.

"You're sure?" he asks.

I watch as he fists his cock and guides it through my arousal to the hole he's stretched. There's no way he'll fit back there without a bit of a struggle, but I'm prepared for the hurt. He wouldn't do anything to me that he thought I couldn't handle.

Parting my legs, I nod. "Yes."

His jaw pulses with the strength of his clenching before he's bending forward and spitting between my legs twice. Warm liquid drips down my ass, and he presses his cock to the hole, pushing forward the slightest bit. Our eyes hold, a throttling intensity keeping them fused.

The pressure of him sliding further inside steals my breath. It's not pain, but it's definitely discomfort. I can feel every vein along the shaft as he slowly pushes in, taking my virginity and filling me—

"Niko," I gasp, my voice breaking.

Desperate for something to hold on to, I grip his biceps and blink up at him with wide eyes. He pulls out before pushing back in, further this time.

His fingers find my clit and begin rolling it in gentle circles, resurrecting the pleasure that's faded. I relax again, and he slips further inside, spitting a pained exhale.

"Nearly there, baby."

I can do nothing but nod and hand over everything to him. My heart, soul, mind. Body. They're his. I'm just taking the pleasure he's giving, knowing that I'm the only one who'll ever experience this side of him.

Once he's in completely, I'm so full that I'm almost scared to move. But then he's the one doing the moving for the both of us, and sparks start popping and sizzling beneath my skin. Suddenly, the fingers on my clit aren't the only thing bringing me pleasure.

Niko tears his eyes away to stare between us. I attempt to push up on my elbows so I can see past my breasts, but I'm too weak.

"Never felt anythin' like this, baby girl. You're so good for me, so fuckin' tight and hot. This ass was made to be fucked by my cock," he groans, his movements speeding up.

I swallow a whine for more and pluck at my nipples. I'm so stimulated a second orgasm is already approaching. It's endless bliss with Niko. A promise of a very, very happy forever.

With a rough curse, he holds himself up with one hand and drops enough that he can bury his face between my cleavage. A huge hand covers one breast, massaging it while he sucks and licks at me, worshiping every inch of my chest.

I'm approaching release too swiftly to be paying much attention to our surroundings. The creak of the door doesn't register until I'm watching it open.

Niko takes my nipple into his mouth, and my eyes roll, making the shape that appears at the end of the bed blurry. I try to blink, desperate to clear my vision. We're not alone . . . but I don't care. The intruder can watch in jealousy.

With my man thrusting into my ass and feasting on my breasts, the only thing I can focus on is the blast of another orgasm. Even as I make out the features of the man at the end of the bed.

Travis stares at me, watching me with horror in his eyes as I come with a scream that could shatter a glass tower. One he's certainly never pulled from me.

Niko finds his pleasure a few thrusts after and fills my ass with cum. I can only hold on to him, seeking the comforting weight of his body on mine.

My ex-boyfriend spins on his heels and stalks out of the room before slamming the door shut behind him. The loud noise jolts through my system, waking me from the daze Niko found himself in alongside me.

I fall down from the high with a startling realization. Pawing at Niko's shoulders, I shove him from my chest and press a hand to my mouth.

"Oh, my god."

"Gonna take a shot in the dark and guess the wind didn't blow that door shut," he mutters, swiping his hair from his face.

"More like a storm."

And now we've got to go withstand its incoming blows.

14

Niko

My son hasn't taken me by surprise in over a decade.

Being handed Tanya's positive pregnancy test beneath rusted football field bleachers had me wondering if I'd shit my pants from utter shock. The sight of Travis's first scraped and bloody knee at two years old was enough to have me rushing us to the hospital, only to be scolded for overreacting.

I was expecting Tanya to leave me and for our son to choose to move in with only her. When he stopped accepting my invites to hang out on a rare weekend when I wasn't working, I took it on the chin as if it was a fair punishment for my lack of free time. Maybe he had wanted me to fight his mother for split custody, and I'd let him down by allowing her to have her way, or maybe he just simply didn't like me.

Regardless of the why, I learned to stop expecting much from our relationship. We're strangers forced together by social events and holidays.

I take the small moments he offers me to try and learn something about him, but he's never shared that initiative. I've failed us, and I wear that with a deep sense of shame.

If I thought he cared about closing the chasm between us, I'd try harder. But after this long, I know that's not something he's interested in. What he walked in on only reinforced his disappointment in me.

I can't apologize for this choice, though. It's not a mistake, and I refuse to make it into one.

Ivy's worried frown has my annoyance with my son growing tenfold. She's lost in her head while she dresses, her movements rushed and anxious after telling me it was Travis who caught us in the act.

Sure, it doesn't help that she doesn't have any clothes here besides the dress she showed up in yesterday. I'm caveman enough to have suggested she put my shirt back on.

She didn't entertain me with a reply to that. Hell, I barely got confirmation that it was my son who walked in on us, so I knew not to push for anything else.

My jeans are constricting as I sit perched on the edge of the bed and scrape a hand over my bearded jaw. It's scraggly from not being groomed in two days, but fuck it. My son just saw me balls-deep in his ex-girlfriend's ass, so something tells me an untrimmed beard won't matter much.

"Why is he even here?" Ivy asks accusingly, but it's hard to tell who or what she's actually accusing.

"I didn't invite him, angel. I'm surprised the roads were plowed enough for him to get here. They must have been out before the snow even stopped."

She sighs heavily and pushes her hair behind her shoulders. It's messy and knotted but still glossy. Beneath the mess of old makeup, under-eye circles, and pale skin, there's something different about her now than there was three weeks ago. It's obvious to me. She's happy.

I did that. I've made her happy.

And Travis being here is not only a reminder of a time in her life when she was hurting, but it also ruins my plans of ravaging her all fucking day until she demanded we finish getting everything ready for the Christmas event. It's only one day away, and with the storm, everything is going to be rushed.

I'm prepared to do everything I can to help her get it figured out.

"I'm sorry he saw us like that," she murmurs, fidgeting with the sleeve of her dress.

I release a disgruntled noise. "Don't be. Fuckin' awkward as it is, I didn't miss the irony of it."

"Irony?"

"He hates anal and big tits but caught me takin' your ass's virginity while suckin' on your nipples."

There's a beat of silence, and then she's belting out in loud, unabashed laughter. Something tight releases in my chest at the sight and sound, and I let myself smile.

"This is going to be the weirdest conversation I've ever had," she wheezes, slowly coming back down to earth.

"You're tellin' me."

"What are we going to say to him?"

I slide a hand into my pocket. "The truth."

"All of it?"

"He's goin' to learn about the baby anyway, Ivy. Better to tell him now and deal with the brunt of the backlash while he's already here."

She chews on her lip before nodding. "You're right. I'm just—I don't feel guilty about what we've done, even though I probably should. It's just my inability to not people please that's upsetting me. Travis may not deserve my kindness, but he's still your son. And while that's so damn complicated, it also makes it harder to hate him. He could become my family in a really weird way."

I cross the room and wrap an arm around her shoulders, tucking her into my chest. She holds my middle and buries her face in my chest, exhaling slowly.

"Just remember that you don't owe him anythin'. If he disrespects you, he can fuck off. Son or not, I won't stand here and listen to anyone mouthin' off about you."

"Thank you."

"Don't got to thank me for takin' care of you."

"Yes, I do," she whispers.

"Goin' to keep doin' it."

"And I'll take care of you, too, Niko. If he thinks he can be rude to you like he was the last few times you were around us, I'll tell him off."

She was always scolding him for his lowball comments and attitude when they were together. If he knew that it made me hard to see her standing up for me, he would have put an end to me ever coming near her.

I set my chin on the top of her head and huff a soft laugh. "Thank you, baby girl."

Her hands sweep up and down my back in comforting motions that have me ready to barrel down this door and tell my son to fuck right off. But I don't.

Easing back, I pinch Ivy's chin and drop my head for a kiss. She hums against my lips and blinks up at me with twinkling eyes.

A clang sounds from out in the bar, and I stiffen, eyeing up the closed office door. "Think he's shatterin' glasses out there?"

She snorts. "More like drinking all your beer."

"Can't believe you were pretendin' to like that shit for so long."

"Not anymore," she sings, bumping me with her hip on her way to open the door.

Before she can open it, I'm palming her ass through her dress. "Never again."

"Is it too early for a virgin peppermint daiquiri?" she asks.

I close my hand over hers on the door handle, and we twist it together. With my mouth grazing the back of her ear, I mutter, "Not at all."

She'd be damn near skipping out of the room if it weren't for my son waiting for us. We're too quiet as we make our way down the hall and into the bar.

Travis is waiting for us with a long neck in his hand despite the early morning setting. There's a trail of snow leading to where he's perched over the bar, glaring at the shelves of alcohol on the wall.

His shaggy blond hair hangs in his eyes and curls at his neck, in desperate need of a trim. The stubble on his jaw has been there since he was sixteen and boasting about sprouting hair on his face before I did. In reality, I'd started growing a mustache at the exact same age, but I let him believe he was just better than me.

In a well-fitted, red henley shirt and dark jeans that don't rise above his ankles when he sits, he appears well-dressed, as if he either stopped here on his way somewhere else or has magically started caring about the way he dresses. Usually, he's in sweatpants and a hoodie.

"What are you doin' here?" I ask gruffly, pulling a stool out at the end of the bar for Ivy.

Once she's taken it with a pat on my forearm, I start on her drink. I'm taking advantage of her lack of sickness so far this morning, even if I'd rather use the chance to get some food in her belly instead of a slushy drink.

Travis doesn't flinch at my tone. He's so busy staring down Ivy where she sits that I doubt he even heard me. His curling lip has me on alert.

"Hey, Travis," Ivy says, offering a half-smile.

"Hey, Travis? That's what you want your first words to be?" he snaps, shaking his head incredulously.

Ivy lays her hand flat on the bar. "What would you prefer I say?"

"Fuck, I dunno. I'm sorry for fucking your dad? What the shit!" he thunders, smacking his bottle onto the bar. His head is on a swivel when he adds, "How are the two of you so calm right now? You do know that I caught you sleeping together, right? How are you making a fucking drink right now!"

I wet my lips and finish pouring the syrup into the blender.

His outburst is expected, and I try to remind myself of that even as my own temper flares.

"I'm only calm because I'm not ashamed, Travis. I didn't do anything wrong as far as I'm concerned. We broke up months ago, and you were a total asshole to me," Ivy says, shoulders straightening.

My son laughs cruelly. "So, I should go fuck your mom, then?"

"Travis," I spit, slamming the lid on the blender. "Watch your mouth."

Ivy winces when Travis puts all his focus on me now. A storm rages in his brown eyes, and then he opens his mouth and spews everything I was expecting.

"So, Ivy's not ashamed. What about you, old man? Are you feeling guilty, considering you're not only fucking my ex-girlfriend but someone way too young for you?"

"I'm *not* too young for him. He can keep up with me better than you could," Ivy attacks, cheeks flushing red with anger.

It's the worst time for my cock to get hard, but fuck, she's such a sweet little thing. So protective of her man.

My son pins her beneath a glare, and she meets him with one of her own. I choose this moment to start the blender. The noise rips through the bar, forcing everyone to take a breath.

"I'll ask you again, Travis, what are you doin' here? Did I miss a text or call?" I ask once I've finished with the blender.

The collection of daiquiri glasses I picked up for Ivy the morning after she left three weeks ago sit on the bar top, and I take one to fill with her drink.

"I was here looking at a new place and saw them finishing up with the plow out front. Figured you'd be here like you always are," he answers tightly.

Him considering moving here is news to me. Didn't think he'd ever do that.

Ivy takes her drink with a soft smile, and I force myself not to take her right here on the bar with how beautiful she looks. And when she slips the straw into her mouth . . . Fuck me.

"Don't take cheap shots at your dad right now," she tells Travis, frowning.

He rolls his jaw. "I don't need you to lecture me, Ivy. You're not my mother despite fucking my father."

"I'm not goin' to tell you again to watch your mouth," I warn, coming to Ivy's side.

Travis watches me closely, inspecting every single twitch of my limbs. And when I set a reassuring hand on her back, he cocks his head.

"How long?"

"Not long," I answer.

Ivy rests a hand on the one I place beside her on the bar. "A few weeks."

"Just fucking?" Travis's throat strains with an uncomfortable swallow.

I meet his gaze and hold it. "No."

"For fuck's sake."

"Why does it bother you so much? You haven't given a shit about your *old man* in years." Ivy puts air quotes around the old man.

"Don't try to tell me what I should or shouldn't give a shit about. This isn't right," Travis states.

She narrows her eyes. "Says who? You?"

"Yes, me. Your boyfriend's son. It's not right to be fucking a father and a son."

"Good thing I'm not fucking the both of you, then," she sasses.

He looks at me now, disbelief heavy in his gaze. "This doesn't bother you at all?"

"That she's had us both?"

"Obviously."

I stroke her spine, leaning toward her. "No. And I'd suggest you leave it at that before I get into the specific reason as to why.

You've already seen more than you ever should have, and I'd like to move on and forget that that ever happened."

"Unlikely. That shit is burned into my fucking memory!"

"Then unburn it," Ivy mutters before taking another sip of her drink.

Travis looks up at the ceiling. "This is bizarre and so messed up."

"I'd try to make peace with it. It's not going to just disappear now that you know. Especially since Ivy's pregnant," I say.

She tenses beneath my hand and whips her head around to gape up at me. "Niko! You don't have to be so blunt about it."

The legs of Travis's bar stool screech across the floor when he stumbles to his feet. I see the move coming before he can make it. As soon as he's reeling his arm back to punch me in the face, I've got it pulled back behind his back and the front of his body pressed to the bar.

"Don't be a fool, Travis. Think your shit through," I grunt.

"I've thought it through! And I'm going to punch you!" he shouts, even as his cheek is smooshed to the bar.

Ivy's standing now, her cup pressed to her chest. Guilt lines her pretty eyes, and I wait until my son has stopped thrashing in my hold before releasing him.

He stands and immediately spins around, huffing like a bull. When he stabs a finger into my chest, I let him.

"You're not allowed to fuck my girlfriends and knock them up! That's not something fathers do! What the fuck is wrong with you?"

My nostrils flare as I struggle to keep my cool. "You haven't wanted anything to do with me for a long time, Travis. Am I even a father to you at this point or just the man you got your genes from? That choice has been up to you for a long damn time."

"This isn't about our past shit, Dad. This is about you and your current actions!"

"His actions don't have anything to do with you. Sorry. You

weren't a thought in my head when this started, and even if you had been the closest father-and-son duo out there, it wouldn't have kept me from Niko. Sure, I would have considered my choices a bit more out of respect for you, but at the same time, where was your respect for me when you were telling your friends all of those things about me? You don't get to treat people poorly and expect to be given special treatment from them in return," Ivy says, stepping in.

Travis's problem isn't with her, regardless of what he's saying. His issues are with me, and I don't blame him for them. I'm the one who's betrayed him. Even if we're not close, Ivy is someone that at one point, I do believe he cared for.

If he had treated her well the entire time they were together and hadn't been an asshole and hurt her the way he did, I'd have been more reluctant to pursue her.

She still would have been mine, though. I wasn't going to let her go a second time, and I don't expect him to ever understand that. If I were him, I wouldn't. Hell, I wouldn't even bother trying to.

I'm the one who has to live with the consequences of my decisions, even if I stand behind them.

"I'm sorry, Travis. I know it's upsettin', and I don't expect you to be okay with it," I say, drawing his attention. He grits his teeth, his grip white-knuckled on his bar stool. "Feel how you need to feel. But I do hope you'll warm up to us eventually."

"Don't hold your fucking breath," he spits, reaching for the thick jacket that's been slung over the closest booth and slipping it on.

Ivy grabs my hand, squeezing it tight. "For what it's worth, Travis, I didn't set out to do this."

"You expect me to believe that?"

"It doesn't matter what you believe because it's the truth."

He flicks his eyes to me, frustration swirling. "You know, I always wondered if you wanted her. Thought you were just putting on a show with the gentle tone and offers to help all the damn time. Turns out you were just panting after my girlfriend."

"*Ex*-girlfriend," I correct coldly. "And the woman I'm goin' to be raisin' a baby with."

Travis clears his throat and lets loose a dark laugh. "Good luck, Ivy. Lord knows he fucked it up with the first woman he tried that with."

"Get out," Ivy orders before I can get any words out. She takes three steps forward and gets into his face, spine straight and teeth bared. "I hope you get a lifetime's worth of therapy sessions for Christmas. Maybe then you can work through your abundance of issues. Learn some self-love techniques while you're at it, too. Until then, you can see yourself out."

"You're going to let her kick me out, Dad?" he guffaws.

"You were already leavin'."

"Ridiculous. When Mom hears about this—"

Ivy jolts forward, and he jumps back. "Make sure you give her my number while you're at it. I'd love to chat with her."

"You're both insane."

My girl beams up at him and wiggles her fingers directly in his face. "Merry Christmas, Travis."

Travis shakes his head at her, disgust rippling over his expression before he glances at me and tosses a few parting words.

"Hope you're happy."

I move to rest at Ivy's back and palm her hip while holding his gaze. "I am. And I hope you find your happiness soon."

He doesn't reply. Instead, he simply zips his jacket up and storms out of the bar, leaving nothing but a cold wind and another pile of snow in his wake.

The door doesn't close behind him, so Ivy rushes to push it against the snow falling in through the doorway. It's high on the sidewalk, the snowdrifts coming up to the window in the door. Travis would have had to force his way through just to reach it.

Guilt nips at me, knowing that he came here without being

forced and found what he did. I can count on one hand the number of times he's come to visit me here, even if that wasn't why he came to town.

I'd love to know why he's considering moving here of all places, but I doubt I'll have the chance to ask.

"That was absolutely terrible," Ivy mutters, spinning to face me with her back to the now closed door. "He tried to punch you."

"Don't blame him."

"I do! Violence isn't the answer to this."

"There isn't an answer for him. Not for somethin' like this."

She tips her chin up stubbornly. "Well, he'll need to find one. You're family."

I take her face in my hands and dip my head to kiss her forehead. "Until he does, I've got another family to focus on. And while I'd like for him to fit into it soon, I got a feelin' that's wishful thinkin'."

"He'll come around. I know I gave him a hard time . . . I'm sorry. It's just the way he was talking to you reminded me of when we were together."

"I know. My protective angel," I coo, bringing my mouth to hers and nipping at her bottom lip. "I'm sure you scared him shitless."

"We can try to talk to him again. After Christmas and everyone's had a chance to cool down. He might be an ass, but he's your son," she says on a breath.

"Thank you."

"No, thank you, Niko. I'm excited for the future because of you."

"A future together," I confirm.

She grins, and I replicate it. "I've never heard of anything better than that."

EPILOGUE

Ivy

Jill rushes over to my makeshift booth with a gift-wrapped box in her arms and a giant smile on her face. Her lipstick is a bright Christmas red and is slightly smeared at the corner in an *I've just been kissed* kind of way. With all the mistletoe I hung in the bar, I wouldn't be surprised if she found herself smacking on someone.

"Look at all of this!" she cries, pointing the box at my little table in the corner of the Frosty Mug.

It was Niko's idea. Since the snowfall had kept most Snowbell Ridge residents locked inside their homes last night, the Christmas Market was moved to today. Now, on this blue-skyed Christmas Eve, a few small booths have been set up in the bar for those who still wanted to have a chance to sell some goodies.

The decorations we set up during the power outage cast a cozy, multicoloured hue in the bar, making it feel homey and warm. I've nearly sold out of my slippers and only have a handful of sweaters left.

"Merry Christmas, Jill," I say, opening my arms for a hug when she reaches me. "You look beautiful."

"So do you! I love this dress. You look like a Christmas elf."

I glance down at myself and the green-and-red dress I'm

wearing. It reaches my knees and has a full skirt that poofs out when I spin. Niko's already had his head up it and his mouth all over me . . . my panties never getting returned afterward. I'm pretty sure they're in the pocket of his pants.

"Thank you." My cheeks warm as I smooth down the skirt. "I wasn't expecting such a turnout today. It's been crazy."

"Have you been outside lately? It's even wilder out there. The line for the sleigh rides was over an hour long!"

I blink in surprise. "That's incredible."

"You've totally killed it, Ivy. Grayson was asking me earlier if you were planning on sticking around for next year."

"Really? I mean, yes, I am. But wow. I'm flattered."

Suddenly, she's shoving the wrapped box into my arms. "Open it! It's from the office."

Laughing, I tug at the bow of ribbon at the top. The paper is metallic red with Santa hats on it, and I almost feel bad when I rip it open.

"You could have been a gift wrapper in another life, Jill," I tease.

She eagerly takes the paper from me. "Maybe I'll get a booth next year and earn some extra money."

"I support it."

The box is plain and doesn't hint as to what's inside. I pull at the top and peel the tape away before opening the flaps. The tree ornament inside steals my breath.

"Oh, it's beautiful," I whisper, lifting it out of the box.

In the light, all of the small details are visible. From the elegant lace handle meant for hanging on a branch, the way the ornament has been shaped into a chunky ball of yarn, and the sparkles giving it a shine in the low lights, it's stunning.

"I was shopping a few days ago and found it in the cutest little shop. Usually, we do a Secret Santa in the office, but with how busy this year has been, there just wasn't the time to organize anything, so I grabbed it, and everyone chipped in," she explains.

"But I didn't get you anything. This is too much, honestly. It's gorgeous," I gush, shaking my head.

She closes her hand around mine, keeping the ornament tucked against my palm. "It's not too much. Your first year at the office should be remembered, especially with how hard you've worked to make this event a success. It makes all of us look good."

"It wasn't much of a burden," I admit, already searching for Niko in the crowded bar.

He's been busy all morning working behind the bar, and I'm already expecting to hear about how he never wants to make another drink again. Poor guy.

And poor *me*, honestly. Considering my love for peppermint daiquiris, I really hope he'll make an exception where I'm concerned.

"I thought I noticed something earlier! You've been holding out on me!" Jill scolds.

"What?"

"Don't play coy. You're totally boinking Scrooge."

My laugh is so loud and weird, more a snort than anything else. "Boinking?"

"Yes, boinking. Or should I say, you've found someone to shovel your sidewalks!"

"Okay, yes. But it's kind of complicated—"

"What's complicated?" Niko's gruff voice has fireworks exploding in my belly.

Jill's brows dance as she releases my hands and cocks a hip. "You've been shovelling my friend's sidewalks, Niko."

"Is that a sexual innuendo?"

I step beneath Niko's lifted arm and let him pull me close. His warmth and the scent of his cologne provide a sense of comfort that I hope I never go a day without.

It's only been a day since we found ourselves snowed in, but it feels like it's been months. Years, even. I've always believed that the honeymoon phase can last forever if you put the effort in, and that's what I plan to do.

"I think you were a bit too obvious earlier when you were trying to make my clothes burst into flame from behind the bar," I tell him.

He brushes a kiss over my temple. "Not obvious enough, considerin' you're still dressed."

I roll my lips, an eyebrow lifting. "You'd prefer me be walking around here naked?"

"No." His scowl is evident enough in his voice, but seeing it makes me giggle.

"That's what I thought."

"Maybe I should go give this to someone else if you're goin' to keep teasin' me," he threatens and lifts the cup in his hand toward me.

The scent of peppermint hits when he brings it up to my nose. I snatch the cup like a raccoon taking scraps and gulp it back.

"I'll have whatever the hell she is," Jill says.

"Ivy's Winter Kiss."

Goosebumps pebble across my arms, a warm smile forming around my swirly straw.

Jill sighs heavily and pats my arm. "Well, I'm incredibly single. Merry Ho-Ho-Ho it is. I'll see you in the office soon, yeah?"

I nod, unable to stop drinking.

Niko and I both discussed keeping my pregnancy to ourselves for a couple more weeks, considering how early it still is. But I can't wait to announce it to everyone as soon as we can.

"Don't forget to climb Scrooge's lap and tell him what you want for Christmas," Jill whispers while passing by me, a coy smirk on her face.

I giggle into my drink and let her leave.

"The drink good, angel? I tried to bring one around earlier, but it was so fuckin' busy," Niko grunts.

Easing away from the straw, I pat my mouth dry and find his waiting eyes. "I think I could survive on only these for the rest of my life."

"Not happenin', but I'm glad you like it."

"What a buzzkill," I tease.

His chest rumbles when he hums, taking my hand to guide us from my table and through the crowded bar. I don't question where we're going, already knowing. There's only one place we'll have any semblance of privacy.

A couple of minutes later, he's opening the door to his office for me and ushering me inside. He closes us in and lingers by the door, fidgeting with his belt buckle.

"I'm good to have an office quickie, but with how fast I drank that daiquiri, I might have to go to the washroom first," I warn lightly.

"As much as I'd like to take you right now, I don't want anyone here to hear you. Just missed you, baby girl. Wanted a minute with just us."

My heart attempts to fly straight out of my chest. Suddenly, he's too far away, and he must share that feeling because he comes right to me. I'm scooped into his arms before I can blink and carried to the bed.

A sense of déjà vu hits when he sits us on the edge and steadies me on his lap.

I drag my nails over the clean edge of his beard and kiss the tip of his nose. "I missed you, too."

"You've sold almost all of your slippers."

"Don't worry, I saved you a pair."

Genuine interest flares in his eyes. "Yeah?"

"The biggest pair I had. I hope they fit."

"I'd squish."

"I don't know how anyone could ever consider you a grump. You're such a teddy bear."

"Only to you, Ivy," he declares, as if I don't already know that.

"Mmhmm, I'm so lucky."

His expression grows serious, and I move my hands to the back of his neck, toying with the hair there.

"When I was growin' up, my mother used to try and get me to write a wish and stick it on the Christmas tree. I always thought it was a crock of shit. She told me that I could wish for anythin' in the entire world, and it might come true one day. A million dollars or a signed jersey from my favourite football player. If I could go back and choose to write somethin' on a slip of paper, there's only one thing I'd wish for," he says, his voice softer than I've ever heard it.

"What?"

"This. All of this. You." He pauses, moving a hand between us to rub my belly. "The baby we're goin' to have."

Tears well in my eyes, and I sniff while blinking them away. His beard scrapes against my palms when I take his face into my hands and bring us nose to nose.

"I'd wish for this, too."

Every single time.

Thank you for reading Snow Harm, No Foul! If you enjoyed it, please leave a review on Amazon and Goodreads.

This is not the last time you'll see Niko and Ivy or a few of the side characters! Their story continues in Till Cupid Do Us Part

While you're waiting for more of these characters, jump into my backlist or start from the beginning!

For hockey romance, jump into Lucky Hit or Her Greatest Mistake. If you prefer small-town romance, Strung Along and the town of Cherry Peak can be your first stop.
P.S A few of the characters from the Cherry Peak series were briefly mentioned in Ivy + Niko's story ;)

To be kept up to date on all my releases, check out my website and Facebook reader group! Hannah's hotties and www. hannahcowanauthor.com

Acknowledgements

This book was so, so fun. I had a blast with it and can't wait for more from these characters!

Thank you to my amazing group of alpha readers for having a great time alongside me. Sierra, Becci, Nicole, I love you from now til forever.

To Mitchell, look! You're in the acknowledgments again, you needy bugger. I love you.

Thank you to Sonia and Mel for this gorg cover! It absolutely sleighs. And my editor Sandra @oneloveediting for fixing all the mistakes that I still can't seem to stop making 16 books in LOL.

Thank you to Jordan @jordanburns_designs for the interior graphics. You're a queen.

A major thank you to every member of my Patreon for collaborating with me on this one. From the names of the characters to the tropes and title, you helped this one come together.

Thank you to Tori and Maddy @the.bubbly.bookshelf for not only being 2 of my biggest cheerleaders and friends, but for the stunning PR box work you did for this story.

Thank you to Cassie @cassiescreatives for your friendship and the graphics you've created for these two! I appreciate you endlessly.

Thank you to my influencer team and ARC readers, you are such superstars, and I am so grateful for your support every day. To every single person who's spread the word about this book, thank you.

And finally, thank you to Vic @artwithvica for the stunning character artwork you've created for Ivy and Niko. MUAH!!

About The Author

Hannah is a twenty-something-year-old indie author from Canada. Obsessed with swoon-worthy romance, she decided to take a leap and try her hand at creating stories that will have you fanning your face and giggling in the most embarrassing way possible. Hopefully, that's exactly what her stories have done!

Hannah loves to hear from her readers, and can be reached on any of her social media accounts.

Instagram : Hannahcowanauthor
Twitter, Facebook : Hannahdcowan
Facebook Group : Hannah's Hotties
Website : www.hannahcowanauthor.com